T0246156

WHERE
RIVERS
PART

ALSO BY KAO KALIA YANG

Somewhere in the Unknown World: A Collective Refugee Memoir

The Song Poet: A Memoir of My Father

The Latehomecomer: A Hmong Family Memoir

WHERE RIVERS PART

— A Story of My Mother's Life —

Kao Kalia Yang

ATRIA BOOKS

New York London Toronto Sydney New Delhi

ATRIA
BOOKS

An Imprint of Simon & Schuster, LLC
1230 Avenue of the Americas
New York, NY 10020

First Atria Books hardcover edition March 2024

ATRIA BOOKS and colophon are trademarks of Simon & Schuster, LLC

Simon & Schuster: Celebrating 100 Years of Publishing in 2024

For information about special discounts for bulk purchases, please contact Simon &
Schuster Special Sales at 1-866-506-1949 or business@simonandschuster.com.

The Simon & Schuster Speakers Bureau can bring authors to your live event. For
more information or to book an event, contact the Simon & Schuster Speakers
Bureau at 1-866-248-3049 or visit our website at www.simonspeakers.com.

Interior design by Jill Putorti

Manufactured in the United States of America

1   3   5   7   9   10   8   6   4   2

Library of Congress Cataloging-in-Publication Data
Names: Yang, Kao Kalia, 1980– author.
Title: Where rivers part : a story of my mother's life / Kao Kalia Yang.
Description: First Atria Books hardcover edition. |
New York ; London : Atria Books, 2024.
Identifiers: LCCN 2023026221 | ISBN 9781982185299 (hardcover) |
ISBN 9781982185305 (paperback) | ISBN 9781982185312 (ebook)
Subjects: LCSH: Yang, Kao Kalia, 1980– —Family. | Yang, Chue. | Hmong
Americans—Minnesota—Biography. | Refugees—Minnesota—Biography. |
Hmong (Asian people)—Laos—Biography. | Refugees—Laos—Biography. |
Mothers and daughters—Minnesota. | Hmong (Asian people)—Social life
and customs. | Yang, Bee, 1958– | Vietnam War, 1961–1975—Refugees. |
Vietnam War, 1961–1975—Campaigns—Laos. | Vietnam War, 1961–1975—
Aerial operations, American.
Classification: LCC E184.H55 Y375 2024 | DDC 959.704/33594092 [B]—dc23/
eng/20230630
LC record available at https://lccn.loc.gov/2023026221

ISBN 978-1-9821-8529-9
ISBN 978-1-9821-8531-2 (ebook)

Prologue

I did not know how to love or miss my niam tais, my mother's mother. My mother had left her long ago in Laos. I knew that their parting was not by choice; there was a war, and the Hmong, our people, were forced to flee into the jungle to escape persecution for having helped the Americans in Southeast Asia.

Growing up, I heard Niam Tais's voice on old cassette tapes she'd sent from Laos to us in the refugee camps of Thailand. In each recording, she said the same things, her voice trembling across the scratches of the used and reused tapes: "Me Kablia, I am your niam tais, your mother's mother. Although you don't know me, I love you."

My mother asked me to record my voice for Niam Tais, saying, "My mother would like to hear your voice, I'm sure." I never knew what to say. I didn't want to tell my mother that her mother was a stranger to me, so each time, I'd say, "Tell me what to say." In each recording we sent back to Laos, I ended up repeating the words my mother offered me. I said, "Niam Tais, this is Kablia. Although you don't know me, I am your daughter's daughter. I am three, four, five, six years old now. I'm only saying a few words so that you'd know the sound of my voice."

In each recording, I was afraid to say that I loved my niam tais because I didn't know what that would feel like, and my mother, even if she wished for me to love her mother, did not want me to say things that I didn't mean. Still, each time I heard my mother's mother's voice telling me she loved me, I wished I could return her words in a way that was serious and true. I had no way of imagining her place in my life.

I grew up with only one grandmother, my father's mother, my pog. Both of my grandfathers had died when my parents were children. My pog was a force to be reckoned with. She had many grandchildren. We only had her. We raced each other to be by her side, to hold her hands, to sit at her feet, to be bathed in her scent, Tiger Balm and medicinal herbs. I knew the feel of her hand, dry like paper, fingers strong and straight, blue veins like rolling vines soft underneath her skin. I knew her voice, too, rough and low, steady and slow. And so, I thought it was enough—to have one powerful grandmother, to live in a life where the other was a scratchy voice coming from the turning of circles in a small rectangular borrowed box.

It was not until . . .

. . . I was thirty years old. I had lived with my parents right up until then, except for stints at Carleton College, Columbia University, and the University of Wisconsin–Eau Claire. I had known that all three departures were temporary ways of bringing me more fully back to Mom and Dad and the dreams we shared for my goal of becoming a writer, learning how to teach, and living within that combination in the world. In my late twenties, I met a man, felt comforted by his presence and sleepy by his side, and so in the run of my life, I thought I should find a reasonable way of resting beside him. We agreed to marriage.

One summery evening, in the thirtieth year of my life, shortly after my marriage, I visited my mom and dad. Dad was at work. Mom was in her garden in the backyard of the house in Andover. It was a fenced garden my father had made for her, a patch of dug prairie where he had devised a system for watering so she wouldn't have to drag the heavy hose from the house each time her plants grew thirsty; he'd threaded the uneven plot with a long stretch of hose and pricked it at different points with a hot needle so that when the water was turned on, water leaked left and right. He had hoped that it would spray forth like a sprinkler but that is not what happened. Still, it was as romantic as my father got. That summer's eve, my mother stood among her Hmong cilantro, grown wiry and old with little white flowers bursting in clusters about her thigh.

When my mother saw me, she smiled, delighted by my impromptu visit. She started talking and I started weeding close by. A cool evening wind blew. The horseflies and black gnats were few and far between. The scent of mint and basil mingled with the cilantro in the air. My mother, wearing a loose long-sleeved shirt, looked at the earth in front of her as she bent at the waist, pulling at clumps of grass and the fat purslane stalks in between her beloved mustard greens. I followed her example as I had countless times before.

I saw how humble our hands were: small hands, small fingers, middle finger and ring finger bending toward each other like old friends with secrets to share. My mother's movements were sure and fast, unlike my own. My hands tangled unproductively against the deep-rooted dandelions. I wrapped my fingers tightly around the base of the green plants right where the white roots were showing and pulled hard. When the earth gave way and I held the broken roots, I knew that they would sprout again in a couple of weeks. I sighed quietly to myself but did not complain or voice my observation. Instead, I listened as my mother told me stories of how she'd once, long ago, weeded alongside her own mother.

She talked and talked, more than she'd ever talked before, keeping me close, keeping me listening until the cool breeze turned colder and small goose bumps appeared on my arms as the sun disappeared, leaving in its glow a tangerine sky. The cicadas in the nearby trees sang their high-pitched songs, like the buzz of electricity but louder and alive. Alas, I told her that I had to leave. I felt her presence holding me still. I knew my new husband waited in the house, probably eager now to go home and start dinner. I had learned he was a man secured by simple routines, but I lingered, helping her with the harvest: Hmong cucumbers the size of newborn babies, young squash with warts the size of my thumbs all over their skin except for the damp parts that rested on the brown earth, bundles of mustard greens with stalks as thick as leeks, gallon buckets filled with green beans, ropes of snake beans, handfuls of spicy chili peppers, and an assortment of green and purple eggplants.

At the driveway, beneath the old oak trees, my mother filled brown paper bags with produce for me and my new husband as we headed back to the home we now shared. The weight of the bags grew heavy in my hands. It was too much for the both of us to eat, but I did not know how to stop her hands from pushing the vegetables in mine. I accepted them all knowing we would never finish them. I understood them for what they were: a wish for my marriage, for my life ahead, one in which she would not be at the same table sharing my meals.

In that moment, I missed my mother. I didn't want to leave her. My heart lingered even as my body moved away from hers. In the car home, looking out the window at the expanse of prairie grass by the side of the road, I began to understand how hard it was for my mother to leave Niam Tais that other evening, lifetimes ago. As my husband turned on the music, jazz, one of his favorites, a collaboration between Charlie Parker and Dizzy Gillespie, I was swept into a space where the wind inside my own chest felt constricted. It tickled the back of my throat. I swallowed what I thought was breath but knew as tears in the dark of expanding night, as the tires of our car rolled further and further from the house of my mom and dad.

. . . I had just delivered my dead baby into the world. I was thirty-one years old. Baby Jules was nineteen weeks. He was my first pregnancy. He died suddenly inside me somewhere in Alaska. My husband and I had been on a trip to see Denali. On the peak of a minor hill, breathing in the glory of the surrounding mountains, looking down at earth that looked scorched, upon rivers flowing like veins, I felt his last kick. I pressed a hand to my belly. I told him, "Breathe, Baby. The air here is so light it can lift you."

In the hospital back in Minnesota, a week after our return, I was afraid to see my dead baby, scared to feel the weight of him in my arms. My husband, as nervous as I was, caught up in his own grief, his own sea of sorrow, shook beside me. It was my mother who reached first for our son. When I could not bear to look, it was her voice, even and straight, that said, "He's so cute."

In these words, my mother gave me the courage to turn toward the sound of her voice, to look at the little baby wrapped in a blanket in her arms. In the crumpled cloth I looked upon the face of my dead child and I saw some version of myself: eyes closed, mouth open, little nose, the slight brow, a fine chin. My mother's words released me from my fear. I reached for the baby. She handed him to me with both hands. I pulled him to my chest, a baby born so light he could never have held me down. The whole time, my mother crooned behind me, "Baby, you are so cute. You are so cute."

In that hospital room, now aglow in the embers of memory, I learned the power of my mother, not only over me but over the lives that would emerge from me, however their stories would go. Awash in waves of her fearless love, I was able to say goodbye to Baby Jules, send him off to a world beyond the one I breathed in, knowing that he would be cradled already by those who've loved my mother, her mother before her, so on and so forth.

. . . I heard in the background a cry so loud and piercing it cut through the chattering of my teeth. I was thirty-two. I had just given birth, a living birth to a slippery baby, her hands fisted on either side of her head. My placenta had not come out the way it should have. The doctors had decided to do a manual extraction. I lay on the hospital bed, teeth hitting each other so hard and uncontrollably, my body shook in response. I heard my mother's voice, once again, even and straight, saying "Seeyees, my Seeyees. You are here. Your niam tais loves you so much."

It was then in that other hospital room, streaked by the early morning light, depleted of strength, that I knew what I had been missing my whole life, the power of my niam tais's love, contained by a war waged before I was born, a war that severed not only my relationship to her but my own mother's.

. . . I heard nothing but the silence of a clock that should have been ticking, that was clearly working fine for the nurses and doctors moving quickly around me in the operating room. I was thirty-four. I had just delivered a set of twins into the world. Once again, the placenta had not detached, and a manual extraction had been completed. Only this time, it had all taken too long and I could feel myself leaving.

I asked my nurse, I said, "Jen, am I going to die?"

She said, "No, sweetheart. The hard part is done. I'm going to clean you up and then we're going to wheel you out of here to join those babies."

I nodded.

The clock on the white operating wall was still not moving for me. It stared silently back at me, its hands frozen between two and three in the afternoon.

Jen cleaned me up. They wheeled me out of the operating room.

In the hallway, the wheels slowed. I saw my mother above me.

She placed her hands on my heart. My heart stopped beating. I coded.

I woke up after the chest compressions so that I could throw up.

I woke up again in the intensive care unit. I woke up to the figure of my mother at the foot of my hospital bed. She was speaking quietly.

My mother was begging, pleading, bargaining for my life with her own.

Somewhere after all of this, I told myself that when I could, I would take something back from that war for my mother. I would travel on the winds of her memories and together we would sift through the pieces of her life, salvage the loves whose stories were buried in the debris of everything, find the moments of light and laughter, confront the hurt and confusion, the not knowing and forgetting. I would flee with her to Thailand as a young mother with an infant in her arms, and then we would leave for America as refugees together, hands holding fast to each other. Here I would stand with her along the assembly lines, rushing to keep up with the machines. Here we would stand in the grocery store with the WIC vouchers in our hands to buy milk and bread for the children. Here we would wait on Christmas day in a long line of mothers outside the Salvation Army on the east side of St. Paul so that before the day was over, those same children could say that they had gotten something from Santa, too. I wanted to claim the legacy of the woman I come from, the women who had to define for themselves what it meant to live in a world where luck was not on your side.

Where Rivers Part tells the story of Tswb Muas, my mother, the daughter of Ntshuab Thoj, my grandmother, two women who lived quietly, loved fiercely, and raised daughters who carry and continue their stories and the lessons of their lives across oceans, continents, and generations. I have taken on my mother's voice in the telling of her story. These pages, like the long-ago tapes of my childhood from the grandmother I never got to meet, are a message from my heart to my mother's, my way of saying: although time will not hold us close together forever, our feelings for each other will live on long after we are gone.

Niam, I am sorry that I never got to meet your mother.

Niam, I am lucky that I get to be your daughter in this lifetime.

Niam, in all the lifetimes to come, if I get to choose, let me be your daughter again.

There is no life that does not contribute to history.

—DOROTHY WEST

There was once a Hmong house that sat where two rivers met.

The house was made of wood.

There was a shingled bamboo roof on top.

Out back, there was a garden filled with herbs and spices.

In my memories, the house fills my heart.

Remembering it makes me weep.

One day, I will return.

This Hmong house will be full of people again.

Mother will sit among the flowering mint in the garden.

Father will stand by the door underneath the overhang of the roof.

My brothers and sisters will abound.

The living and the dead will be together,

at long last.

There was once a Hmong house that sat where two rivers met.

Tswb's Family

The family she came from:

Tswb's mother

Tswb's father

Tswb's father's five children from previous marriages (including
   Maiv and Npib)

Tswb's three brothers (Vaj, Looj, and Soob)

Tswb's four sisters (Huab, Nplooj, Little Cucumber, and Xis)

*The five siblings who died without names, whose names have
   been forgotten.

The family she married into:

Npis (husband)

Npis's mother

Npis's six older brothers (including Eev)

Npis's nine sisters-in-law

All the nieces and nephews with their colorful names.

The family she made:

Tswb and Npis

Dawb and Kablia (first set of daughters)

Txuj and Sibhlub (second set of children)

Zuabli and Ntxhais (third set of children)

Hwm (the last born)

*The seven miscarriages, all unnamed.

Pronunciation Note

Tswb is pronounced "chew."

Npis is pronounced "bee."

All the names in this book are spelled in Hmong. Some names have been changed in accordance with Tswb Muas's wishes.

A Map of Tswb's Life in Laos

dej tshuam
phou khao
phou bia
Long tieng
ban xon
a parting place

nplog teb,
1961–1979

Because the places where she lived cannot be found on any map of Laos, because the country's maps changed after the communist party came into power following the wars in Southeast Asia, this one was made in discussion with Tswb and Npis with the help of Google Earth.

Map source images by Aaron R. M. Hokanson and Maxwell Hwm Yaj; map illustration by Alexis Seabrook.

Contents

TRY TO IMAGINE

CHAPTER 1

Bad Luck Woman

When Mother married Father he took her home to a house full of people. He had been married twice before her. His first wife, the true love of his life, had given him five children, four boys and a girl, but he had not been faithful to her. As a provincial leader, he traveled frequently across the mountainous villages of Xieng Khouang Province. In his travels, he'd met another woman, gotten her pregnant, and made the decision to take a second wife despite the protests of his first. His second wife gave him two more daughters but could not give him the rest of her life. She divorced Father shortly after her second child was born. She left both girls with him. After her departure, he remembered his love for his first wife, but by then the heartache had taken over her body. She lost her appetite, grew frail, turned away from his offerings of rice and soup. She lost her ability to pull her children in her arms and hold them close to her beating heart. That heart, which had been loyal and true, torn asunder. She died on a quiet morning, surrounded by my weeping father and his children. After her death, Father was full of sorrow and remorse. But his feelings of loss, as strong as they were, could not bring her back to life nor could they attend to the house filled with children. His oldest sons were already married at the time. His youngest ones still cried for a mother's breasts. A year after her death, Father decided he would marry again. He was in his early forties by then. Mother was seventeen.

Mother, like Father, had been married twice before. Her first husband, in a practice of old, had kidnapped her against her will to be his bride. He was the son of a relative. They had played together as children. In their early teenage years, he'd professed his love. She'd denied it. In a fit of frustration, he'd gathered his family and clan. They caught her alone on her way down to a village stream and carried her home, like a pig to the slaughter. By the time her parents were informed, there was little to be done. The sacred chicken had been flung above their heads, her spirit had been severed from her ancestral home and welcomed into his. Mother fought him for four months, turning away from him in their marriage bed, sitting as far as she could from him at the dinner table. In a fit of despair, the young, unwanted husband left the mountain village where his family lived to go buy salt from the lowlands. There, he contracted a sickness and died upon his return. She was a fifteen-year-old widow.

Her circumstances were not unique. It was 1932. Laos was a French protectorate. Mother and Father and their families lived in the high villages surrounding the peak of Phou Bia Mountain. Once a year the French levied taxes on the farming families. In order to pay the high taxes, the families worked hard, tilling the land. Numbers mattered profoundly. Young girls and young boys married in the name of love and in the name of family, but more often than both, they married in the name of survival. Fate was in the hands of the rich and powerful. Widows abounded, and there were practices that had been created to continue the possibilities of life.

When the young man died, his family decided to marry Mother off to another of their sons. In the time she'd spent with them, they had learned that she was not only beautiful but also a most determined and hardworking young woman. They believed that she would give the family strong children. She protested once again, but to no avail. In her heart, she was able to recuse her second husband of any personal wrongdoing. He had nothing to do with her first marriage. In fact, she wondered if he had any say in his own marriage to her. Despite the budding affection between the two, her second husband, a healthy young man with an easy laugh, fell suddenly ill after six months of marriage. He died quickly and painfully. She contracted whatever illness had befallen him but did not die. His family grew afraid of her: now a thin young woman full of sorrow and sickness. When news of her health and the family's fear reached her father, he came to collect her, knowing his daughter was now considered a Bad Luck Woman.

Grandfather was not a typical man of his times. He was a humble man who had married an unexpectedly beautiful woman, a woman who was smart and able though rumored to be promiscuous. There were vicious suggestions that their oldest, my mother, was not his biological child. Village folk wondered out loud, close to his family and friends, how such a short man with no bridge on his nose to speak of could have conceived of a child as lovely as her? Her hair was the color of the winged birds that sat high on the tall trees, so black it appeared blue in the bright light of morning. She had eyes to match, deep and dark, open wide and unafraid. Her slender body was long and strong. There was a grace in the curve of her neck, a refinement in the turn of her head. The villagers worried that my mother looked more like the child of the village chief than the poor farmer who raised her with devotion. Grandfather didn't care. He was committed to his daughter, his firstborn, his champion. From a young age, whenever Grandmother lost her patience with him, it'd always been their firstborn who would silence her: "Mother, do not speak to my father in that fashion."

As a child, Mother often accompanied Grandfather into the fields when the striped-chested, yellow-beaked migratory birds flew into the mountain villages on the east wind, announcing, "Pob kws ua kauv kaus, pob kws ua kauv kaus." She walked in front of her father, carrying a small woven bamboo basket that he'd fashioned just for her, marveling at how the birds were speaking in Hmong, letting all the farmers know that it was now corn planting season, singing, "The corn has rooted, the corn has rooted." Mother had always been Grandfather's dearest companion.

When Grandfather took his oldest child home by the hand, her few belongings in that same woven bamboo basket from her childhood, he did not stop to look at the villagers who gawked as he walked by with his daughter. Her feet meandered behind his own, her head bowed low. She who had always walked a straight line did not know where to place first one foot and then the other. She was not yet sixteen, and yet in the eyes of the villagers she was a full-grown woman, led home by her father, the weight of multiple tragedies on her shoulders. At home, he tucked her into the warm bed of her youth. He called shamans from far and near to find her frightened spirit and return it to her body.

Mother spent a year living happily with her parents and siblings in the house where she had been born. During the day, she tended to her younger brothers and sisters, helping with the hard work of subsistence farming, feeding the hungry pigs in their pen and giving corn and rice grains to the chickens in the yard. She had no desire to marry again. Neither her first nor her second marriage had been her choice. Being home with her family after the ordeal of both, hearing her mother's sharp voice call with the rooster's crow early each morning, was a comfort. At the family field, her father offered her the tenderest ends of the sweetest sugarcane stalks. Mouth full of fiber, throat sweetened with its juice, she told her mother and father that she would never marry again. The elderly couple accepted her words as a matter of course. Who would want to marry again after all that she had been through? Their love of her and support softened the bite of the gossipmongers who suggested that something more ominous had happened to Mother in her time away from the village.

News of my mother's return to her family home traveled with different people as they trekked from one village to the next, visiting family, attending funerals and weddings, spirit releases, and hand-tying ceremonies to bless those in need. It did not take long for the news of the beautiful bad luck woman to reach Father's village. One of Father's relatives knew Grandfather and thought highly of him. He brought up the possibility of a union between Father and Mother, saying, "Her father is a kind and thoughtful man. I understand that she has these same quali-

ties, this bad luck daughter." At first, Father was not interested in marrying a seventeen-year-old. She was younger than his oldest child by five
years. What did she know about the responsibilities of a mother? She'd
barely been a wife. And then he heard a detail about her that he kept
coming back to: she was stubborn, refusing to look the villagers in the
eyes. Some felt it was an act of resistance and not shame.

Father agreed to visit Mother's village with a marriage contingent. He
was not a poor man. He made the trip with two male relatives, each of
them pulling the reins of a horse, all three walking in a line. When they
entered the edge of the village, the children ran to different houses, speaking quickly: "There are men in our village with horses!" The little ones did
not know what this meant but the elders understood it was a formal visit,
one that would end in marriage. Old folks peeked out of their doorways as
the men passed. Some called out greetings, others asked questions about
how far the men had traveled and if they needed water for the animals or
a place to rest for the night. Father responded, "No, we are fine. Thank you
for your hospitality. We've come to visit with the Thoj Clan."

There were no surprises when the men came to Grandfather's house.
In fact, Grandfather and Grandmother both stood in the open doorway
waiting to invite them inside. The men were offered water to quench
their thirst and wooden stools to sit on by the family's fire ring. They
talked of people they knew in common, of the weather, the coming harvest, and then Father broached the topic of marriage.

Mother was aware of the commotion in the village. She had observed
the group of men walk into her family's home, and yet she was surprised by the formal proposition of marriage. She was taken aback by
the heavy satin of Father's clothes, the soft-soled shoes that he wore on
his feet. She was a farmer's daughter. They walked the earth with their
feet bare. Father, no longer a provincial leader, had established himself
as a respected merchant. Although never formally educated, he spoke
four languages: Hmong, Lao, Mien, and Mandarin Chinese. He was over
twenty years her senior. Though such marriages were not unheard of, it
was clear to her that there was a gulf between them beyond the years
that separated their births.

When her mother called her to the fire ring, she kept her head low though her eyes did not remain on the hard-packed floor of her family home. On a wooden stool beside her father, she looked at the aging man across the family's fire without reservation. She was surprised when he dropped his eyes and granted her space to study him. He was a slender man, tall enough, but thin faced, fine boned. She'd always favored men with a bit of meat on their bodies, men whose hands were strong and fingers long. My father had a merchant's hands. His hands were small and elegant. His fingers were delicate, tapered at the tips. Those fingers moved over the satin of his pants, nervous before the young woman's gaze.

Mother had grown comfortable with her reputation as a Bad Luck Woman. Who was this person, and didn't he know of her past? She was certain he would run once her father told him the truth of her history. She was wrong about him. When Grandfather told the wealthy merchant of her two dead husbands, he accepted the words with a gentle nod of his head, communicated an understanding beyond fear. He said, "I believe then that your daughter and I are well suited. I also know what it is like to have bad luck in love."

Grandfather meditated upon these words. In the end, he decided that two bad luck individuals could perhaps neutralize each other, and maybe, just maybe, they could even foster good luck. When he spoke, it was directly to his daughter. He said, "Here is a man who has gone through a lot in his search for partnership. He can care for you while you care for his youngest children. Unlike your first marriages, this time it could be a marriage without pretense or protestations."

Mother shifted her gaze to the low flames of her family's fire. She looked at the flickering light, chased the yellow sparks with her gaze, listened to the crackle of the burnt wood for long moments. As the flames of the fire danced higher with each piece of new wood Grandfather fed into its center, she listened to Father's honest conversation with her parents. He told them that he had a total of seven children at home. He gestured in her direction and said that his oldest sons were older than she was. Three of them were married and two had children already. He extended both hands toward the heat of the fire, palms up, as he explained that the remaining four were young. The youngest child was just a baby, still hungry for breast milk. Mother looked at his open palms, tried to read the spread of the lines across their surface, but to no avail. The lines on his palms were too faint to read. In her search for some direction in his hands, she found herself making a decision, telling herself that if she could not be a good wife, then she could perhaps learn how to be a good mother. Unlike his palms, her own were etched with deep lines, an indication of a long life. She clasped them tightly when she looked up at the two men before her, her father and the stranger in the satin outfit.

On the first night of her marriage, Mother found a baby at her dry breast, sucking hard for comfort. She winced from the pain of the child's hold on her tender flesh but dared not push the infant away. The baby girl's hungry hands held her body fast, clung to her as if she were a lost mother. Throughout the course of the long night, she endeavored to become one with small, steadying breaths to control the throbbing pain in her breasts.

Beside her, the slender man slept on his back, still and silent. Together they listened to the sounds of his large family falling asleep across the connected houses, welcomed the deep, even breathing of the child in their bed and the chirping crickets from the other side of the wall. A strong wind blew and seeped in through the cracks. A chill entered the room, and the two adults in the bed shifted closer together. A heat grew where their bodies met. Outside, the clouds grew heavy with moisture. They covered the light of the moon and rain fell in the dark night. Inside, hushed breaths filled the room.

Mother's eyes were wide open before the early-morning rooster's crow announcing the new day. She untangled herself from the sleeping child. In the gray, she studied the straight line of her new husband's nose, saw the shadows beneath his cheekbone. There was no room to be angry, no feelings of betrayal or hurt. Here was a man she had agreed to marry. Here was her husband. Her heart thudded in her chest loud as the rooster crowing from outside.

On her first day as Father's wife, Mother chose to wear a sensible outfit. She wore the traditional black wide-legged pants and the black shirt of the White Hmong, pulled the fabric together in front to cross above her breasts. She tied red and green sashes around her waist with a firm grip. She pulled her long hair back and secured the heavy bundle with a clip. On her feet, she wore her only pair of shoes, blue flip-flops. The only aspect of her body that she adorned were her ears; she wore the heavy silver hoops her parents had gifted her.

In the main part of the house, Mother started the fire for the morning meal, a routine she knew well. Once the scent of smoke filled the house, her new daughters-in-law each entered one by one. There were three of them, all shorter than her. The youngest looked her age. The oldest, a baby tied to her front, looked older. Each was shy before her, calling her Niam and asking questions about how much rice to rinse, if they should butcher three or four chickens for their first meal together. Mother told them, "It will take me time to learn how much rice this family eats and how much meat is needed to feed everyone. You will each show me what you know and together we will make this family work."

My mother and father lived in the original structure, a wooden house set into the edge of a village of split bamboo huts. Connected to their house were others, the houses of my father's grown sons and their families. While each tended their own fire, the main fire pit was in Mother and Father's house. Each morning and evening, the large family gathered for meals together around their long wooden table. It was Mother's job to supervise the preparation of the meals, the youngest girl strapped to her chest, her new daughters hanging on to either end of the red sash at her waist, her daughters-in-law moving around her in accordance with their age and place in the family, teaching her the norms of the family she had married into. Although she was young, Mother's voice did not contain the uncertainty of girlhood. She spoke with the experience of one who had been a daughter-in-law, as someone who understood the fragility of the situation. Her voice rang with a somber confidence that afforded her respect. The oldest sons looked at her from the corners of their eyes, unsure of this young woman who they were to call Niam but ceding to their father, who had married her. Father watched her movements silently, without judgment or malice, only patience.

CHAPTER 2

The Unlikely Sisters

Mother inherited three daughters. The oldest one, a ten-year-old, was named Maiv. She was short and round, slow in her walk and talk, soft in her features and gestures. She was Father's first wife's only daughter. The second girl was Npib. The three-year-old was named after a silver coin the Hmong used both as a currency for goods and decoration on their clothing. She was the oldest of Father's second wife's children. Then, there was the baby. Everyone called the child Me Mos with her pale skin and round eyes peaking from light brows. The two older girls, half sisters, were as unlike as two sisters could be in the speed of their movements, their temperaments, and their regard for themselves and others, but both took to Mother immediately. They accompanied her everywhere like personal guards, holding fast with their hands and eyes, afraid she'd leave if they freed her up to go to the bathroom in the nearby jungle or down to the wide river to bathe.

Their fear pulled at my mother. She found opportunity for them to be with her throughout the day. In fact, much of her days were spent with the three sisters. One on her back, secured by a child-carrying cloth, while the other two were weights by her side, anchors to the big life she now occupied, continual reminders that hers was a position carved out by the women before. In her previous relationships, my mother had been expected to play the role of a young daughter-in-law, to show deference and to serve as an asset to a family. She found herself, as my father's wife, a matriarch, the one to set the tone for the group, to serve as an example to the young girls eager for her embrace.

In the dawn, when it was time to feed the pigs, it was Maiv who helped Mother cut down and carry the young banana trees from the grove behind the house. Together, they peeled away the tougher, reddish purple outer skin of the banana trunks until they got to the creamy white center, its sap like spiderwebs on their fingers. The girl watched as Mother wielded the big Hmong knife, one hand firmly holding the wooden handle, its dark metal blade long as a child's arm, the other holding fast to the banana trunk. The knife was heavy. Maiv closed her eyes each time the knife sliced through the air. The wooden block they chopped on was old, marked by the bites of uncountable years of blades. The sound the work created was hypnotic. The swoosh of the knife through air, the *kwush* of the blade slicing through the banana trunk, the motions repeated time and again as the pile of chopped banana trunk grew in a heap on the chopping block and fell off the sides. The tight closing of Maiv's eyes, her face round as an egg, charmed Mother.

Near dusk, when it was time to do the dishes after the family's meals, Mother carried the big bowl full of dirty plates and bowls to one of the two rivers that surrounded the village and set them on the flat rocks for Npib to wash along with her. Unlike her older sister, Npib was fast, her eyes following Mother's motions while her hands mirrored them, her palm moving in a circular pattern at the bottoms of the enameled plates. Every few minutes Mother smiled at the child in an encouraging way. Often, Mother had to take hold of a little hand to show her how to use her fingers to feel for the hard bits of dried food off the edge of a spoon or at the center of a rice bowl. Each time, Mother was patient because she could see that the girl was already impatient with herself, her thin chest rising and falling in the exhalation of her breath.

Mother had no tender words for her new daughters, no motherly wisdoms to bestow. Denied a constant motherly presence, the three girls made few demands on my mother beyond their physical needs and their hunger to be loved. Day by day the girls and the woman learned how to move and behave like a team. When the heavy Hmong knife slipped and nipped Mother on a finger, it was Maiv who searched the house to find a piece of clean cloth to stem the flow of blood. When Npib slipped on the high incline up from the river back to the house, it was Mother who lifted her off the ground, pulled up the fabric of the girl's Hmong pants to inspect the scrape, to wipe it clean with a soothing leaf, and to blow cool breath on the heated skin. Across the stretch of the loneliest nights when she heard Father search in his sleep for the figures he'd lost to the past, it was the baby, Mos, who held Mother fast as my mother tried to find sleep and enter into the space of her own dreams.

In the early years of their marriage, Mother discovered that Father was a gentle man and a dignified person. He spoke softly, the hint of a tremble in his words. He ate slowly, lightly, paying close attention to his food, gravitating toward freshly boiled vegetables and away from the oily meats. He was abnormally clean despite their lives close to the hard ground. His clothes carried no crumbs or smears of dirt. His breath was scented by the smell of red bark tree and fresh coffee. He carried a flowery thermos filled with the dark liquid from dawn till dusk, offering cups to his merchant friends who visited the house frequently. In the beginning of their marriage, he had offered her sips but she refused, unsure of the components of the hot, murky water. Mother had never met anybody who drank coffee before, never known a healthy person who took hot sips of the bitter brew slowly through the unfolding day, savoring it as if it were precious, necessary medicine. She found herself in an arrangement that was unlike anything she'd known of marriage, her parents' or her own brief and tumultuous ones. Father conducted himself with a measure of dignity and expected the same from her. For all the things she had been offered in her young life, dignity was not among them. Before she learned how to love him, he won her respect.

In fact, the whole of the family treasured him. His sons ensured he didn't have to do the heavy work of managing a household, the cutting and stacking of firewood or the carrying of water from the rivers. His daughters-in-law were full of praise for his kindness to them and his patience with their children. His youngest daughters raced each other to carry the evening bowl of warm water to wash his feet before bed each night. Both his children and grandchildren clamored close to hear his songs around the family's evening fire, hushing themselves so he would not have to raise his voice.

Father sang in the fashion of his generation, his voice holding the quivering notes of his past. A song he sang across the span of his life, documenting his own story as an orphan goes like this . . .

Every year the world collects its taxes,
It'll take three bars of silver,
This year the heavens collect its tax, it will take Mother,
Father will accompany her.
When the world collects its taxes,
It'll take three bars of gold,
When the heavens collect its tax, it will take the spirits of Mother
*   and Father,*
Dissipate them like the shells of rice in the wind.
When the world collects its taxes,
It'll take money to fill its coffers,
When the heavens collect its tax, it will take the spirits of Mother
*   and Father,*
Disappear them into the air like the fumes of opium.
Mother and Father will be dressed in the garbs of death,
They will climb the shiny stairway to its twelfth step.
Mother and Father will leave their bodies cold on the earth,
As their spirits climb the blue-green sky,
Their orphaned children will wander from house to house without
*   a home.*
Mother and Father will leave their bodies stiff in the ground,
As their spirits climb the bright, sun-filled sky,
Their orphaned children will keen from kin to kin, unable to
*   make a family.*

His tears soaked his words and created a tickle in the throats of the children listening, made them feel for their parents and themselves, the lives they had and the lives they knew others lived. In these evening songs, Father was vulnerable, a man who inhabited the wisdom of grief.

Father had raised himself and five of his younger brothers into manhood. On this journey he had learned, among other things, to be careful in his speech, slow in his feelings, and steady in the places where others might shake. He garnered a reputation for the way he treated others and held himself. Beyond the immediate family, relatives and acquaintances visited the long house throughout the day, seeking his perspective and insights, asking for his counsel.

Though he did not push, Mother knew that he anticipated more children. Although older, he was not yet too old to raise more sons and daughters. He was wealthy enough to do so. She herself had never been pregnant. After two marriages, she was concerned that she might not be able to conceive. But within the first two years of their marriage, they gave birth to their firstborn together, a son. As each old year departed and a new one arrived, a bounty of children came to them. In total, Mother delivered eleven children in her marriage with Father, four boys and seven girls. One of the boys and four of the girls would die, and the rest of us children would learn how to live without them. Each pregnancy gave Mother more stability in her place at Father's side, gave her the time and experience to be his third and final wife.

The girls grew under my mother's care. Maiv became a young woman, her features soft and round. The halt in her speech and her actions as a child exacerbated with the years. Her eyesight and her hearing were poor. When she became a young woman, there were a few offers for her hand in marriage, but none of them were acceptable. All the men who came knocking at our door for Maiv had first and second wives. Many of them were as old as Father and needed a maid more than a matron for their homes. Father understood their needs, but he refused to let his daughter fulfill it. He turned down their offers. He had all his sons promise that they would care for Maiv always. Even Mother gave him her word. She told him that when he was gone, she would love Maiv for the both of them. Npib though was a separate issue entirely. Young men and their parents clamored at Mother and Father's door with marriage proposals for Npib. Before they could reach Father, she waved them aside herself. She was not interested. They need not bother her parents with offers. Npib had grown into a practical beauty. She wore her dark hair pulled back into a clean scarf without nonsense. The bones in her face were strong. Her tan skin was smooth and clear. She spoke to people with unabashed intelligence. She was unafraid of other people and the world, and it showed. Npib felt strongly that she had a life purpose and a vision, and she would do everything to live it.

At the dining table, she jokingly told the family, "One day I'll marry a man worthy of my time or else I'll never marry at all."

Npib was a wonder to Mother. Npib, unlike Maiv, unlike Mother herself, was proudly and openly defiant in a culture that liked the appearance of obedience. Npib delighted my mother and scared her at once.

A bite of rice at her mouth, she told Father, "I'll arrange my own marriages. You don't have to."

The soup he'd just taken down came out. He gestured for a cloth to wipe his mouth.

He said, "Marriages?"

She ate the rice slowly and said, "Yes, the expectation that the first one goes well seems unrealistic to me considering who you and Mother are and your failed marriages."

Short of talking about good and bad luck, they could not deny her truth.

Late at night, Mother asked Father, "Do you think Npib will really do it? Marry herself off to someone?"

Father sighed and said, "We'll see."

They didn't have to wait long. Npib really did arrange her own marriage.

The war effort had reached the high mountains of Laos. General Vang Pao and the Americans had started recruiting Hmong men. There were now Hmong men who earned their living not from farming or trade, but war. Npib found herself such a man.

One day, a warplane came to our village and unloaded more soda than any villager knew how to dream of: there was orange soda, yellow soda, green soda, brown soda, and white soda. All of them fizzed with bubbles when the children snuck close, grabbed a bottle, and shook it. A Hmong man in a uniform stepped down from the plane with two soldiers at his back. They walked straight to the wooden house on heavy boots, called at its open door. When Father approached, the man spoke stiffly, letting his words fall, one at a time, not to Father but to the village at large. He announced that he was going to be Npib's husband. She and he had agreed to marriage. They had already settled the details. The soda was for the ceremony. She'd requested as much for the children in the village. Father and Mother had no choice but to accept their new son-in-law. Npib was the first girl in our village to wave happily from a plane as she took off into the air with her new husband.

Unfortunately, Npib did not like her new husband's sense of entitlement. He refused to accompany her to visit our parents. He felt that life on an army base was far more exciting, the people so much more worldly. After just a few months of marriage, Npib arranged her own divorce and returned home as a passenger on a smaller plane. Though the villagers had gathered at the sight of the plane, there were no sodas to unload. Npib climbed down from the plane and walked herself home, returning with just the simple woven basket on her back, hands swinging at her sides. She announced she was now a divorced woman to all who gathered. Some of the villagers were in awe. Others were scandalized. Npib could not have cared less.

Mother was quiet. She offered no judgment, made no criticisms. When asked about Npib, she offered only a wish in response, a mother's wish that her daughter find certain love in this life. Father asked if she'd done anything disrespectful in her marriage, given her husband cause to let go of his commitment to her, to which she replied, "I've not done anything wrong. He was simply wrong for me."

Out of deference to the fact that she had arranged her own marriage and it had failed, Npib did not ask to return to our familial house. She made herself a little hut behind the main house, on the edge of the back garden near the banana grove. She kept it clean and free of pests. She made her own meals and invited her nieces and nephews to join her at her modest table. She said by way of explanation, "This house is temporary. If I want to, I might marry again."

Her second marriage happened as suddenly as the first. It, too, did not work out. Npib agreed to be someone's second wife, another wealthy man, except this one wore gold rings across his fingers and no fewer than two watches around his left wrist. While the husband treated her fine, his first wife did not. Npib found herself more servant than wife in the busy home they kept. While she understood the disrespect from the first wife, she could not help but notice how little control the husband had over the household, how little attention he paid to everyone under his roof, including her. He entertained one minor dignitary after the other. Each time, he wanted her to be the one to serve the drinks and stand by to fill them. His first wife relished seeing the younger woman, the one who came to them with such assurance, positioned in such a manner. One day, around the six-month mark, Npib decided that her new position had no room to grow. Just as she'd left by herself, Npib came home on her own. Again, with hands swinging at her sides. Neither Father, nor Mother, nor the villagers were surprised the second time around. They did not approve of her choices, but she had made it clear that her decisions were not theirs.

It was not until her third marriage that Npib found a man and a love that she truly believed was worthy of her time. He, too, was a military man. He came to our house in a respectful way to ask Father for Npib's hand. He shared that he had never been married before and that his father had died when he was just a boy. He was raised by a strong mother. He liked Npib because he sensed in her the same kind of strength that his mother had, an ability to raise children on her own if need be. Like Npib, he was smart. He knew the helicopters that carried the dead to the air base in Long Tieng. He knew that the life of a soldier could be a brief one. He wanted a woman who could survive with and without him. He was proud of the fact that Npib was pursuing a life and love she wanted and not what others thought she should have. Npib nodded her head as he spoke. Father and Mother were moved by the accuracy of his perceptions of their rebellious daughter, filled not with judgment but with approval. They were sad to see Npib travel once more a long distance from the village to begin her married life but were assured at the doorway when Npib held both their hands tight and said, "I have good feelings about this one. He wants from me what I can happily deliver."

Far away from the village, in a place where the warplanes flew across the skies like flocks of birds, Npib and her husband created a home for themselves, along with his strong mother. In that home, they had three healthy children. They lived for a time in a life of Npib's choosing until the war took that choice away.

It was a cool, sunny morning. The man Npib loved had a meeting with General Vang Pao and his men about a special assignment for an impending mission. He was going to wear his officer's uniform, but Npib insisted that he wear instead the new Hmong outfit she had made for him. It was of the finest, heaviest velvet she could afford. He was bashful in the finery, but she insisted that being the love and the pride of your wife's eye was nothing to be ashamed of. Unable to argue with her, he agreed to put on the outfit.

From the house, Npib heard a series of gunshots around noon. She didn't think much of it with the day spreading out before her, her young children calling attention to their hunger for the afternoon meal. She spooned out fresh rice into bowls, mixed in chicken broth and meat, settled down to feed them. Near evening, it was her mother-in-law who wanted to know what was taking her son so long to return home. What kind of meeting lasted hours and hours if there was no fighting involved? General Vang Pao did not have that kind of time. Npib was not concerned; often one meeting bled into another.

When her husband did not return by nightfall, Npib started worrying. She told her mother-in-law to stay home with the children. She visited several of her husband's friends and colleagues with inquiries. In the last house she visited, one of his friends was distraught, full of tears and nerves, incapable of speech, pointing only toward the edges of a field.

It was a moonless night. Npib knew that field to be empty but for a few posts on the outer edges. The local boys and girls liked playing on the even ground. The boys chased a ball. The girls held stretches of rubber band braided together and jumped across varying heights in teams. A sinking feeling filled her heart, but she knew what she needed to do.

Npib returned to the house to put the children to bed. Once the youngest had fallen asleep, she untangled herself from the hold of her child, not yet six months old. In the quiet house, lit only by kerosene lamps, Npib called her mother-in-law close and whispered that she feared the worst had happened. In a louder voice, she asked the older woman to accompany her to the open field.

The two women had one flashlight. Npib walked in front of her mother-in-law. The batteries were nearly at their end and the weak beam of light kept going out. Each time it went dark, Npib slapped the plastic against her open palm. Beneath the heavy cover of clouds, the women walked the dirt road to the field. On the stretch of grassland, they stumbled over mole hills and craters as they made their way toward its edge. Once there, they found that the earth was soft, freshly dug around the wooden posts. Without talking, they started digging with their hands. The women worked quickly, the night closing in around them, nearby crickets and frogs singing their tunes. The beam from the flashlight gave out. Underneath the weight of a lowering sky, they heard each other's breathing grow loud with their exertions, the muscles around their throats tightening as their hands crawled deeper into the hole in the ground. It was Npib who first felt the thick velvet with her hands, clenched it tight with her fingers. It was her cries that erupted into the night. Lights came on in the houses closest to the field, but no one came out to help.

Npib told Mother and Father that she buried her husband, the love of her life, with her own hands on the very same night that she dug him out of the makeshift grave. His mother watched and wailed. The old woman sat in the dark of the dirt, beneath the moonless sky, holding her child in her arms, as her daughter-in-law dug his grave. Npib's voice grew thick with her tears, but she did not allow them to fall. She sat rigid on the stool close to our fire ring. Her hands held fast to the sleeping child in her lap, her youngest. She told Mother and Father that she finished burying his body with the rise of the sun. She told them that this time she was home to stay.

A new day, a dark day had dawned. There would be no more marriages for Npib. She and her children had returned to the village for
good. In the coming seasons, her children died one by one, all taken by
diseases no one had a cure for. Their spirits had wandered too far for a
shaman to call back home. The villagers labeled her—just as they had
Mother—a Bad Luck Woman.

In the end, Npib was a widow. She was an example for Mother and
Father and everyone else who had witnessed her defiance, her journey,
her effort to write her own story of what happens when a woman takes
on love, marriage, and war. Npib was filled with a grief so deep and a
loneliness so thick that even those who loved her were afraid to get
close to her, unsure how to penetrate the fog of sorrow that held her
captive; she had walked the world with a brave heart, and now that
heart was rotting away day by day. Though her body remained in our
world, it was obvious to all that her spirit had chased her dead children
and husband to the land of the ancestors.

It was Maiv who comforted and cared for Npib in her final days. It
was the older, slower sister who made sure that her heartbroken little
sister died peacefully despite the tumult of her life. Npib died before
Father. Her death reawakened in both Mother and Father something
they had feared from the beginning: that their union couldn't produce
anything but bad luck. Neither could voice this to the other. Unable to
speak their fears to each other, they harbored them alone.

In the end, Npib existed only as a ghost sister to all of us younger
ones. The only person who spoke of Npib often was Maiv, who remembered her as the bravest and most courageous of individuals. It was
Maiv who told us of Npib's life and marriages not as a warning but as a
reminder, who shared the details of her sister's life not as a tale of woe
but as a wondrous gift to those who knew and loved her.

In a halting voice, hand to her mouth, touching her lips then her throat,
each time Maiv spoke of Npib, she began, "Npib was the smartest of us
all. She learned quickly of the world. She didn't wait for people to tell her
what they thought or what they wanted. She knew her own mind. Her
whole life was fast because she was faster than the world we lived in."

CHAPTER 3

Little Cucumber

Me Dib, Little Cucumber, was Mother's third-youngest child. She had light brown hair and light brown eyes. Her eyes were huge on her thin face. The sides of her mouth tipped up, in a perpetual smile. When she learned to talk, the family discovered that her words came out in songs, the words trailing each other, no pauses in between.

From the bed, for she was often bedridden, she'd say, "Niamthiabtxiv-kuvnconebos." MotherandFatherImissyoutwooooo.

Her voice was a song everyone loved, old and young. Mother and Father would come running at the sound of her voice. It was a voice that came from far away, this girl who was here now but all feared would not be for long.

Little Cucumber suffered from ear infections. Often, one side of her ear, the right side, would stink. By the time she turned four, she knew of its stench. She said often, with a hint of laughter in her words, "I'drun-frommyselfiftherewasroomtorunfromyourself."

Nothing Mother or Father did could cure the infected ear. Father traded bars of silver for Western medication, but nothing worked. Mother, who had become a reputable medicine woman in the hopes of curing her daughter, tried all the herbs and medicinal brews but none of them could cure the sick child. At their best, the medicines eased the girl's pain for a week or two, then the horrible itching would commence, followed by the stench of rot in her ears.

Because of the fragile state of Little Cucumber's health, both Mother and Father did everything they could to bring her joy. They savored the sound of her singsong voice saying, "Oh,thismakesmesoveryhappy,the-happiestlittlegirlever." It was for these words that Mother sewed Little Cucumber the jacket.

The jacket was intricate and far too ornate for a child. It consisted of the familiar designs found on the outfits of young men and women, usually worn during the New Year's festivities. Unlike the jackets that most children wore, simple black cloth with a few jingling coins for decoration, my mother spent months sewing the jacket with bright red and green threads, depicting the swirl of snail shells, the burst of flowers.

Mother made the jacket by layering fabric so it would keep Little Cucumber warm across seasons. The thin girl was perpetually cold, shaking even when others were sweating. Mother made the jacket long. It covered Little Cucumber from her neck all the way to her knees. The girl often wore both the jacket and a blanket in her place on the bed, a bed she'd requested be kept like a nest, surrounding herself with a mound of clothes and spare blankets. The little bird at its center only wore the jacket through a single monsoon season.

Little Cucumber, in the very last days of her life, asked all who loved her to hold her close. She said, her voice no louder than a whisper, "Please-holdmetightforawhileignorethesmellofmyearandletmerestinyour-arms." Everyone held her, soaking the top of her thin hair with their tears, filling her ears with words of love and gratitude for the time she'd given them. She blinked her understanding with those large eyes in that sliver of a face.

When Little Cucumber died in her nest after a series of long days and sleepless nights, Mother could not bury the jacket with her. Most Hmong mothers would have used the jacket to soften the bottom of the coffin for their child. But Mother could not bear the thought of a life in which there would be no keepsakes of her little girl. She folded the jacket up and stored it at the bottom of a chest Father had traded for, a place where she kept only the family's most valuable possessions. Mother buried her daughter in a nest made of the girl's other clothes, pieces of embroidery she'd sewn so that one day the girl would know how to look for and find the mother who would miss her always.

I was born two years after Little Cucumber's death. At my birth, as is customary, I was given a name. No one alive now remembers my first name. Whatever it was, it was most certainly an ugly name. Ugly names were common. Babies were given ugly names in the hopes of tricking evil spirits from coming after them. An adorable baby girl would be called "Spoon" and a handsome little boy would be called "Table," a child whose eyes darted quickly after words and images might be called "Stupid." By the time I was born, Mother and Father were both on alert for all the possible dangers in the world around me. They had lost too many children.

Mother and Father did everything they could to keep me healthy and well. They were afraid I might catch colds. They worried evil spirits might come for me. They were concerned about the rivers that flowed on either side of our village, the only way out a single dirt road. When it rained, they kept me indoors. When the mountain winds blew through our village, they tucked me into warm blankets and held me by the blazing flames of the family's fire. Father, a much older man by the time I came along, had been recused from most of his duties; I became his main responsibility.

When I turned two, Mother got pregnant again. It would be her last pregnancy. She found that unlike her earlier pregnancies, this final one was far more difficult. Her body struggled to hold the life inside her. By day's end, she could barely walk on her swollen feet. Each time the pressure shifted, she felt pain low in her back. Even at the start of a new day, she found her head was light with exhaustion. Her thoughts were scattered and impossible to chase down. Even the names of her children were hard to remember, let alone her grandchildren. Through the whole stretch of the hot season, she could not muster the energy to sew me, her toddler, a jacket—even as the weather was turning. The rains had begun to fall. The rivers on either side of our village surged over their banks. Families whose houses were close to the rivers prepared to flee to higher ground.

On a particularly dreary and windy day, Mother searched deep into her small pile of clothes but could not find anything suitable. Suddenly, she remembered Little Cucumber's jacket. A hand to her swollen belly, Mother reached up and grabbed the key from the high shelf off the bedroom wall she shared with Father. She knelt down carefully to unlock the chest. Her hands trembled as she made her way deeper into its contents, through her formal Hmong dress, the heavy silver necklace that Father had made for her, the precious bar of silver her mother and father had gifted her upon her marriage. At the very bottom, she found Little Cucumber's jacket carefully folded—as precious as her little girl had been. Mother put the jacket on me to keep me warm.

My older brothers and their wives were at the fields taking in the last of the harvest. Even Maiv had gone with them that day to see to their children. The house was empty but for Mother, Father, and me. That day, Father was sick with a cold and stayed in bed. Mother was making lunch for me at our fire. She had me playing by the opened door with several wooden tops. She moved slowly, a hand supporting her large belly, so things were taking longer than normal. Mother said that she'd just turned away for a few minutes to wash some mustard greens. When a cold gust of wind entered the house, she turned toward the door to see that I was gone.

It had rained. The ground was wet. If I had somehow ventured outside, there would be footprints leading away from the house, but there were none to be found. Mother searched the whole of our house, woke up my father, and together they scoured the connecting houses, going from one sleeping quarter to the other, calling for me. They were greeted by silence. Father searched the perimeter of the house, looking for clues. There were none to be found. The garden was empty, the leaves of the plants sagging beneath the weight of the rain. The only footprints in the slippery earth were his own.

After several hours of searching fruitlessly, asking neighbors to help,

Father set off for the family fields to enlist my brothers and their families to organize a search party. Mother and the rest of the villagers walked along the riverbanks calling for me all afternoon, looking for any indication that perhaps I had fallen into the raging rivers. The rain gave way to a light drizzle. Mother started crying helplessly.

When Father got to the fields and notified the family, everyone raced home. The road was empty, just grass tall as grown men on either side. Before the entry into the village, there was a large puddle of rain that had formed in the dip of the road. The family got home soaking wet from trudging across the pool.

My quickest brother, the eldest of Mother's children, Vaj, decided that he would take a horse and go look for me beyond the village before the dark set in. In the night, all the adults knew—wherever I was—I would be impossible to find. The adults were aware of the wild creatures that lurked in the jungle, from the poisonous snakes to the prowling tigers. The drizzle shifted again; this time it became a full torrent. My brother started crying, imagining how he might find me if he did. Except for the sheets of rain that fell in front of him, the world was eerily quiet. There was no flutter of wings or rustle of leaves. The whole of the sky had turned into a single gray cloud as far as he could see. Lightning flashed from the heavens. Visibility was waning. As Vaj thundered down the road out of our village toward the pool of water, his horse stopped hard. My brother was nearly thrown off. Once he steadied his mount, he made out a small figure in front of him across the wide pool of water in the road. One hand holding the rein, the other wiped his eyes so he could see better.

There I was kneeling at the edge of the pool of water in Little Cucumber's jacket, long hair pulled back neat as it had been in the morning. I was playing, hitting the water's surface with the palms of my hand as if I was drumming. My brother called to me. I looked up, dazed. He said in a careful voice, "Stay where you are. Big brother is coming to get you."

At these words, my expression shifted, and I started to cry, reaching toward him.

Vaj tried to remain calm: "Stay put. I'm coming."

He forced the reluctant horse into the water. When Vaj reached me, he dropped from the horse and gathered me close. He was surprised to find that I was dry. How had I crossed the pool on my own? Where had I been all day? What was I doing there, by myself, alone on the road? I, who was so easy to scare, so afraid of the things in the jungle, the creatures that lived away from the village? There was no time for any of it. This was not the right place. He asked no questions out loud, cognizant that there may well be spirits involved. Vaj picked me up, climbed back on the horse, and made haste for the village.

Once home, fed and warmed, when asked where I was and who had taken me away from the village, to everyone's bafflement, I said, "Little Cucumber."

No one had spoken her name to me. There was no way I could have known my older sister's name, and yet there it was, plain as day for all to hear.

Mother and Father called a shaman that very night despite the storm raging overhead and the lightning that flashed through the cracks in our walls. After a long ceremony, the old woman with a red hood pulled up to cover the top of her head told my family that my name needed to be changed immediately. It was the only way she could safeguard my spirit, keep the threads of my destiny from breaking under the weight of grief. Whatever I had been called was no longer who I would be. After long hours of divining, she named me Tswb, "bell" in Hmong, a call to come, a signal for the living to gather around and pay attention and for the dead to proceed with an awareness that the living were close by. Mother took Little Cucumber's jacket off of me, and no one ever saw it again.

CHAPTER 4

Among the Fallen Flowers

Father sleeps underneath the blanket of fallen citrus flowers. The mound of river rocks on top of him levels bit by bit as the seasons shift. I imagine that soon the softness of the petals will rest on the softness of his closed lids. I tell myself that he is dreaming away, taking his time. He now has forever. Time has stopped for him. Beside him, I feel the invitation to slow down, to breathe deep, to sleep. I was nine when he died. It has been five long years. I'm now fourteen and already tired of a world in which I have no father to call my own.

There is no need to hurry. I want everyone to know this. But nobody cares. Mother is afraid again. She knows the soldiers are coming our way. It is a matter of days. My brothers and their wives are in an uproar, chiding their children, gathering their things, packing up the last of the grains, the smoked meats, the salt. Everyone who passes by me, sitting in the orchard, beside my sleeping father, shakes their head. They all say the same thing: "Go pack your things."

My family is preparing to leave the village but I'm not ready to leave. Although Father has been dead for some time now, I feel as if we would be leaving him. This was his village. This was his life. I don't want to leave any of that behind. I have imagined, on numerous occasions, that one day I would take my children here, show them his resting place, let them see what remains of him here on earth. But the life I'm caught in is not the life I had been preparing for.

My education is over. The village school has been bombed. Inside our wooden house, its color gray like the day, are my schoolbooks full of copied lessons. They are useless now. Even from here, in the spread of the citrus orchard, I can hear the mayhem in the line of connected houses. I know Mother is looking for me.

"Where is Tswb?"

"Where is Tswb?"

"Where is that girl?"

I should get up and go home and do what everyone else is doing, but the citrus petals on the ground are soft. They smell sweet and clean. If this is a goodbye, if I'm never to return, then I should be sad but I'm more tired than anything else.

I was exhausted the day my father died, too. He had been sick. All my older brothers and sisters had been worried through long days and even longer nights. I was afraid to sleep, afraid of being awake in a world where Father was no more. I went to him in those final days to hold his hand. His hands, bigger than my own, were warm and light. His skin was dry like the spiritual parchment that we made using the fermented pulp of young bamboo. I held one hand close to my heart, tight with both of mine. I held it above his own chest, rising and falling with his wavering breaths, trying gently to lift him up. When it was clear I wouldn't be able to, I allowed his hand to fall. It fell soundlessly on the wool blanket that covered his body. Beneath the cover, his body was nearly flat as the bed we slept on. I knew that on the day my father died, my mother fell apart. All the pieces of her were still there, but some invisible wall she'd been able to rest on had broken down. In the days following his death, she became unstable, holding others to stand straight, holding me tight when I was close enough for her reach, tighter than she'd ever held me before. The part of me that wanted to go to sleep forever in those days was my beating heart.

I speak to Father now in my head. When he was alive, I listened to him more than I talked. When I did, it was always some question that he could answer. Father had stories to share, songs to sing, advice to give, admonishments to offer. Perhaps this is why in our brief time together, somehow my father had managed to answer most of my life's questions for him. So now that he is gone, I speak to him in such a way where there are no question marks between us.

Dearest Father, I will remember you always. I'll tell my children of the future that they should never sleep after a full meal. It is not good for their health. It will make them fat and teach their bodies how to be slow in all things essential.

Dearest Father, I can still feel your tender feet, soft as a baby's, in my hands. When I hold my children's feet in the future, I'll think of you with your shoes on, always going places but never too fast for the people you love to follow.

Dearest Father, the New Year's flowers you so loved bloomed this year across the mountainsides, and the wind carried their scent to me. I breathed in the sweet smell deeply, held my breath for as long as I could imagining that I was perfuming my body with their scent. No matter where we end up, no matter where I go, I'll always look for those yellow flowers, wild and free—as I felt under your care.

"Tswb, Mother wants you."

Xis is staring down at me. At eleven, she is more child than adult, my little sister. I feel grown looking up at her. She's short and round. I'm short, too, but I'm slender. Her hair is uncommonly light; it is barely brown. In fact, it is reddish brown, strands so light they travel with the slightest breeze unlike my own black hair, thick and so heavy its strands fall directly down, resisting all but the strongest winds. In fact, it cushions my head on the ground soft as a blanket. Xis's skin, like her hair, is uncommon. She's pink. Her cheeks are rosy. They show the flush of youth, again unlike my own. My skin is fair and my cheeks hold little color. As I study Xis, her top teeth are worrying her bottom lip. Here,

I smile. Our teeth are the same, slightly crooked on top and bottom. Her deep dimples show on either side of her mouth as her lips flatten. Like everyone else, she is worried. I have no dimples, but I mirror the straight line of her mouth. I'm partially annoyed with this rush to run away, even though I understand danger is close to us.

I use my arms to push my body up from the ground until I'm sitting. I know my palms are bruising the petals underneath them. I feel the sharp pebbles underneath pushing into the flesh of my palms. Although I'm not touching the dirt, I feel connected to the earth. As if my hands themselves can swim through the layers until they connect with my father's. Xis was too young when our father died. She had less time with him. Her grief is different from mine, and mine is different from my older brothers' and sisters', so there is a loneliness we share as the youngest of Mother and Father's children.

I tell Xis, "I don't have much to pack. Just a few of the newer outfits and my shoes."

She says, "Mother wants you inside."

I nod. I extend my left hand to her. I'm nearly three years older. She grabs my outstretched hand with both of hers. I feel a world older than Xis, but our hands are the same size—though hers are soft and plump, and mine are firmer. She pulls and I rise. On my own feet, I don't let go of her one hand. I squeeze it a little. She squeezes back. We walk away from the citrus orchard and the sound of the rushing rivers, the place where our father is buried, the beloved site of many childhood games. We played tag here with our friends in the village at dusk. We were chased and we ran fast, and those who could climbed the tall trees. Is this what we will be doing once we enter the jungle? This year, we will not be here to harvest from the fruit trees. How I will miss the tangelos, the tangerines, the pink grapefruits, and the green pomelos, the thin-fleshed oranges filled with sugary juices, sweeter than any other in these parts.

Inside the house, everything is a mess. Everyone is looking for the most valuable things to take with them. Maiv is choosing among the gardening hoes hanging along one side of the communal room. Mother is deciding between two cooking pots. The larger one that feeds more than our family or the medium one, which would be easier to carry? Would we have guests in the jungle? she wants to know. Xis says, "Take the bigger one. We will find plenty to eat and to share."

I shrug at her optimism. She's too young to know that we might run out of food. Other families have. Strangers passing by our village ask for food all the time. I kneel on the hard-packed dirt floor. A nephew, Mien by birth, but orphaned and adopted into our family as a baby, lunges himself at me. I pull him close. His thick, tight curls tickle my chin. I lift him up. His small body is compact, more muscles than anything else. He's heavier than he looks. I tell him, "You're going to be so strong one day." He laughs and starts punching at my face with his fists. I put him down on his feet and he runs to his mother.

True to my word, it does not take me long to pack. I am not very fast but there's not much to gather. Mother does not want me to carry more than my back can handle. She says that the elderly neighbor woman beside us walks with her head forward, her back a curved bench, because she carried too heavy of a pack in her younger days. I take three outfits, all traditional, all made by Mother, the stitches so small and even they are invisible to the eyes. I pack two simple sarongs, one green and one blue, both printed with flowers, vines twisting and twirling. I pack my flip-flops and a pair of plastic shoes with a little rise at the heels. I decide that I will leave my village with the sturdy canvas shoes I used to wear to school on my feet. I put on one of my bead necklaces. I twirl the other around the bun high on my head. In the little square mirror I will leave behind, I examine myself.

There is a group of thirteen sisters in our village, and they tell me that I'm beautiful. I agree with them for the most part. My skin is smooth. My hair thick and straight. My chin is tapered. My neck isn't very long—nothing like Mother's—but it is thin, so it doesn't look too short. My mouth is neat and clean, tucked in a line I work to keep as straight as possible. My nose is big, but my nose bridge is high enough to balance it out. My brows are my least favorite part of my face. They are light. They angle a little over my eyes. I sigh and I tuck a thick strand of hair behind my ear. I hear a familiar voice asking for me at our open door.

It is Tub, our neighbor. He is four years older than me, nearly eighteen already, studying to become a teacher. He would have been a good one. But all that is over now. Tub likes me. He has always liked me. I don't like him but he's one of my true friends. When we were younger we used to spend hours catching rockfish in the rivers that converged around our village. He used to cut fat stalks of mature bamboo into their natural segments, and we would put the little fish in whole, season it with salt and chilies, lemongrass and fish mint, green onion and cilantro from my mother's back garden, and cook it in the center of the fire ring until the bamboo segments turned dark, and liquid sizzled out through the cracked sides. The scent of the cooked fish called both the children and adults close for a taste of our harvest. I miss those days.

At our door, I stand before Tub, my canvas shoes on my feet, my woven bamboo basket filled with clothes beside me. I know his family is not leaving. They will surrender when the Pathet Lao and North Vietnamese soldiers come. His grandmother is frail and sick. His mother and father worry she will not make it in a run through the dense jungle and mountainous terrain beyond our village. I stare at Tub. The longer I look at him, the more nervous he gets. He shifts on his feet. His gaze falls to his brown, sandaled feet.

Finally, he stammers out, "Take this."

He offers the gift with both hands. I look at the small parcel wrapped in a piece of slippery blue fabric. I shake my head. I don't want to take anything of his. This is our goodbye and what I want most is a clean parting. My heart is already crying for the place of my birth; I don't want my eyes to follow suit for a person beyond my father.

I tell him, "I don't want it. Whatever it is, it's yours. Keep it for a new friend. This old one needs nothing more from you."

I have no trouble saying what I feel, so I continue to put more words in between us: "I'll miss you. Thank you for being a good friend to me all these years."

Tub starts to cry. He is embarrassed. We both are. He tries to hide his tears, but they fall in a line down his lean face. His hair, straight and thick, falls over his eyes when his chin goes down.

He says, "It's my watch."

It is his most expensive possession, his favorite thing.

"I can't and I won't take your watch. Your family might need it in the days to come to trade for food or a favor or something."

Tub does not look up at me, but his words are clear and assertive: "I want you to have it."

I shake my head. I straighten my mouth even more. I lift my chin and my chest, and I tell him, "Be safe. Maybe we will see each other again when this war ends."

I turn around with a sigh and I make it clear that our goodbye is over.

I don't hear him, but I know the exact moment he walks away because my heart slows down, and I have to tilt my chin even higher than before in the hopes that the angle will keep the tears I feel from spilling out. I tighten the line of my mouth and look toward the earthen jar at the corner of our house to focus my gaze and keep it clear.

On the walk away from our village, on that single road away from our home, I don't look back. Mother walks in front of me. Like me, she's wearing a woven bamboo basket heaped with pots and pans and other necessities for our journey. Maiv holds tight to one of Mother's hands, weeping out loud for our father and our sister Npib, lamenting the war and the leaving. Xis holds fast to Mother's other hand, but her head is turned toward me, checking on me, the sister closest to her in age and circumstance. I walk by myself on the road. Although my family is with me, the moment is painfully lonely. My back is only slightly bent by the weight of the bamboo basket as I look down at my feet. I'd only ever worn these shoes to go to school. Ahead of us, I can hear my brothers hastening their wives and their children along. Our three dogs make no sound, following the men.

When my feet take me to the familiar dip in the road, I stop for a moment. The tall grass on either side wave in the rising evening wind.

There is a sound like a high whistle coming from the shifting walls of green on either side. The sky overhead is thick with purple clouds. The whole world is misty. Here, is where I lost my name from birth. Here, was where I was found again and renamed. Here, is where the ghost of the sister I never knew, Little Cucumber, had been. I don't look back at the village, but I close my eyes and I see our now abandoned house by its edge. I know its gray wooden walls with small spaces in between each board, the bamboo shingled roof that we replace every few seasons, the herb garden out back, and, close to the bamboo grove, the remains of the hut that Npib had built for herself all those long years ago.

As we walk further away from everything we've ever known, the village of Dej Tshuam, the Village Where the Rivers Meet, my last thought is that if it storms tonight, the citrus blooms will fall and the harvest of fruits will be small.

Dearest Father, tomorrow the scent of your orange trees, your tangerines, your grapefruits, all of them will be so lovely. Although I will not be here to breathe in their smell, my heart will carry their scent within me forever. In my dreams, I'll harvest their fruits, peel away the skin of each, tear into the segments of flesh, taste the sour and sweet, and I will never forget that I was lucky to have been born the daughter of a kind and loving man.

CHAPTER 5

The Chinese Man

The Chinese man came with a marriage proposal. I was fifteen. He had followed my family for two days and two nights from the village where we had stopped to barter for food. He'd seen me a week before that when we'd passed through his sleepy town on the edge of morning. He'd seen refugees making the trek. He'd opened the heavy doors to his shop many times, given them food and water. He'd done the same for us. But then, in the light of his flickering candle, his eyes had rested for far too long on me. When we left his shop with our gratitude and goodbyes, he'd offered parting words that struck me as strange in a time of war when people passed each other by and often never saw each other again: "I'll see you all again soon." None of us knew then that this meant that he would follow us.

In the village where we next stopped to barter for goods, he'd been waiting. On his horse and the well-traveled roads, he'd beaten us to the place. We traveled mainly at night and through the heaviest thickets of jungle. The whole family was surprised to see the kindly merchant. However, he was not surprised to see us.

He wanted to marry me. He said that he had never seen anyone so beautiful. He promised my brothers that he'd keep me safe. He wouldn't touch me. Instead, he'd educate me. He'd wait until I was ready to be a woman to do anything marital in nature. He shared his intentions and ideas with Mother as well. His Hmong was excellent. He'd traded among our people since he was a boy helping his father.

The merchant had traveled with riches, more gold than any of us had ever seen. A velvet bag the size of my cupped palms full of jewelry: golden necklaces, rings with glittering rocks, beads that were white as eggs; so many beads. I loved jewelry. I twirled the strand of beads at my neck. I raised my hand to feel the strand of beads I'd twirled about my bun. I tried not to stare at his offering or let my admiration for the gold necklaces and rings show. I straightened my mouth even more and tipped my chin up as I averted my gaze. I looked at the tree line with particular interest in the lavender light of early morning.

My family had been in the jungle for a year. We had lived in many places, among different people, all fleeing from the North Vietnamese and Pathet Lao soldiers hunting our people down. Unlike other family groups, we were not yet hungry. We still had enough valuables to barter for rice. We were not yet eating corn mush. We still had a supply of salt. Many women and children had come begging Mother for salt on the journey. She was sharing small handfuls. Now, each time they came, she offered a pinch or two. We had been homeless for many months but I was with my family. I was where I needed to be.

As a family unit, we all declined the marriage proposal. We told him that we had a far distance yet to travel before we might feel safe enough to settle down. We told him once again of our gratitude for his generosity. My older brothers shared that our own father had been a merchant and that we understood the importance of good relationships. They thanked him and we continued on our way.

To everyone's further surprise, he followed us. He left his horse behind. On foot, he carried the bag of jewelry and a backpack, walking a friendly distance behind the family group. At mealtimes, Mother invited him to dine with us. He'd kept his quiet but now after two full nights of walking, of resting against the trunks of trees in shadows of endless growth, he was once again bringing up the proposal to my brothers.

The Chinese man was tall and well built. His eyes were open and honest. His hair was cut short and neatly combed to the side. He wore Westernized pants and a brown belt. He was completely fluent in Lao and Hmong. He hadn't once complained or lost track of our family group despite the respectful distance he kept. He told my mother, a ball of rice in his hand, that he had never been married before. He explained that he came from a family as large as ours and that they lived in the lowlands of China. He was the son of a prosperous merchant and had worked among different ethnic groups in the high mountains of Laos and Vietnam for much of his life. He was incredibly moved by the plight of the Hmong and other minorities, victims of this horrid war. He shared that he owned a shop in the capital city, Vientiane, in addition to the place in the town where we had met him. If I agreed to his proposal, he was going to take me there, far away from Xieng Khouang Province and the dangers that awaited our people here. He looked directly at me, as I sat in the circle of my nieces and nephews, and said, "If your daughter wants to marry anyone at all, I have every reason to believe that I am the best prospect at this moment in time."

He spoke slowly and seriously. In fact, the speed of his speech reminded me of my father.

I did not wait for Mother to respond. I answered him from where I sat, my voice perhaps colder and more careless than I had anticipated, "I don't need or want a marriage prospect at the moment."

I knew no one would force me. Father had ensured that I would get to choose my husband. He said as much on his deathbed. More importantly, I knew Mother was not going to marry me off. She had her own history of marriages, followed by the tragedies of my older sisters.

Npib had made her own decisions. In the end, she lived and died with them. Although heartbreaking, her death was beyond the scope of what Mother and Father were responsible for. While they lived with the sorrow she left behind, they felt no guilt. Since Father's death, Mother had learned other painful lessons about daughters and marriages and all the ways in which bad luck had lived—despite and because of all the dying around us.

In our year in the jungle, Mother had heard news that her eldest biological daughter, Huab, and her husband had both died from an untreatable sickness. Huab was still young. I did not know her well because she had married when I was a child. All I know is that her marriage was a love match. She visited my parents once or twice a year. Each time, she brought a freshly killed chicken, a basket of newly harvested rice, sweet potatoes she'd dug up from fields she tended. She was kind enough to me on these visits, brought a buzz of excitement to our home, and joy to Mother and Father, but I felt shy toward her, this stranger sister of mine. Every once in a while, Mother remarked, "It is good that Huab doesn't visit me so often. It must mean that her life is going well, that she is well loved." I knew that on these occasions she missed Huab. When news of Huab's death reached my mother, she grieved like so many other mothers in that jungle—empty hands facing up toward falling skies, no body to hold, no one to pull close.

Nplooj, my mother's second biological daughter, was another story. She had not wanted to marry our first cousin on our mother's side, but ever obedient, she'd listened to the advice of Father and our older brothers. While it must have been difficult for Mother, she did not fight Father and her sons. The marriage was a disaster. While Nplooj had not liked him as a cousin, she hated him as a husband. Her feelings for him grew so strong that it colored her relationship with her own uncle and his wife, the whole of Mother's family. Nplooj returned home from that marriage full of bitterness, anger, hurt, and, worse, a sense of betrayal. She stayed with my parents only for a few silent months before another man passed by our village and saw her. He kidnapped her to be his bride. If Father had been younger and my older brothers stronger, less afraid of the consequences, they could have gone to his house and demanded his family return her, but they were afraid of injuring clan relationships, questioning the other family's intentions, and so they had done nothing, and counseled Nplooj, "You will learn how to love him." She did not. The life they shared was fine. They had children and the little ones were beautiful. But he was always just him: a man who wanted her so he kidnapped her, a man who instead of asking or winning her favors, had forced them.

The truth of this violence governed their moments together. Long after Nplooj's second marriage, Mother and Father wept for her, even as they held on to the hope that somehow love might flower in her life.

After this, they both agreed that they would never force me or Xis into a marriage we did not want. My brothers respected their decision. Instead of telling us who we might marry, Mother offered insights so we would be better positioned to make our own decisions when the time came.

"I learned from marrying your father that a woman needs to choose a man with meat. In old age, thin men tend to become nothing more than skin on bones."

"Men who laugh too often and too fast are unsure of their own feelings. It is more important for a man to know how he feels than what he thinks."

"Young men who smell bad will only smell worse with age."

These words of advice from Mother had a deep impact on me. I found men who were too thin, laughed too easily, or smelled unclean, unattractive.

But the Chinese man was none of these things. In his plea for my hand, there were no smiles, no weaknesses of feelings expressed. Here was a man who was sure of himself and his place in the world. And yet I was fifteen. I was well loved by my family, and I loved them deeply in return. Why would I want to leave that for a life far from them, where wealth and security would be mine alone? If he had offered Mother, my brothers, my older and unmarried sister Maiv, and my younger sister Xis some pathway into a shared life of safety and prosperity, his proposal would have been of interest to me. As it was, his show of wealth and the offering of beautiful objects did little more than to support a reputation that was growing among those who had encountered me in our year in the jungle: Tswb, although pretty, believed she was better than the circumstances around her.

The Chinese man was disappointed, but he took my words as I had spoken them. He nodded and headed back on the trail we had come from, his velvet bag of jewelry safely hidden in the pack he carried high against his back. I did not look at his exit from my life too closely, uncertain of what awaited my family in the days to come.

Soon, we needed more food. The rice was diminishing.

In a temporary home, in the depths of the jungle, our life resumed—the running, the hiding, the bartering—but our needs had grown more urgent. Surrounded by the towering trees with their tangle of vines and the calls of wild monkeys, we lived in small gatherings of refugees. The men kept watch over us, taking shifts from morning through night. Us women and children gathered food and attended to each other as best we could. A cold stream ran close to the base camp supplying us with essential water where we bathed and washed our hair.

We had long run out of shampoo. Mother created a mixture out of a specific kind of jungle leaf with red veins. Xis and I helped her, harvesting from the trees. After Mother rinsed the leaves clean with water from the stream, she boiled them in our big pot until a reddish residue unleashed into the water. She used fern leaves as a filter, holding a smaller pot underneath, slowly pouring the hot liquid through the overlapping leaves. I liked the long ferns with their stiff leaves, each decorated on both sides by little black dots that rose against the pads of my fingers. The final product was a liquid clear as water that created suds in our hair and gave off a smell like moss.

On a splendid warm day, Mother and I went to dig for cassava several hours' walk away from the camp by the river. My eldest brother had scouted and found an abandoned field on the edge of a bombed-out village. We'd passed many villages in our year in the jungle and while a few were intact, most were filled with the darkened remains of once-standing houses, animal shelters, and grain sheds. Like us, many of the villagers had taken flight in fear, freeing their animals, leaving their planted fields. This one contained a field of the sought-after plant with leaves opened wide like fingers. He made the gathering trip quite exciting: "The cassava plants are taller than grown men."

Mother and I had no trouble finding the place with his directions, and he was right—the field was large, the leaves green and healthy. The plants themselves towered over us. The stalks were as big as my arms. The earth was red and hard.

We took turns digging into the dry soil. The umbrella of the thick leaves had grown so wide that the ground underneath was mostly bare even though the field had not seen a gardening hoe in months. The cassava roots themselves were the size of our legs, thick and round. Halfway to filling our baskets, I heard a quivering breath, then a small hiccup of cries escaping from my mother. When I turned, I saw Mother surveying the remains of the village, blackened out spaces where families had been. On the rise of a hill behind the village, we could still make out the heaps of earth, now grown over with grass, that had been grave sites. Mother wiped her tears on the red sash at her waist. I knew she must be thinking about Father, Npib, Dib, and Huab and other family and friends buried and unburied. The weight of her emotions and my own brought the corners of my mouth down.

Right up until I turned fifteen, I saw my mother simply as a mother. I had not noticed her as a woman in the world, a woman of beauty and grace. When she became my father's widow, the third time in her life, she was only in her late forties. She'd say every so often, "I don't know how to dress today. If I dress well, people might think that now that my husband is dead, I am trying to garner the attention of others. If I dress messily, people might think that now that my husband is dead, I've let go of my self-respect and no longer care how I look." When my father was alive, Mother had never communicated this kind of insecurity. Whatever she was wearing or however she looked, she was always the same person to me, the one I was born to, the one whose hands had swept my hair away from my face, tucked it behind my ears. These words she spoke changed the way I saw her. In many ways, they allowed me to see her as an independent body, one who had suffered losses I could not imagine for myself.

I marveled at how clean and put-together my mother looked despite our year in the jungle, her clothes intact, sewn and sewn over some more, her hair pulled back and tucked beneath the blue scarf she wore on her head. Mother was taller than I would ever be. Even with her head bent, shoulders curved, tears seeping down her face, and lines creasing her forehead, I knew my mother had somehow remained beautiful despite the ugliness of the war.

I felt a wave of love sweep over me. A gratitude for my choice not to leave with the Chinese man, my choice not to leave her. A knowledge that others had. I felt a certainty that I had made the right choice because it was mine to make. I said, "Mother, we'll tell the other women and girls about this field. It'll get harvested by Hmong hands. It was planted by them."

She nodded and got back to work, pulling the hoe far behind her back and swinging it forward into the base of a cassava trunk.

On our way back to the family's site, baskets heavy with cassava roots, we passed a funeral. There was a family living in a shack in a clearing. The door to the makeshift home was open. Inside, there were dark figures hovering over the body of the deceased. We heard the rise and fall of many voices wailing. A woman lamented, "How can you go? You are leaving behind your children, your daughter and your sons!" Mother wanted to go inside to offer her respects, a practice from a time before. I wouldn't let her go. I didn't want to see her fallen by the grief of others; I was already afraid she'd fall under the weight of her own. I saw in the hunch of her shoulders, how she was now bent forward by something more than the full basket of cassava roots on her back. Besides, the person who had died was a stranger to us. We didn't even know the family. I was pulling my mother away when I heard a single sob that halted my feet.

Beside the structure, at its corner, was a young woman my age or just a year or two older. Her skin was tan. Her forehead smooth and wide and round. Her clothes were torn and dirty. The shirt was missing buttons. Her hem was torn and mended many times over. The young woman had no shoes on her dusty feet. Her brows were light and nearly absent above deep-set eyes. Though it was her cry that had called out to me, I saw that her gaze was clear and eyes dried. Her mouth trembled. She stood on the eastern corner of the house where the body inside was hung in the traditional Hmong way of preparing the dead for their journey to the afterlife. A thin wall separated them.

We stared at each other. Her hands clenched at her sides and she braced herself. It was as if she thought I might attack—me, another young woman, Hmong like her, caught in the same jungle but whose circumstances were less dire because my mother was beside me and there were shoes on my feet and beads around my hair. It was I who looked away first, dragging my mother from the clearing in front of their grieving hut onto the dirt path and then into the heavy growth of the jungle. Her gaze followed us until we disappeared into the foliage. I could feel the heat of her emotions on my back.

Among the calls of the birds and the cries of the monkeys in the high canopy of green above us, I lost myself to my fantasies with the speed of youth, the basket of the cassava roots keeping my gaze low.

I imagined a time when the run would be over. I saw myself as a nurse in a hospital. I felt my small hands and saw them dancing over the keys of a typewriter, quick and efficient. On a long-ago visit to Long Tieng, an airstrip in the mountains made by the Americans and operated by Hmong folk, I had once seen a nurse typing at a military hospital. On my own accord, the small hands at my side started moving, my fingers clicking on invisible keys. Then and there, I made a promise to myself: one day, my own small hands would type on such a machine. Thoughts of an orphan girl's weeping with her mouth and fighting with her eyes were replaced with one of me in the future, sitting at a table with a typewriter in front of me.

The sky had taken on the deep purple hues of opium poppies in between the leaves of the tall trees overhead. The wind was rising. The cassava roots in our baskets were slowing us down. Mother walked in front of me, one hand braced against the basket at her back, the other at her side holding fast to her gardening hoe. I followed behind her on the narrow trail, trying to keep my back as straight as I could.

When she stopped suddenly, I stumbled into her.

There were two young men out hunting. One carried an old American gun strapped to his back. In his hands, he held a slingshot. He appeared as startled as we felt. He recovered quickly. He nodded to my mother. When he looked at me, his mouth opened and then closed. The second man, a few steps behind him, called out a casual greeting. Such encounters were common in the jungle because we were all running from the

North Vietnamese soldiers and the Pathet Lao soldiers who were looking for Hmong people and killing us. We were using the trails we'd learned from the animals who inhabited these mountains and jungles long before us. In this truth, there was a sense of community, of mutual care.

My eyes did not move from the first man. He was in rags. There were smudges of dirt across his face. His hair was thick and full and it stood up on his head like a boy's, but his shoulders were broad. His whole body filled the trail even though he was not very tall and certainly wasn't fat. His eyes admired me. Usually, I liked to look through men, but I found myself unable to be my normal self. The sky overhead had suddenly fallen on me; my thoughts were covered beneath a blanket of fog I'd never experienced before. My throat felt dry. *Yes, Tswb, he is a handsome young man, but nothing less and nothing more. He is certainly not the best-looking person you've ever seen.* This truth gave me the strength I needed to straighten my mouth to a more familiar position. I gave him the look I had mastered: a look I hoped would show him that although he was in front of me, the world around him was more interesting. He cleared his throat. Evidently, mine was not the only dry one. My gaze found its way back to his face. There was a smile in his eyes then his lips parted, and I was struck by the whiteness of his teeth, his straight, even, perfect smile.

The two men stepped into the thick bushes so that Mother and I could pass on the sliver of a trail we shared.

As Mother and I walked away from the two men, I could not help but think of the Chinese man, the hasty memory of it all. What had just happened? Nothing, and yet it felt like everything all at once.

How could I know then, in that jungle, on that narrow trail full of thorns, that this person would be the one I would leave my mother for? That the Chinese man, with his velvet bag of jewelry, his promise of an education, his careful talk, would be little compared to the forces now swirling inside me, the heat erupting in the heart of who I was and would be?

CHAPTER 6

Sweet Everything

We are shy with our hearts. If possible, we are even more shy with our bodies. When we first meet, it is just our voices talking quietly in the background of my family's camp life. My mother moving from one task to the next, calling me along. I'm at the stream washing clothes. He stands nearby underneath an overhang of wide banana leaves that casts his skin in a soft green-gray light. I'm at the makeshift fire cooking rice porridge for my nieces and nephews, stirring with a wooden spoon my eldest brother has fashioned for just this purpose, so the rice does not stick to the bottom of the large pot and burn. The thick white porridge bubbles and burns my hands but I don't flinch or show that it bothers me. He crouches nearby, helping stoke the fire as I cook. In the rising smoke of the flames, he looks like a figure from a dream. And we talk, or more honestly: he talks, and I listen and I judge, and sometimes I just feel the words he speaks like I'm basking in a scented breeze though of course it isn't the same as being in the citrus orchard where my father waits.

Tswb, I like your brother Soob's chicken. I can't believe that in a war, he is still able to keep such a beautiful bird alive.

Npis, the young man with the spiky, childish hair my mother and I had met in passing after our cassava run, gestures toward the rooster my brother has in a bamboo cage by the stout tree where he sleeps with his wife and children beneath its canopy, jungle vines falling low from its branches. The rooster is insignificant to me, but I hear from Soob that he is prized because of his heritage. I am not particularly fond of the hobby of raising prized chickens. I have grown used to the discord it causes in my brother's life. His wife despises the beloved bird. It eats precious grains of rice. In the runs we make, it slows us down. It crows and draws attention. It's dangerous and unnecessary, this pet of his. It is an indulgence, a recall to a life that is impossible now. I'm quiet when they argue because it is one of those spaces in their marriage that remain intimate and intact even though we are in a war and on the run.

In fact, Npis does not tell me about his own prized pet chicken. He does not tell me about how when he ran away from his burning village, he'd tucked a beloved rooster into his shirt. How all through that first year in the jungle, even when his family was hungry, he refused to let people eat it. He does not tell me about the night an enemy plane flew through the skies and how the earth splattered around the family's hideout. He does not tell me about how he ran to his bird, lifted the bamboo cage from the ground, and freed it. How the rooster fled for its life and did not look back.

If Npis had told me, I would not have married him. His actions were not sensible. Why save a chicken when your family was starving? If he had told me, I would have known that here was a man whose dreams were too close to the ground, afraid to take flight like my own. Plus, it would have clued me in on the sacrifices he would make for the animals in his life, even when our jackets had been worn thin by the hard seasons of our life together. His commitment to the animals, especially the chickens, would be a continual source of sacrifice in my life with him. But I did not know it then; all I knew was that he'd taken the time to admire and to see something beautiful in what my brother Soob has achieved in keeping an animal safe despite everything.

I prefer to work with the women. I don't like to take care of the nieces and nephews so much. It is a task that has fallen on Xis. Perhaps disproportionately.

I share these things because they are true. I'm an honest person. I've always been. Each time, there was an opportunity to lie, to make myself sound better, to make someone sound worse, I have chosen to be honest—even at a cost to me. It is a quality that I respect about my mother. It is a quality I want to carry over to my daughters. Chasing children around all day is not my preference. Because I'm older than Xis, I have more say about where I'm situated in a day's work. Besides: she's better with the children. She laughs with them. She plays with them. There is more joy around the camp when she is the one taking care of them. Everything is less tense, less dangerous somehow. Her rosy cheeks bloom and blossom with the little ones in her arms and lap, their once plump bodies squirm, sharp elbows and knees poking out.

Npis will tell this story to our daughters many years later as an indication, from our earliest days, that I was spoiled and could choose the jobs I wanted even in a poor country, even in a country wrecked by war. He will laugh and use it to tease me, and I will hate it. I will feel injured and betrayed. I will regret that in my youth, I shared such facts with him—not knowing that one day they would be deployed as an arsenal against my personality and the essence of my character, however playfully.

I will be the first to admit that I was loved by my family and cherished. I will be the first to proclaim to the world that I had options other girls did not. I was able to go to school. I did well in school. I was the first girl in my village to be literate. In fact, in our two-room schoolhouse, I ran far ahead of all the boys in my age group on lessons in history, math, and especially memorizing and reciting the literary passages from Lao books. I will remember how one of my teachers, a Lao woman from the provincial city, loved me. She used to walk me to my family's house after a long day of school, holding my hand in hers. She used to laugh and tell me stories of her life in the city, the reasons why she journeyed so far away from her home to educate mountain girls like me, girls whose smiles are so bright and beautiful they make all the world a better place. These are not things I'm ashamed of, these tender memories of having choices and being loved for them—of being valued.

And yet: it will hurt me one day when Npis repeats these truths to my girls, his eyes naughty like a version of himself he could never have been beside that fire in the jungle with me, teasing me because he knows he can and because the life we will share will leave little room for laughter; in this far-off future, far from the bubbles of white porridge rising to the surface of the blackened pot, I will have nowhere to run or hide beside him.

But we were still young, and in that jungle, beside that fire, the thick scent of cooking rice and water in the air, his eyes were full of wonder. He nodded his head like he understood the monotony of caring for the little ones, how much more productive and useful it was to be a pair of helpful hands in the work of finding food, washing clothes, tending to the fire, ensuring that meals were eaten with clean spoons and bowls.

My father died when I was just a toddler. I have no memories of him. I hear he was a good man. At least, this is what the people in my life tell me when I ask questions. Or when I used to ask them. I don't anymore. There's nothing new they have to share with me about him anymore.

I, too, lost my father when I was young. I was not as young as Npis but young all the same, and yet I never spoke those words with that kind of yearning, that kind of despair, that sadness that swims out of his mouth and cloaks the world in an invisible, shared space of sorrow. I know no one else who can do this. Npis tells me he sings songs. He is a traditional song poet. I've spoken with a few of the young women in the camp and they tell me that he is not just a regular song poet, but a great one. He can carry not only his own feelings of grief, of fatherlessness, but other people's as well in his songs. I have not heard him sing and I won't until we are married, and we are in Thailand and the women and girls clamor for him to raise his voice at the New Year's celebrations in the camp. Like everyone else, I will be spellbound by the soft cry in his voice as he sings of our communal sorrows and joys. But even as he is talking about his own father, I am missing mine. I hear again that quivering long-ago voice by the fire, singing a song about being an orphan, about the taxes the heavens take. The steady ache in my heart grows, my throat clenching. I know I am in imminent danger of letting him see me cry for the first time.

My father planted a citrus orchard for our family when he was a

younger man, when he was healthier and stronger than the man who took
care of me. When he died, we buried him beneath his flowering fruit trees.
I am afraid of death and dying, bodies and burial grounds. But I'm not
afraid of the place where my father rests or the remains of his body. I used
to go and play close to him there. Sometimes, when I was tired, I would rest
my head among the fallen petals. When I think of my father in that place,
I think only of the beginnings of the rainy season. The earthy smells rising
from the green things that grow on the ground and the clouds above low-
ering themselves bit by bit, and somewhere in their meeting, how moisture
forms, scented by both earth and sky. I breathe in the memory, looking for
the smell of orange blossoms, sweet and spicy, and a return to that time in
our lives when sweet and sour was within a hand's reach.

I don't talk very much. I'm not a talker but with Npis, in the circle of
his feelings, the words inside me float out of me. I can't control them.
They rise and rise and erupt like the songs I don't sing into the world.
He lets me feel my way into the world. This realization makes me look
at him and look at him some more and it tells me clear as day, *You'll*
never tire of looking at him.

I must go home now. My mother must be wondering where I am. She
can get very worried. My mother—here he laughs and raises his brows a
little—*is not the gentlest woman when her worries overcome her.*

I have only ever seen his mother in passing once or twice. She does
not wear a scarf over her hair like my own mother. Her hair is not long
like my mother's. Her hair is dark and thin and curly. She pulls it back
and ties it with a rubber band. Tendrils escape and they twirl around her
face. His mother isn't beautiful like mine. She's a wide woman, wide of
face and form; even her feet, shoeless on the dirt path, are wide. They
don't cling to the earth like other shoeless women I've seen; they lay on
it the way a tree emerges out of the ground. His mother scares me. Her
eyes are always assessing though her mouth is soft. She moves slowly
and steadily. Her voice, the one time I heard her talk to a grandchild,
was deep. It was nearly as deep as Npis's. She terrifies me.

Yes, you should go home.

I despise women who display their feelings unnecessarily for a man.

I've seen it before in the village. The older village girls volunteering to wash the clothes of young men they like or saving a sweet yam from the fire to give to a lover on the cooler nights. Even as a girl I knew I would never become this type of woman. And I am not. If Npis needs to go home, he should go. I won't ask for him to linger or stay. I won't say, I'll look forward to the next time you visit. I won't ever tell him that as I fall asleep, it is often his voice and his words that accompany me into the dark of my slumber—where once it was the pull of exhaustion, the struggle of trying to survive for another day.

I make it a point to straighten my mouth. I raise my chin. I nod my goodbye. Before Npis gets up or wipes his hands, dirty from the soot of our fire, on his once-black pants, I turn my shoulders away from him and busy myself more earnestly with the bubbling porridge—perhaps now too soft because we've spoken too long. A piece of me is angry at myself.

I don't look as he departs. I hear him make his excuses to my brothers and Mother. She, in Hmong fashion, invites him to stay and have a bowl of porridge. *Tswb is making porridge.* He declines. I know his family group is out of rice. Porridge is a memory from the more plentiful times. He probably really wants porridge. We have enough to share a bowl or two. I shake my head at myself. I'm not that kind of woman. I'll never be. Why pretend to be what I'm not for this man?

After Npis departs, his words linger. They accompany me as I spoon out bowls of hot porridge, now growing thinner by the day, for the nieces and nephews. His words stay with me when I collect the bowls to wash by the stream, my hands making the stream cloudy. I see tiny minnows emerge out of the rocks to grab the bits of rice swimming with the current. I let my fingers linger in the water, allow them to dance for a bit in the direction of its flow as I breathe and breathe and breathe, knowing the preciousness of breath in this war where death waits shamelessly for both the young and old alike.

Deep inside my chest, in a place I have never felt before, a transformation is happening. Without my realizing it, the river of love that lives there for Mother, Maiv, Xis, my brothers, my sisters-in-law, and their children flows with a bright new current.

CHAPTER 7

Among Strangers, He Is My Friend

Like so much else in that dreaded war, my marriage happened without our knowing.

There was a pattern that we lived. Every few days, weeks, months, we'd relocate for our family's safety. The network of Hmong families allowed each unit to know when and where the Pathet Lao and North Vietnamese soldiers were traveling. My brothers decided when we'd move and where we would go next.

My marriage disrupted the course of our lives.

It was a regular evening. The dark had settled across the jungle. The night animals had just started their scurrying. We'd had our meal of roasted cassava. I loved the steam that rose from the fibrous white root. It recalled the roasted potatoes of my youth and the scent of sticky rice, which I had never liked but am now hungry for. The women and girls were laying out the old blankets for sleep when the men reported that we had to leave. We had been in the same place for nearly three months. There was news that a large group of enemy soldiers, hundreds, maybe even thousands, were planning an attack. They told us, always in a voice of urgency, to pack up and gather the children.

Mother, Maiv, and Xis started packing, stumbling in their haste. They were racing to roll together the bedding, to get the pots and pans into our baskets. All I kept thinking was, *If we leave tonight, Npis won't know where to find me in the morning. How am I ever going to see him again?*

Mother said, "Tswb, hurry up. We have no time to waste. Once you are done, go help your sisters-in-law gather the little ones."

I did as Mother asked. It didn't take me long to pull my few belongings together in my basket. I was about to go and help the sisters-in-law when I heard Npis's voice calling my name, a whisper across the chaos of the camp. It was now full dark. I didn't know where to focus in the havoc of our impending departure, but then I sensed a flicker of movement. I was that sensitive to his presence.

Npis stood half hidden by a towering tree at the edge of our sleeping area. His whole body was gesturing for me to come closer.

No one was paying attention to me. I walked far too quickly to him, stumbling in my haste. He stretched his hands for me. Without thinking, I put my own hands in his. It was our first touch. It felt natural and appropriate. My hands were cold and his were warm. He pulled me further into the growth behind the tree. He let go of my hands, suddenly self-conscious. My hands felt heavy away from his hold, like the blood had pooled in my fingers. They dangled uselessly at my sides.

He said, "Your family is going toward the east. Mine is headed south. We are going to go to Thailand. We are leaving Laos. My brothers have decided this war is over for the bigger world, and the longer we stay in this jungle, the fewer of us there will be."

He said, "I want to marry you. I have nothing to offer you. I am the youngest son of a family on the brink of starvation."

He said, "If you don't want to marry me, I am in no position to force you. My family has little, if anything, to offer as a bride-price for your hand. All I have is me."

His voice was grave, and the words were heavy as rocks. They fell with force on my heart. They shook me and my world.

All of a sudden, I felt confused. The voices of my family, the women looking for their children, grew loud. I struggled to focus.

I had a mother to think of. I had an older sister who moved too slowly for the regular rhythms of life, who would need lifelong care. I had a younger sister who admired me and looked toward me as an example. I had brothers. I had a family.

I looked down at our feet, though I saw nothing. I knew we were standing on top of leaves, brown and heavy, a mat on the floor of the jungle. Even though I couldn't see anything in the dark, I tried to focus on the fact that I had shoes. I knew he had none. I knew his feet, a younger version of his mother's, were thick and wide and rested on the ground in some elemental way that seemed to be one with the earth. I scrunched my toes, felt the instability of my own feet.

A wind blew and I swayed. Npis braced me with his hands on either side of my arms. I felt their heat through the fabric of my shirt. I wanted time to stop. I wanted the wind to settle. The evening to stand. I wanted this moment for myself, for always. But everything was reeling. I wanted to think about my dreams and responsibilities but all I felt was this fear that I would never see Npis again. My throat was thick with words I should say but didn't want to. Above all else, I didn't want to break his heart. That is what happened. After all these years, I know the truth: I fell into my marriage because I could not bear the thought of breaking Npis's heart even as pieces of my own shattered inside.

I whispered, "I don't know what to do. This is not a good time to make a decision like this."

He said, "Come with me. Marry me."

I allowed the firm hands that held my arms to turn me toward the thick darkness of the jungle, to lead me away from my family, all in a disarray, all preparing to run once again so that we could be together tomorrow, so the soldiers wouldn't take us and kill us, or worse, make us want to die. I left my family, a fumbling step at a time in a night so dark that I lost sight of all the world, but for those hands on my flesh. Come the morning light, my mother would see that I was no longer by her side.

In another life, away from the pain of a war, perhaps we could have been married in a normal fashion. Npis might have come to my house with his family, and they could have offered for my hand in a respectable fashion. They might have come bearing a bride-price and promises of my well-being. If that dream is too lofty, perhaps I could have happily walked with him on that single dirt road that led away from my childhood village, the place where rivers meet, the tall wall of grass on either side waving us into a shared life. We would have the hours between my village and his to talk of a life together, dream our way into the future. At his village, there'd be a ceremony to welcome me into his family, a chicken waved across our bowed heads, my spirit freed from my ancestral home and welcomed into his. His family representatives would have sent news of our marriage to my own family. The appropriate elders and clan leaders would gather, and the ancestral spirits notified. All of it would have been so different.

In this life, the life we live, he took me home to his family camp. On the way, we were afraid of the soldiers coming so we ran and hid whenever there was a noise coming close. I felt shame and sadness that I had not gone back to the camp to tell Mother or said a thing to my sisters. I could not even bear to think of my brothers. How concerned and scared they would be when they found out that I was no longer in the camp. As we walked further away, I grew more uncertain. What had I done? There were points when my feet halted on the jungle floor and I looked behind me at the curtain of darkness that enveloped us, unsure of how to return. His hands pulled at mine each time I hesitated. I stumbled forward, his hands and my errant heart my only guides in the night. I was sixteen years old. Npis was nineteen. We had done something reckless and dangerous: in a time of great despair and uncertainty, we'd chosen to carve out a life together that aspired to a future.

When we got close to his family camp, I could smell the lingering fires. The first person we met was his mother. Npis's mother was out looking for him with a flashlight. When she saw that his hands held another's, she stopped and stood very still, the light on our faces. We were like children caught doing something wrong, something with grave consequences.

He said, "Mother."

She said slowly, "You've brought a wife home."

It was she who found a thin rooster to perform the age-old ritual of welcoming me into his family. Near the light of a small fire, I saw the cluster of banana leaf tents that made up the family's encampment. Out of everywhere, little children with messy hair gathered to look at us, some wiping their eyes from sleep. Men and women, mostly young, stood close by and welcomed me into their midst. Usually it was the father's job to perform the marriage blessing, but in Npis's family his mother had long taken on the role of both mother and father. Npis's mother, my new mother-in-law, waved the chicken over our bowed heads. I'd untangled my hands from Npis's. They were now clasped in front of me, gripping each other. My heart pounded. I had heard the familiar words before when each of my older brothers had brought their wives into our home.

Npis's mother's deep voice said the words that severed me from my ancestral place in the Moua Clan and settled me as a member of the Yang Clan. I knew she was a respected shaman and medicine woman, like my mother. The blessing she offered on that day, she did so with force and intention. Whoever I was, wherever I came from, it was clear to me that Npis's mother was anchoring us together to live this life as one.

She chanted the old words, made new again for us on that tumultuous night:

Today, I bless my son and his new wife not toward ill health or misfortune. I bless them not against the spirits of wealth or prosperity. I bless them not against pens full of animals or harvests of rice grains. Today, I bless my son and his new wife against ill health and misfortune, against disappearances and disturbances, against the falling of tears and the swelling of fears, against big problems and harsh words, against the worries of the heart and the failures of hard work. Let these things disappear into the holes where dragons dwell. I'm blessing you and burning your future sorrows into the flames of a fire so that your ears will not hear and your eyes will not see heartache. I'm blessing you and sending your future sadnesses into the currents of rivers so that they travel far beyond the edge of darkness, that cloak that keeps the world cold. From today into the future, may my son and his new wife in their shared life eat of joy and drink of generosity. Today, may their life together take them high as the heavens, fill their lives with children and their homes with love. May my son and his new wife live a life free from ill health, live to a hundred years without exhaustion.

That night, Npis's huge family made us a meal on the hot embers of their small fire. Each offered what food they had to me graciously with open palms. I could not eat. I missed my mother.

All around me, everyone referred to Npis's mother as Mother.

I knew the age-old expectation that I was now to call his mother mine. I would not fight it. But inside, I felt I had jumped off a steep cliff.

For the first time that night, my own mother was no longer *Mother*.

In the circle of strangers who I knew surrounded me only because of their voices and their breaths, I decided that I would never give up my mother's place in my life. That in fact, she would become more fully mine because now I was also someone else's daughter. In all my immaturity, I knew that some bonds had to be reinforced or else they would break, and among them, the most important relationship I had ever known, mine with my mother.

Npis's mother moved around me, talking to different men whom I recognized as Npis's brothers. She wanted to make sure that someone would go and find my family group to let them know where I was. Though customs dictated we wait three days, she said we were in a war and if one of her daughters had disappeared suddenly, she would want to know that she was safe. She didn't want my mother to worry unnecessarily. Hearing this concern for my mother from Npis's mother made me feel smaller than I was. I felt shame pushing my neck low. I tried to dig into the soft jungle floor with the toe of one of my canvas shoes.

Around me, people called me Nyab Npis, "Npis's wife." I had called all of my sisters-in-law in relation to their husbands for as long I've known them. It was not strange. It was customary. But I felt alone all the same answering to these words, two words pieced together, in place of my name, Tswb.

I heard a multitude of voices and perspectives that first night and the many others to come. Each time, it reminded me of my status in the family as a newcomer, showed me how little I knew of this family's history and circumstances. It brought forth waves of loneliness that took my breath away.

Nyab Npis's skin is as smooth and pale as an egg. You get skin like that only if you have been afforded time and space away from the hot sun in the fields.

I hear that Nyab Npis knows how to read and write. Before the war reached us, she spent much of her days in school, not in the fields.

Nyab Npis has a reputation for not smiling often. There were people who worked to give her joy who received nothing in response.

Nyab Npis's hands and feet are so small and soft looking. She has not had to exercise them much, to work them hard.

Nyab Npis still has shoes.

There is a strand of beads in Nyab Npis's hair.

Nyab Npis is so fragile. In these times, Npis needs a strong woman by his side, we need a strong member in this family.

When the voices died down and the fire became little more than embers in the night, Npis and I slept side by side in a small banana leaf–covered area in the circle of everyone.

I whispered, "How many people are in your family group?"

Npis whispered back, "We have eighty-one. Including you now, there's eighty-two."

I whispered, "There are so many of you."

Npis whispered, "We'd like to keep it that way."

He shushed me without meaning to.

The banana leaves sheltered us, but I knew we slept beneath the greater protection of the tall canopy of the leaves high above in the night. Whatever light there might have been from the moon and the stars in the sky, beneath everything, where we were, I felt only the depth of night. On a thin, scratchy blanket, a stranger to my back, I missed my bedroll. My blanket. My mother. My mother more than anything else. But I made no noises when the tears leaked from my eyes. There were too many ears listening in the dark, too many eyes for me to see myself through in the morning. A breath escaped. Npis's right hand reached for my left. He squeezed lightly, just enough for me to know he was there, that he knew that I was lonely for the life I'd left behind.

He whispered, "I'm your friend."

It was those words that allowed sleep to visit me that night and countless others. I told my quivering heart, "I'm with my friend."

My husband was my friend. He will remain my friend throughout the course of our long life together, a friend who will change on me and with me, who will become weak even as I become strong. When the sorrows of our shared life grew thorns that poked into the bubble of our love and in the moments when we both fell hard to the earth, grasped for safety nets that were not there, it was always the reminder that when we rose again, if we rose again, we would still choose to be friends that kept our stories chasing each other, walking beside each other, waiting for one another.

CHAPTER 8

Parting Gifts

My mother was not mad at me when we visited on the third morn-ing of our marriage. She missed me even more than I had missed her. It was apparent that she had not slept much in the time since I'd been away. The worry lines were deep on her forehead and either side of her mouth. The area underneath her eyes was dark and the space above them, beneath her brow, was hollow. My family had made a new camp several hours away from where we had all been together. They were now in the middle of a towering bamboo grove. She waited for me at its edge. The moment she saw me, she called out to me, by name, "Tswb."

My mother ran to me and I to her. She pulled me close. Her familiar smell, dry leaves and the smoke of countless fires, brought forth the cries I had struggled to contain at Npis's family camp for the last three days. I cried like a child who had done something wrong. I felt like a child who had misbehaved and in doing so had injured the people closest to them. I wanted to say sorry and explain to her that I had no idea what I had done or what to do next, but she shushed me and pulled the hair away from my face. She tucked the strands behind my ear, smoothed them with the flats of her palms, again and again, then she stepped back away from me. I was now wearing an outfit that Npis's mother had given me, an outfit that identified me as a member of their clan. Our own family outfits were not that different. Instead of the traditional purple turban, we preferred the hats with balls of red yarn stitched to the edge. I was wearing, for the first time in my life, a traditional Hmong outfit that my mother's hands had not sewn. She wiped away her tears and gestured for all of us to walk forward into the bamboo grove.

My second brother, Looj, came to talk to me. He told me that when they realized I was gone, he went searching for me. He couldn't find me anywhere. In the morning, they noticed that one of the family dogs had also gone missing. In the late afternoon, the female dog came bounding after the family, but I was nowhere in sight. He had never felt so bereft in his life. He pulled me tight and said, "The most important thing is my sister is alive." He gave me three rings, all silver, that he had made with his own hands.

As Npis and the representative members of his family met with my own, the women in my family pulled me aside. Xis stood to the edge of the group. She was suddenly shy with me in a way she'd never been. Her light brown eyes studied my face, seeing changes I had not known were there. Maiv acted normally, coming close, wiping the fabric on my right arm with her slow hands, telling me in her slow way, "Tswb, you didn't listen to Mother. You should have told us where you were going. We were so worried until the strange men came to tell us you had married. You could have saved us a lot of worrying. I was afraid for you. I have been afraid before with the other sisters. I didn't think I'd have to be afraid for you, too." I nodded because she was right. I said, "I am so sorry. I was not thinking straight. I'm sorry I made you afraid."

She said, "Npib used to do that to me; you know this."

I could only nod, pull my gaze low.

My mother waved away my apologies. Her tears fell for my actions, but her words supported me in them: "I knew you'd eventually marry someone of your choosing. It happened at a most unpredictable moment but isn't that the life we live? Don't apologize. Make your actions count."

She said, "If your father were here, he would have many words to offer you. But he is not. You have me and your brothers. Your brothers will tell you all the things that have always been told to Hmong women about loving your new family as if it is the one you were born to, how his mother is your mother now, and his brothers yours, his sisters, too. They will tell you to live modestly and honestly, to think about your words before you say them, and for you to act with love and kindness as your trusted guides. They will tell you that you are a woman now and your job will be to stand where Npis's mother stood, accept her responsibilities and serve the Yang Clan. These things have all been said before. There is truth to them, of course. But they are men's words. I have only one thing to say to you, Tswb."

She took a quivering breath, a steadying breath. "I want you to understand that all your life, I've wanted good luck for you."

It seemed there was more she wanted to say but couldn't. My mother looked away from me. I said to her profile, the high bridge of her nose, the wrinkles that curved about her mouth, "Mother, you don't have to say everything right now. I'll visit you often. We can talk then if it is easier."

My mother shook her head. I saw the veins in her neck. I watched my mother swallow down her words. I saw that she was now even thinner than she had been just a few days ago. A sister-in-law said to her, "Mother, it's okay. Let's not burden the young with our worries. Let's send our Tswb off in the best way we can."

My family sent me into marriage with far more than I will ever be able to return to them—in this life or another. My mother, from the depths of her basket, the vessel for the contents of that long-ago chest of prized possessions, produced a traditional xauv, the heavy, silver draping necklace that Hmong women wear on our finest days. She said that she'd had it especially made for me and had carried it for many years, for the day I might marry. She gave me embroidery she'd sewn, pieces and parcels I might one day pull together into a traditional Hmong outfit. Sitting in that circle, accepting the gifts my mother had saved for me, I could only think: *How heavy her basket must have been*. How come I had not asked, even once, to help her carry it across the stretch of these long years?

I saw Npis's shoulders drop with each gift my family presented me as part of my bridal dowry. The bride-price his family had come up with was paltry in comparison. At some point, he stopped making eye contact with me entirely. I wanted him to see that I was entering this marriage with strong foundations from my family—even if the world we lived in was an unsteady one.

That evening, at dinner, I sat beside him on the thick trunk of a fallen bamboo. He said nothing to me. I did not know what to say to his silence. I refused to apologize for the bounty of my family's love. I banked the tears that swelled up inside me, waves pushing at the surface of who I wanted desperately to be in the moment: a more mature version of myself. I flattened my lips and bit them on the inside to contain the cries that I knew had the power to crack me open. This was not how I had expected my wedding day to go.

At some point, my mother joined us, and said to Npis, "Tswb is a very light eater. She's picky. I know how hard it is to find food in this jungle. But I wanted to tell you this. All of her life with me, I've worked to give her the more tender morsels. Now, she's under your care."

I was embarrassed by my mother's words. His family was nearly starving. Although my family was not wealthy, it was clear that we were doing better than their family group. And yet, something held me back from stopping my mother. I looked directly at Npis. As I had wanted him to bear witness to the gifts my family was giving me, I wanted him to hear my mother's words, and understand the depth of her love for me. I wanted him to know that I had been born and raised with love and that my life was valued by those who knew me best.

One of Npis's older brothers was close by and heard my mother's words. He glanced at me, a hint of anger and judgment sparking his gaze. I did not look his way again that day and would avoid it for many more days, unsure of how to respond.

Npis kept his own eyes down, his hands clasped in between his knees. He refused to look at my mother, not even once. He nodded his head slowly three times to acknowledge that he'd heard her words. He said nothing. In his silence, it occurred to me then that he might see me now as a burden and a responsibility. The thought made me uncomfortable.

My mother sat down beside me. She picked up my right hand. Her fingers were longer than mine. Her hands were thin. The skin above them was tinted with spots of gray. She enveloped my small hand in both of hers. Her hold was dry. I leaned into her shoulder, and she held me for a moment so I could close my eyes.

I don't know what I thought marriage would be like. I was not a girl who lived her life dreaming of a wedding day. What person imagines their family fleeing through the jungle? What person imagines a life where black balls of smoke rain down from the sky? What human being imagines that this is how their great love story will begin? A husband, shy and uncertain, a husband wearing his best clothes that were little more than rags, a husband with a pair of flip-flops his mother had found from somewhere, nodding before the words of your mother, unable and unwilling to make a promise he knows he can't keep. I thought: *At least he isn't a liar.*

Into the warmth of my mother's shoulder, I shook my head. She whispered words into my ear: "Npis is young, too. He'll grow with you. You'll both learn how to live together—even without promises spoken out loud. What matters is that you are with the person you want to be with. Everything else is just that."

To both Npis and me, she said, "Marriage is not easy. Give yourself opportunities to try and try again, to be good to each other."

We spent the customary night at my family's camp. We brushed our teeth side by side at a cold mountain stream where the water rippled over the rocks like sheer fabric. We dipped our worn toothbrushes into a small, blackened pot filled with a slippery concoction that my mother had made. I'd used it countless times. In fact, I'd helped her peel the bananas, thrown the peels into the fire, watched them grow dark as charcoals, fished them out with sticks, rinsed them, then boiled them in water until the water grew slippery like soap. Where there were mouth sores, the liquid caused pain, but it also kept our teeth healthy and clean. Npis and I didn't talk, both of us administering our toothbrushes with vigor, and then gurgling the clear water from the stream in our mouths, swishing the liquid to the front and back, from one side to the other, rinsing our toothbrushes with exaggerated care and attention before coming back to the circle of my family.

In the dawn, we would set out for Npis's family's hiding place, a cave. In the light of day, my family would move further away. The only reason they had stopped in this bamboo grove was to settle my marriage as best they could with Npis's family. That night, my mother brought me my woven basket, filled with my other outfits, my remaining shoes.

She said, "You'll need these things. If you get hungry away from me, trade these outfits for food."

That night, Npis and I slept close to the embers of my family's fire on the bedroll I had so missed. He said nothing to me. He kept his hands clasped behind his head and his feet crossed at the ankles. Beneath the rustling leaves of the tall bamboo trees, we both looked toward a sliver of sky above us. A single star sat in that window of darkness, shining its light down. By the light of the tempered fire, I saw my young husband with his eyes closed so tightly that the line in between his eyes was creased like a ravine. His breathing was shallow and uneven. Somehow in the quiet of my family, knowing my mother, my sisters, my brothers, and their wives and children were near, I fell into a deep, comfortable sleep. I felt their love around me. It was everything I wanted: my new husband and me with my family. It was as whole as my heart would be—until decades later when we were grandparents and our children and grandchildren visited and filled the house of our future with their sleep, their snores, their twists and turns.

The next morning, we parted with the rise of the sun. I could tell my husband could not wait to leave my family group behind. I could tell he was impatient. My whole family could see his eagerness to depart. He couldn't hide how his feet shifted from side to side. They allowed our parting to be brief. I promised my mother I would visit her—no matter where she was. She nodded and told me, when I wouldn't let go of her hands, what she'd spent my life telling me: "Tswb, hurry."

We visited my family several more times before that final moment when the parting between my mother and me was forever. Each time we visited, we had to travel further to get to them. The families were both moving in different directions, scaling mountainous terrain, sliding down slippery ravines into green valleys crowded with growth. Each time we visited, Npis was quiet and awkward. He felt he was among strangers. I told him, to be with him, I lived among strangers. He got defensive. I got angry. We walked sometimes as far apart as we could on the trails through the jungle on our way to the rivers to bathe, to the abandoned fields to forage for food, to visit my family and to return to his. I walked behind him as slow as possible. He walked in front of me as furiously and fast as he could. When I lost sight of him, I'd grow scared. As my heartbeat quickened, I'd turn a corner and he'd be there, sulking but waiting for me, standing to one side of the road, arms crossed over his chest, eyes to the growth by his side, examining the greenery.

Npis didn't touch me for the first month of our marriage. He, in fact, helped me when I got my first period weeks after our marriage and I was embarrassed and uncertain about how to proceed. It was he who told his mother. It was his mother who gave me the old swatches of cloth to put in between my legs to hold the blood. It was the only period I ever had in that jungle because within the next month, I got pregnant. Npis, despite all his angst and his worries because of our union, was kind to me in the moments when we were together and not arguing, and somehow to my young heart that was what mattered most.

One afternoon, after we'd gone to a mountain stream to catch fish, and chanced upon a fallen tree, when I wanted to walk on it, he walked beside me, holding one of my hands to balance me. When I took a sudden step and the wet, mildewy bark of the tree came off and I slipped, it was his warm arms that kept me from the ground. He laughed and then lifted me up so I could continue my journey on the same fallen log. What could have been a stupid moment of unnecessary hurt became silly fun, a risk we both chose to take for the sake of laughter.

On another occasion, when he came across a field of dried cucumber vines, he found several edible cucumbers the size of children's arms and legs. One of them, the youngest and most tender one, he saved for me. I found it among the clothes in my basket later that day. He didn't like drawing attention to such acts. In the dark when I thanked him, he waved away my gratitude and shook his head. *It's nothing. Don't make anything of it.*

Whenever his mother had a bit of extra food to offer and called her youngest children close, Npis refused to join them. He wouldn't partake in anything that was not shared with the rest of the family. He never commented about it, but I saw how he moved further away from whatever thing his mother had foraged or found.

And yet: each of those few times we visited my family, we argued. They were the only extended times when we were truly alone and away from others. There were lots of feelings to air and observations to share. I wanted to know because I'd never heard of such nicknames before, "Why do your nieces and nephews have such bad nicknames? Who calls their kids Charcoal and Doggie?" Npis immediately got defensive: "And what does your family call your nieces and nephews?" I'd go on to share the very normal names our family gave each child, names like Cloud and Wind. Npis would act like I was saying we were better than them. We'd argue.

As had become our custom, we were arguing on our final visit to my family group. I believe that if either of us had known it would be the final visit, we wouldn't have argued. Now, neither of us can recall what that argument was about. All we remember is how our hearts had simmered inside our chests. All I can remember is how I was so full of frustration, and how I thought seriously about just staying with my family forever, making the kind of decision that my sister Npib would have made. *How is this man worthy of my time? How is my sacrifice by being with the strangers of his family even rewarded except with anger?* I could come up with plenty of solid reasons for hating Npis in the heat of my frustrations. But then I'd have to contend with certain realities: Did I want to be a divorcée? Did I want to let the beginning of the child in my womb grow up without a father? And the answer was always the same, spoken to me in the words of my mother: "What matters is that you are with the person you want to be with." On that day, we were like angry squirrels, chasing each other with our words, up one trail, down the next.

My family was camping close to the side of a mountain, along the bend of a river. When we got to its edge, I was deflated. My cheeks were hot from the harshness of the terrain and my feet throbbing. The canvas shoes had fallen apart, and I was now wearing the pair of flip-flops. Their thin soles were no match for the landscape.

I had to put up an act of joy at the sight of my family. Xis ran up to me and held me by the waist. She was fourteen and full of excitement. She had spent the morning and afternoon catching small fish with the nieces and nephews. They'd gotten enough to steam for dinner. I was thankful that her previous shyness was gone. Although I was married and no longer with the family, she was coming to terms with the fact that I was still her sister and would always be so. My mother came out at Xis's excitement and greeted both of us. I spent the afternoon with the women in my family, shelling dry corn they'd foraged from some other abandoned field. The family was now out of rice. They had started eating corn mush—just like Npis's family. Although the situation was growing dire, our talk that day was happy.

Near nightfall, as my mother was headed away from camp to get water to make corn mush to accompany the steamed fish Xis and the children had caught for dinner, a group of young men ran into the group with news: a large contingent of North Vietnamese soldiers— estimates ranged from a thousand to ten thousand—were on their way to corner the Hmong. Their counterparts in the air were bombing the jungle indiscriminately and had planted regiments with guns to await scattering families. These warnings were not new. Though the war with the Americans had ended in 1975 when the communist government had taken over Laos, the search for Hmong folk who refused to be reeducated, who continued to fight on behalf of the old royal regime, or Hmong folk who were simply fleeing genocide, continued. Npis talked to them earnestly. He walked over and whispered to me that if we didn't leave immediately, the enemy soldiers would cut us off and we would be unable to return to his family. My mother had stopped at all the commotion. She stood, with the water pail on her back, and looked at us.

I wanted to go and say goodbye. I wanted to stay the night and risk everything in the morning. We'd heard similar news before. This was no reason for us to end the visit to my family early. We hadn't even eaten yet. Xis was excited for us to share the steamed fish. I was hungry.

But Npis would not hear any of it. We started to argue right there in front of everyone, something we had not done before.

My oldest brothers intervened. They said, "Now is not a good time for an argument. We need to proceed with caution." One of them said, "Brother-in-law Npis is right. You both should go home now if you are to reunite safely with the family there."

I looked to my sisters to help me make a decision. Should I fight to stay with them or leave? Maiv was tending to the family's fire. She knelt close to the ground, blowing hard into a piece of smoking wood. Her cheeks ballooned in and out, her mouth like a funnel, seemingly unaware of the news that had befallen the camp or the noise of our argument. Xis had a little niece on her lap, was tickling the girl with light fingers though her eyes were on me. They were helpless in my despair. Even as a child, Xis hated confrontations, heated arguments, outbursts of anger and frustration. They made her afraid. I could see the fear in the width of her eyes.

I said through tight lips, "Fine. We will do what you think is best, Npis."

Npis made some poor apology to my brothers about our argument and told them we'd visit again as soon as it was safe.

He took hold of my right hand and started walking away. I struggled to free myself. I watched my mother's eyebrows raise high and her mouth open in concern. If there were words that she wanted to say to me, they never surfaced. I let myself be led away, thinking, *We'll fight this out on the way.* I turned toward Npis, jerked hard and freed my captive hand, walked on my own feet away from my mother. Like all the other times in my life when I had been angry at my mother or I was trying to hide my hurt from her, I walked away believing my mother would be there when I returned, believing that I would return to her when I was ready, and it would be all right. I believed then that there would be no lifetime in which such a return would be impossible.

There was no more fight. We walked away together. I refused to hurry. Npis refused to leave me, on edge from the news. A gust of wind blew, shuffling the leaves overhead. We moved slowly and stiffly, feet by feet away from everyone who mattered to me. The whole time I was hungry and angry. My mouth, on its own accord, was a straight line, tightening with each step we took. I was walking toward a new reality, one in which I would never see my mother again. I didn't know then that I was dying, that death was not the only thing that could tear apart the love between two people, that wars and the decisions we make in them sever us from the people whose love holds safe our very lives. With each step, the dark grew around and inside me.

It wasn't until we made it safely back to the cave where Npis's family was hiding that the image of my mother standing there, on her way to the stream, made the world around me waver. I saw her, a once-tall woman, standing in surprise, her back slightly bent, strands of her hair falling from the scarf that she wrapped around her head. In memory, I saw how distraught she had been. A wave of nausea hit me. I stumbled toward the sound of water, only there were no rivers by Npis's family camp.

Someone asked, "What's wrong?"

Another person said, "Nyab Npis is pregnant."

My world shook with the sudden fear that the moment I had left behind could be the final time I would have with my mother, the scene I would carry, the last time I would have of being close enough to run to her, to hold her fast, and never let go. I reeled with the force of this possibility; the ground underneath me opened up, revealing all the goodbyes I had buried, the ones I would never be able to return to.

CHAPTER 9

Mothering

I had lived my life like my mother's child. By the time I came along, she'd lost daughters to forces beyond her control, but I had never lost her. In the months after our leaving, I had to learn how to live without my mother, not because I was an orphan but for the bullets that flew in between us, this sad love story that I was now tangled in, this new family that I had now entered.

In the days after I left my mother standing there in the clearing, mouth open, eyes full of questions, I started dreaming about her.

In each dream, my mother was healthy and well. In each dream, my mother was mothering me, pulling out a sweet yam from the ashes of a fire, and blowing at the crusty, burnt skin, sweet juice oozing. In each dream, my mother was offering me a drink from a pot of boiled water, admonishing me for drinking directly from streams. In each dream, she wiped the dirt from my face with light fingers, took strands of my hair and tucked them behind my ear. In each dream, before the moment of waking up, I'd start to cry, my heart twisting inside itself, the syrup of the baked yam on my fingers nothing more than the salt of my own tears.

Right up to the moment the child inside me started moving, I thought more about a reunion with my mother than any other possibility of a future. Even as my thoughts traveled in one direction, the forces of life pulled me in another.

My pregnancy happens the normal way. One night in a run of nights, in the dark of sleep, Npis fumbles for me, feels for me, and I start feeling my way toward him in return. Our hands skim the length of arms and legs, shoulders and backs. We grapple in the dark with our clothing, the tensions in our lives, the war raging around us, and the hunger in our bodies. The place where our baby was conceived I knew was far from normal; she happened on a far-flung night in the depths of a dark jungle, in a crevice of earth, fallen leaves underneath us, twigs poking my backside, the wings of birds and bats flapping from tree to tree overhead.

I was five months pregnant when I felt her move inside me, and I knew that what was a pregnancy would become a person. Though my hands were small, each time I heard a rocket slice the air or felt the earth beneath me shake, I placed a hand over the child I carried and held my breath hoping to salvage hers.

One moonlit night, the family was traveling across yet another river. The Americans had built a bridge of concrete across the glimmering water when their troops still inhabited the country. As we were about to cross, one of Npis's older brothers thought he saw a shadow move. He signaled with his hand for the family to retreat, a push at the air for us to backtrack, but it was too late. Fire flew across the distance between us as gunshots rang out. We scattered. Npis and I rushed for the river below, our feet slipping down the rocky incline. We hid underneath the bridge for a moment. The concrete over our heads created an echo chamber for what transpired above. Our breaths ragged like the night now punctured by wounds. I had been dragging along a sickle, a precious tool when walking through the thick foliage. It fell at the first sight of ambush. Both my hands went to my belly. I clung to the child inside me. At some point in the continued commotion, Npis forced us to move. Fire met our movements. Npis grunted but did not stop pushing at me to walk, run, and flee.

Later, in an alcove with the family members who'd survived the attack, I examined Npis's legs. His pant legs were both torn. Blood was seeping from the hole on his lower left leg. I was afraid at what I would find. My hands shook so hard Npis had to rip up the thin fabric by himself, to remove the soaked cloth to reveal what was underneath: a bullet had grazed his shin. I could see the white of his bone amid the red flesh, the deep purple of clotted blood. He said, "It's not broken." I could only nod and move helplessly to the side when his mother came to clean the wound and dress it, pressing pounded medicinal leaves to stop the flow of blood.

My own mother had been a medicine woman, but I had learned nothing from her of the healing plants. I realized there in that moment that here was another mother I might learn from. I wasn't interested in being a medicine woman myself, but I was about to become a mother, and I saw all around me the ways in which children could get hurt.

For the first time, I studied my mother-in-law, who was now too busy and preoccupied to notice my gaze. She touched Npis's bloody leg with efficiency. His mother, her short curly hair pulled back from her face and tied with an old rubber band. I noticed the strength of her hands, how straight and steady her fingers were as they pressed the leaves into the face of the angry wound. I saw how she looked down on him with concern and care but also resolve. I studied how she tied a length of fabric she'd retrieved from her woven basket around his leg and said, "The bleeding will stop, and it will start healing. Every night, I'll boil an herbal broth for you to clean the wound with, so it does not get infected." Since I had married Npis, I had not seen her touch him. She now placed a hand on his head, and said in her deep voice, "You'll be all right. Your father's spirit will protect you. The ancestors will not let you die in this jungle."

My husband, who had been so adamant to prove himself a man in the early days of our marriage, was rendered a boy by his mother's touch. He nodded his head and softened beneath her hands. Even his lips turned down like a child's. Like her, he had forgotten that I was there and observing.

He said, "Ua li, Niam." As you say, Mother.

As my mother-in-law had said, Npis's leg, bathed with her warm herbal broth each night, healed in the coming days. The wound never got infected. Ridges of skin grew into each other; a scar surfaced where no hair would ever grow again across his shin, like a rise of hills, merging and converging, pushing each other up to form an uneven rise of rounded flesh. For Npis, the scar would be a reminder of the war, but for me it was a show of the power of a mother's love for her child, her call to his dead father and the ancestors to protect him.

In the days after, I asked, "Mother, what did you use to make the herbal press for Npis's wound?"

She said, "I used a combination of pounded pennywort and the leaves from a cinnamon tree."

I said, "They worked well."

She said, "Yes, they do."

I didn't ask her to teach me more and she didn't offer. I didn't know it but I was already beginning to accept that in this new life, she would be present as my mother had been, to help care for us and our children in the moments when we needed her. Npis's mother was a woman who didn't engage in long conversations.

I secretly studied her when she was not looking at me, this older woman who was now caught in the crossroads of everything. She was a different kind of mother from my own—less gentle and less soft. She didn't despair about her clothing and didn't pay particular attention to her appearance. My mother wanted to be clean but never too adorned, wanted to be respectable but was keenly aware of the volume of her dress. Npis's mother did not have much by way of clothing. She moved between several mismatched articles: black traditional wide-legged Hmong pants and a shirt secured in front with a safety pin or an old brown sarong and a dark-colored polyester shirt with white buttons. Around her wide waist, she wore old sashes—once red and green but both colors now gray. She didn't talk much with her daughters-in-law but sometimes joked with her sons and grandchildren. When she laughed, it was a full laugh, mouth open wide, single tooth standing tall. Unlike my own mother, who moved quickly and carefully, Npis's mother was slow and deliberate around the camp. She didn't raise her voice, but she didn't quiet it either—even when the soldiers were close, the volume of her voice remained steady. She was a constant figure in her children's lives, a fixture in all our lives.

I realized that my own mother had also been a steadying force in the lives of my siblings and me, that long before she had her own children, she was a stable presence for my father's. I thought to myself: *A mother must be a dependable presence in her children's lives.*

From the other sisters-in-law I learned other lessons for mothering, possibilities for who I might become once the child inside me was ready to enter the world. Despite the fact that we were in a war, I knew that mothers across time have worked toward only one thing: the survival of their children. But the ways in which they went about the work were different and singular.

One of the sisters-in-law was plainspoken, and the way she spoke to her children was no different than the way she spoke to any other person in the family: gruff and direct. The second one had a singsong voice but she didn't partake in the tender components of motherhood, the blowing of a nose, the wiping of a dirt-stricken face. She sang her commands for her children to attend to themselves. At dinner, she practiced the art of rationing their food like an impartial party. Every time there was a chase from enemy soldiers, she wondered aloud if she should give her youngest opium so the child would go to sleep; each time, her husband chastised her and she agreed with a toss of her shoulder: "Don't blame me if . . ." The third was soft and her children clung to her arms and legs, prohibiting her movements but also giving her comfort. She sniffed a head. She touched a shoulder, tickled a belly, rubbed a sore foot. From each, I saw a different style of mothering.

Another brother's wife was a nagging kind of mother. As we prepared camp each night, her loud voice rang out, naming her children one by one and the tasks that they were supposed to be doing: "Kub, get water! Nplej, boil the water! Vws, measure out the corn! Npaub, wash your little sister's hair!" Each child, like most of the children in that war, attended to their chores like little adults, knowing they had a role to play in each other's survival. For all the unnecessary nagging, each time one of her children stumbled or fell, she wept before their own tears ran. When one had a fever, a chill, diarrhea, or stomach cramps, she lamented and made promises that she'd never nag again once they recovered. She offered chickens for their sick spirits, and promised pigs, goats, and cows—when the war was over—and burned incense sticks to the ancestors, pleading with them to keep her children safe from bullets, from bombs, from bad spirits and other forces, natural and unnatural.

Yet another sister-in-law made it a point to name the trees and animals of the jungle for her children at every opportunity. Without books or pencils, she taught them the names for flowers, the scent of each bloom, and the feel of petals against their skin. She let the children help her cut through the thick trunk of banana trees and feel the sticky sap between the layers, play with their fingers wet with strings of muck that connected and formed webs. Along little mountain streams, she allowed them to play in the mud, re-creating household objects from before the war: makeshift brooms for sweeping houses that no longer existed, dusting pans for picking up debris in a life full of it. I knew that none of the sisters-in-law had been to school, and yet I saw her as a worthy teacher for her children.

In those months of my pregnancy, I watched them all closely. I took a keen interest in the words they shared with their children, in the nature of their touches, and I tried to gauge their effectiveness. In the end, I concluded that the fairest way to judge a mother was through her children, how healthy and content they were, how they laughed and played when the immediate threat of death felt further away. The children in Npis's family, unlike the ones from my own family group, were more ragged but also more eager to slip into laughter or play; they had more playmates and a larger circle of adults to keep them safe.

In moments of danger, any adult with a free hand selected a child, threw them onto their backs, and ran—regardless of parentage. Though of course there were preferences and nicknames. Sticky was a girl of four. She was thin and wiry and clung to the different bodies that carried her easily. Floppy was a challenge because although she too was four, she had no ability to cling or duck from the swaying tree branches; her body sagged in one direction and then the other. Little was short and stocky, older and heavier but helpful in that he could assist the individual who carried him by looking back and around and shout out reports of dangers. Red was particularly fearless, silent and brave at every turn. Crier did nothing but cry and whimper. The adults talked of each child, using their nicknames, with humor and understanding.

I observed Npis's family, the circle of mothers I was surrounded by, and saw how they took care of each other, without seeming order, without the seriousness with which my own family conducted ourselves in our flight into the jungle. I made promises to myself about the kind of mother I would be. Often, I whispered the promises to the baby inside me like a secret, cognizant that she might not hear or understand but wanting to practice being a communicative mother—a little like the teacher mother. I didn't want to be a nagging mother and yet I admired how well behaved and thoughtful her children often were, asking if they could help those around them and each other with loving intention. I saw the importance of physical touch and how it created a magical net between a mother and her child. I wanted to be a mother with light hands who could use a needle and take out thorns from her children's fingers gently without causing fear. I wanted . . .

I wanted to be, even with all these examples, the kind of mother my mother had been to me. I wanted to be well put together like her, to offer my children a quiet pride in the way I cared for myself. I wanted to be the kind of mother a child would always remember as a fountain of love and care.

There were many moments when I wanted to share these thoughts with Npis, but it didn't seem appropriate or fair because I saw how all the women around me were not their dream versions of themselves as mothers, just their most basic and elemental, the parts of them that had survived this war so far.

In the quiet moments when my child moved beneath the warmth of my hands, I whispered to her that I would be the kind of mother to offer her sweet roasted yams with sugary juices running.

CHAPTER 10

The Baby's Arrival

I was too shy to name my daughter when she came. All the preparing I thought I had been doing by looking at other mothers and making choices about how I would be disappeared the moment she was in my arms. I was caught in a state of disbelief. Had I ever held a baby so young? Had I ever been charged with another's survival? How would I even keep her alive, let alone be to her all the things my mother had been to me?

A month before I gave birth, one of Npis's older brothers' wives had also given birth. She gave birth to a baby boy. Mine was a daughter. When she gave birth, we had all rejoiced at the coming of the little boy with a dark birthmark on his behind, like a spill of deep bark juice. We were new arrivals, the women and children, to an enemy camp. His arrival was the first sign that there was a future beyond the pain of the separation in the jungle when we were surrounded by Pathet Lao and North Vietnamese soldiers and the men had to leave.

In a movie of my life, this is one of the moments that will make me tremble and shake. It had been a quiet day, no warnings or alarms. We had washed our clothes. They hung over bushes to dry in the damp jungle. Suddenly, one of the older children yelled, "Enemy soldiers are coming!" There was no time to escape. The soldiers were quickly descending on our group. The men knew that if they stayed, the soldiers would open fire and everyone would be killed indiscriminately. If they left, we would be a group of women and children and there was a chance that we would be taken as prisoners of war. We'd heard news of this happening before with other groups. How some women and children were kept alive as bait for their husbands and brothers in enemy camps and villages. We were more useful alive than slaughtered as traitors to the new communist regime in power. So, the men scattered, and when the enemy soldiers called out their positions, Npis's mother waved a white flag of surrender above our crouched heads. We were like elephants, all of us surrounding the children at our center, my hands flat over my pregnant belly.

The situation in the family had shifted dramatically. We were no longer a family group running through the jungle away from the soldiers. We became a group of women and children led by Npis's mother. We became captives in a small village surrounded by enemy soldiers. We had no idea where the men were, whether they were alive or dead. For their safety and ours, we had no choice but to proceed as if we would never see the men again.

Although we understood that the new government in Laos, interested in killing us, was responsible for our run in the jungle, most of the soldiers we encountered were North Vietnamese, young men who had crossed the border to ensure that America could not return to Southeast Asia. Many of them were fluent in Lao. A few were even able to speak Hmong. To our surprise, the contingent that had captured us was rather orderly and professional. We had met different people who'd had encounters with other soldiers in which innocents had been raped and killed, tortured and maimed. We were afraid and vulnerable. The soldiers saw this and the fragility of our physical conditions and treated us as pawns in the war, not threats. As a group, the young soldiers didn't yell at us or other villagers, though they gestured frequently with their guns, and that was enough to spark our immediate cooperation. They followed the bidding of a leader who wore a clean uniform with stars pinned on his chest, a matching hat on his head, and a gun at his side;

even the leather boots on his feet were well oiled and shiny. As individual soldiers, away from their leader, the men were more unpredictable in their behavior, and this kept us on edge.

One bright day, a North Vietnamese soldier visited our family hut. He spoke in perfect Lao and asked if anyone in our group could translate his message in Hmong. The eyes of several of the sisters-in-law shifted toward me. He stood very straight in the center of our hut, in the light from the open door, as he spoke.

"We found a body in a nearby river and other Hmong folk have identified it as Npis's."

The young soldier, no older than Npis, kept his gaze on Npis's mother's creased face as he spoke slowly.

Her lips quivered. Then, drops of water fell from her eyes, but she made no sound.

I stood slightly behind the soldier so he could not see my face.

Both my hands went to the heavy mound at my center. I pressed my palms hard into the watery world within me. My baby kicked.

I knew the soldier was lying. He had to be. Wouldn't the baby register the death of her father—even within the fabric of me? Surely she would, for I had with my own father. I had felt it to my core the moment he had died.

The soldier bowed his head when his words were through.

He turned toward me on his way out of the hut, still caught in that stream of sunlight, and said quietly, "Please accept my condolences. I understand Npis was your husband."

This soldier had been kind to our family of women and children from the moment we were captured in the jungle. He had been particularly kind to me. On the long trek from the jungle to this village, it was he who asked for a group break when I started limping, the bottom of one flip-flop now sunken and worn thin. I felt every broken limb in the jungle, every jagged pebble on the road. He'd offered me a piece of cloth to wrap around my feet. He had asked, "Are you a daughter-in-law or a daughter?" I hadn't answered him. I hated him. I hated him so much the taste of vomit soured my throat at the sound of his voice, soft and playful—as if we were not captives, as if our very lives were not on the line, as if he and his friends hadn't been chasing us for years, intent on killing us. Even in the months after we'd settled into the enemy village, he visited regularly, each time bringing little gifts, a bar of soap to share or a new lighter, to make our lives easier. He'd never presented it to me because he realized I was a daughter-in-law quickly enough, but he'd look at me on the visits, the liking in his eyes measured only by the hate within my own.

I had never taken a good look at him. But when he offered the formal apology for the supposed death of my husband, I lifted my chin and looked at him from his booted feet up his thin legs, to the heavy brown belt at his waist, to his concave chest underneath the brown of his uniform, to his stick of a neck, up to his angular face. I straightened the line of my mouth. I saw the expectant look in his brown eyes, open wide, to his hair falling boyishly over his brows. His hat was raised high. I saw that he was a decent-looking young man. All I could do was shake my head. How could a decent young man come up with such a vicious lie as the one he'd just told?

He expelled a breath and said, "You're a widow now, young mother."

He looked pointedly at my protruding belly before he turned away from me and walked to the open door, bright with sunlight, ducked his head so he could get through the squat rectangular frame, and walked with his head down, a hand to his chin. On the dusty road, three soldiers waited for him in a military vehicle, each smoking a cigarette.

No one in the hut said a thing. The younger children were outside playing in the dirt. The older children doing errands with their mothers, tending the garden we'd inherited from whoever had lived in the hut before us. Inside, there was just the newborn baby boy, his mother, Npis's mother, and me and my unborn child. There was just the silence. Was Npis dead, or wasn't he?

Npis's mother had turned to her medicinal bag and started sorting through it, little parcels of hard nuts, bundles of bark, shriveled roots, and a collection of dried leaves. Her tears fell silently onto the packages in her hands. She did not wipe them, just sniffed. Her pink lips trembled, showing her single tooth.

I walked to her. I placed my hands on her shoulders, felt their thick softness.

I said, "I think the soldier is lying."

She answered without looking at me, "It is an unbearable lie to tell a mother. When you become one, you will know this."

I let my hands linger for a moment before I moved them. She couldn't see me because she was looking at the medicines in her hands, but I nodded all the same, trying to fortify myself, trying not to misinterpret the words she'd spoken. I couldn't bear more pain in the moment. I thought, though I said nothing, *It is also an unbearable lie to tell a young wife, especially one about to deliver his child.*

I knew that Npis's mother had delivered many dead babies in her life's work as a healer and medicine woman. Among the sisters-in-law alone, I knew there had been difficult deliveries. One of the women had in fact given birth to a baby with no hands or feet though the child was born alive. It took the baby several days to die, unable to feed. When the little body became still and her chest stopped its rise and fall, it was Npis's mother who took the baby away from the arms of her screaming mother. Npis had also told me that before he was born, his mother had lost an infant, a baby girl a few months old. He said his mother never really recovered, that every once in a while, she'd tell the tale of how a jungle spirit had chanced upon her beautiful baby and taken her, replaced her with a dead thing more pig than human. I couldn't fathom such an occurrence. I was too new to ask, too pregnant to contemplate closely the possibilities where things could go wrong with the baby inside me, clinging too desperately to the hope my child would bring with her a new world, not this one where death was happening second by second, minute by minute, day by day.

No one had ever told me that having a baby was like period cramps amplified a million times over. No one had ever told me that I had been nursing a raging storm inside and that the pressure would build until nothing less than my blood spilling would ease it. No one had told me that inside me there were threads of skin, muscle, and fat, and that I was a thing sewn together by the pulsing heat of life, and for me to produce it, I had to come undone. For all the babies I had seen, for all the women I had known, right up until I delivered my first child, I did not know how much bringing life into the world necessitated me placing my own on the line.

I cried without volition. Tears fell from my fiercely closed eyes in messy streams as my body pulsed to a beat more ancient than my seventeen-year-old self could conceive. A rhythm set by the motions of my body held me in its grip. I clenched and unclenched my fist with each breath that I took, the waves of pain rocking my very bones, setting my teeth achatter. Rivulets of sweat ran down my face, neck, chest. Liquid on liquid on liquid. Npis's mother's deep voice guided me through the haze of pain, calm as ever: "Push if you want to, push if you can, pull back on your breath, pull back, hold steady, steadier, steady . . . and here we go again."

It was not pretty. The head came first. I didn't feel it with my hands but the heated core of me knew that it was bone on bone. There was a gush, and the baby slipped out into the world and the arms of her grandmother, and she opened her mouth wide, and a single cry cracked the night air. The women and children in the hut exhaled a collective breath.

When I had wiped down and was able to gingerly take a seat on the bed of straw grass before the warm fire, the wiggling, chubby baby beside me, the women asked, "What do you want to call her?"

The other children peered down at the pale, round thing by my side, their eyes wide with wonder. No matter that they had experienced a birth not long before; this one to them was as special, particularly the nieces, who were excited that their newest cousin would be an addition to their team.

I was too tired to come up with a name at first. When the immediate exhaustion eased away, I felt too shy. I knew that whatever her name would be, in accordance with the practice of our people, I would simply become known as her mother. In essence, unlike when I married Npis, this time I would be naming myself. I licked dry lips and said, "I don't know. What do you all think is best?"

There was a hushed conversation. I know that in the family, Npis's mother had named most of the children. I know that she had been naming children for so long that she was also running out of ideas. One of Npis's sister's sons had been named Chair. A cousin of his had been named Pan. I felt shy but also protective. I didn't want my baby to share a name with furniture or a cooking vessel or a vegetable. I didn't want to be known as the mother to such things—however essential to our life they were, purposeful in design and pure in intention.

The sister-in-law who taught her children the names of everything was the first person to wash the baby. She boiled a pot of water and found a piece of clean fabric. As she held the naked baby to the light of the fire, before the warm bath, she said, "The baby is so fair. Why, we can just call her *white*. Dawb."

I would be known henceforth as Dawb's Mother.

I practiced it to myself, saying the name again and again through the night.

Dawb was a color.

Dawb was the flag of surrender.

Dawb was the beginning of hope in a time of helplessness.

Dawb was my first baby and shall remain so always. The best part about her name is that it echoes in the cavern of the mouth. This child was my call to womanhood, to an identity that I would inhabit for the rest of my life.

With the baby bundled close to me, we fell into a deep sleep that first night of her life and my life beginning anew. I didn't wake up until her cry startled me in the gray of early morning. My whole body felt as if I had been hit by the fall of a towering tree and smashed to the ground. Its phantom weight was on top of me. Every bit of my body was sore. Every bit of me felt broken. And yet, looking at the baby, her thick lids opening slowly, her mouth pink and round, searching, I felt the strong beat of my heart inside my chest.

I shushed her at my breast. I winced when she latched. I felt the sucking hunger of my child. The desperation for life contained in the little body moved me. My eyes grew wet.

I whispered, "Baby, your father is alive."

I said, "Dawb, your father is alive."

I promised her, "You will get to meet him soon."

CHAPTER 11

The Reunion

H ey, hey, get up."

"Hey, hey, get up."

Someone was on the other side of the wall of the hut. Through the slits in the woven bamboo walls, the sister-in-law could feel his hot breath on her face.

She spoke sternly: "I don't care who you are. Leave. I'm a married woman."

The man on the other side of the wall tried to shush her. "Shshshsh . . . quietly. Don't alert anyone. I'm here with a message from your husband and his brothers."

She said, "If you don't stop whispering to me right now, I will scream and alert the soldiers."

We heard scurrying, then silence.

She sighed loudly.

She said to Npis's mother, "I don't know who this man is."

Npis's mother responded in her rough voice, "Probably just an enemy soldier testing your loyalties."

The door to the hut swung open.

All of us prepared to scream from our various sleeping places on the ground.

The person at the door held a flashlight up to his face.

The light amplified features we thought we knew but also the things we feared. I could feel a scream squeaking out my opened mouth.

It was one of the kids who recognized him and shouted, "Uncle Eev, Uncle Eev!"

The air rushed out of my body.

It was one of Npis's older brothers. I could see the wide face, the high cheekbones, the sunken, hungry eyes, even the receding hairline. His voice, serious under normal conditions, was particularly stern and tight: "Don't make a sound. Carry the children. They are waiting for us at the edge of the village. We have to go now before the guards do their nightly checks."

A current shook our little house. Then, the women and children scrambled to their feet, grabbing the items closest to themselves. Uncle Eev had turned off his flashlight. In the dark, we searched for the things that held value. It occurred to us that we couldn't possibly carry all the children. There were more than thirteen who needed to be carried, ages ranging from one to seven.

A chorus of whispers: "How do we get all the children out? What are we going to do?"

The group of children who would need to be carried stood holding the shirttails of the adults closest to them. Each was afraid they would somehow be left behind. The older kids, each with a pack on their back now, huddled close to the door, their eyes clear and wide, unafraid, waiting for a signal to go.

We could hear feet running our way. Eev had an old American gun in his hands. He signaled for the children to move from the door. He braced himself, feet planted far apart in front of us.

He said, "I'll shoot. You run."

We huddled behind him in a heap of bodies. There was no way we could run through walls. In my heart, I thought, *And here is one more person willing to die so we might live in this war*. I clutched my baby close.

The thin door swung open.

Men, our men, familiar faces and forms, rushed in.

All I heard in the desperate moment was that a few of the men were waiting by the edge of the village. We were going to run toward yet another river. They'd prepared rafts of bamboo. I wanted to ask someone, "Where's Npis?"—but I was afraid of the answer, so I made sure again and again that the child-carrying cloth that Npis's mother had given me was secured around my sleeping baby, tied fast to my front. I grabbed the last of my outfits, the small bundle of pictures of my brothers and sisters from before the war, the most precious thing I owned: the heavy silver necklace my mother had given me at my wedding. I pushed everything into my woven bamboo basket, covered it all with an old folded American tarp that Npis had salvaged from somewhere during the first days of our marriage. A chorus of voices whispered, "Run."

Both my hands were braced against the baby tied to my front and I was running with the women and children. A few of the men were carrying two children apiece. We were moving as fast as we could toward the village's edge. A contingent of misshapen shadows in the night with our baskets, heavy packs, some with children thrown on top of both.

There was silence all around us.

There was silence behind us.

There was silence in front of us.

We knew silence as our friend, so we scrambled and scrambled, holding our breath, fast bodies in the dark, older children running in search of their fathers, whom they hadn't seen for nearly five months.

Breathless, I stood at the river's edge with the women and children. Beneath the light of a crescent moon, I saw a figure in the night. His shoulders were wide. His hair, which had been spiky when I'd last seen him, had grown longer. It was wavy. He stood at the edge of the river, holding a bamboo raft steady for the family members. I ran toward this figure of a man.

We exchanged no words. He passed me onto the raft with a tight squeeze of my hands. The unsteady thing swayed. The small group al-

ready on the flat of the bamboo bed moved to balance the rickety structure. None of us said a word.

Then, we heard the first of the grenades exploding in the night. Gun-
fire bloomed in the darkness in flashes of red and orange. The screams
were louder than the explosions. The children were numbed by everything. From youngest to oldest, they made no sounds.

The figure with the broad shoulders pushed us farther into the water,
and the raft started floating away from the shoreline. I was afraid that
we would lose him, but at the final second he jumped on, belly flat
against the platform of bound bamboo. With long sticks, members of the
group pushed us toward the other shore.

Shivering on the other side of the river, we heard engines and boats
in the water. The enemy soldiers were chasing us. This knowledge fueled
us. We scrambled up the edge of the muddy riverbank only to find that
we had to climb up a steep ravine. I kept my left hand cupped around
the globe of my baby's head near my chest. With my right, I grasped at
the ground. I was bent over like an old woman. I felt my feet slipping
on the slick dirt. I couldn't see anything. I pulled at the growth around
me desperately. Handfuls of grass came out. Handfuls of grass held for
me. I slipped but the person behind me, whoever they were, shoved me
up. Along the soft bank of the river, one of Npis's older brothers had
buried grenades in our wake in hopes of slowing down our pursuers.
They started exploding, one by one. Cries of pain, so excruciating the
muscles in my face ticked in response. I winced and clenched my teeth
so hard against each other they would shake for weeks.

Somehow, we all made it to the top of that ravine, and could finally
regroup and run for our lives. The children kept asking, "Are we alive?"
The adults kept reminding them, "Yes, and if you want to stay alive,
don't talk, just run." Despite the active pursuit of the enemy soldiers, by
the third day we knew they had lost track of us.

On the fourth night, Npis's mother burned the last of the incense
sticks she had carried, and thanked the ancestors and Npis's dead father's spirit for guiding us through the harrowing escape, for keeping
her children safe, for helping all of us stay together.

On a misty, gray dawn Npis held our child for the very first time. I looked at them at the mouth of the cave, just him and her. The family was still asleep around us. Some of the men were outside guarding the perimeter. Npis did not say anything to the infant in his arms, but he held her toward the blue light, so heavy with moisture, the air looked like it was water. The lavender mountains visible behind them appeared like clouds in the distance. As I looked at Npis holding our daughter, I believed in the power of the ancestral spirits that had kept watch over us, guarded and guided us, more than I had ever believed before.

Npis had aged in the six months away. The caps of his shoulders rose high on his skeletal frame. The incline in his cheeks had deepened. His eyes were sunken in his face. His shoulders shook in the soft morning, holding the baby, rocking her stiffly from one side to the other.

The men were full of stories of where they had been, what they had been eating, what they had not been eating, how sick this one was or that one had been, or how they were separated and yet somehow managed to find each other with the help of a white antelope, a wild bird, the cry of monkeys. It was all mystical and yet real.

All of us women didn't talk about the different soldiers who were interested in us, who tried to get us to like them by showing us movies of rebel husbands leaving their families and chancing upon new women and falling in love and continuing to live life with their new families. We didn't talk about the soldiers who came to visit our hut, sharing news of bodies being found, how it could be this man or the other. Even Npis's mother was quiet about our ordeal in the enemy camp. None of us knew how to talk about how it was never the immediate threat of death that was scary, or sickness or disease, but the quiet and insidious nature of living at the mercy of your captors.

For myself, I was caught in a thousand places. How do you tell your husband about the pain of childbirth? How do you tell him about the selecting of the baby's name? Or how you wondered whether he would ever meet her? Or how you might raise her without him? Where were you going to go? How would you find your way to your mother and family again? If you escaped? If you didn't?

Npis didn't like the name Dawb. He used to have a girlfriend by that name a very long time ago, before he even met you, before he ever thought that the thatched roofs of his village would blaze in the night.

I didn't tell Npis anything. I just said, "Your sister-in-law chose the name."

I, like the rest of the women, the men, the children, couldn't quite process what was happening, what had happened, what would happen to us. Was what we had gone through horrible or were there more horrors waiting for us?

I listened to one of Npis's older brothers tell everyone the story of the great rescue, again and again. He seemed to be in a trance each time he told it, trapped in a recording he couldn't control. The big brother sat on his haunches, his elbows resting on his thighs, hands clasped in between his legs. His eyes took on a far-off quality, not quite focusing on anyone or anything. The way he looked in his rags, his wide feet, more similar to Npis's than different, spread flat on the earth, the way his voice floated as if it were coming from away; all of it drew our attention.

The men hadn't abandoned the women and children after all. They had fled when the enemy soldiers had arrived. They had regrouped. They had tracked the group to the village. All the long months we thought we were alone, they had been in the nearby jungle playing hide-and-seek with our captors. They weren't the only ones. There were other family groups doing the same thing. They saw lots of shoot-outs, some executions, but they themselves had not engaged in open warfare. The men hid those long months in the jungle, starving and sick, waiting for an opportunity to stage a rescue, to help each other believe again.

The big brother said, "We were waiting on the edge of the river. We had made bamboo rafts by tying cuts of bamboo together. We had hidden them along the banks. For three whole days we sat along the tree line, in the thickest foliage, waiting to see if anyone from the village would come our way. We needed information. We needed to know which hut housed you all. We needed you to know we were alive and waiting.

"The three days were agonizing. We were too close and too afraid to make a fire, to try to find fish or hunt for game. We stationed Npis in a tall tree as a lookout. I stood at its base. The uneventful passing of each day made me more and more angry at the situation, the war, the soldiers, the fact that we had forsaken our wives and children and our elderly mother. The gnawing hunger did not help.

"On the third day, Npis alerted me to two figures walking by the river's edge from the direction of the village. At first, I thought they were women. I thought they were Laotian women in sarongs from the surrounding villages. They carried fishing baskets. Clearly unaware they were being watched, taking their time, making periodic stops to check traps that they'd laid out previously.

"The pair made their way right to the front of where we were hiding. One of them went into the river to check a trap. The other waited by the shore with the fishing basket. Without consulting anyone, I ran toward them with my gun. I was so quiet they didn't hear me approach. I had my gun pointed at the back of one person before the other looked up with a fish in hand.

"I spoke Lao: 'Do anything and die.'

"When the person looked up, I saw that it was a man. The one I held my gun to was also a man. I grunted out again, 'Do anything and die.'

"To my surprise, the one holding the wriggling fish broke into a smile. He said in Hmong, 'Oh, we heard you were dead. It's so good to see you alive.'

"I said, 'What?'

"The one I held the gun to turned around. I was too stunned to do anything. He pushed the gun in my hands to the side and embraced me.

"Both of them had been villagers from our long-ago village. They knew who all of us were. They told us they, too, were captives. But they'd been there so long that the soldiers trusted them, allowed them the freedom to fish at will. They told us that they had been told on numerous occasions that we had died.

"I said, 'We've been starving.'

"They asked, 'How many are you?'

"I said, 'All my brothers and a few friends and allies we've picked up along the way. There's thirteen.'

"They said, 'No one is coming this way. Come out, all of you. We've caught quite a few fish. We'll start a fire and cook and eat. Once you are less hungry, we'll help you out.'

"We were so hungry that the thought of freshly cooked fish pulled us out from the jungle's edge. It was not a question of trust but hunger. I held my gun right up until I was holding a piece of steaming white fish, sucking the flaky flesh from the transparent bones, thinking if these two are tricking us, I'll kill them after I eat.

"The two men went on to tell us everything we needed to know, the schedule of the guard checks, the routes away from the village. They told us that we needn't be afraid. We didn't have to hide or anything. After the meal, they'd lead us right on the dirt road back toward the village. There, we'd wait until darkness came, then one of them would go and tell the women and children to come forth. I said, 'What do you want in return for all this help?' We clearly had no food or money to give. It was too dangerous a task to do for free—this business of helping us free our wives and children.

"They both said, 'Oh, take us with you. We hate the enemy soldiers. We want to be with our people again.'

"And so we came to an agreement. We told them that once we rescued our wives and children, we were headed to Thailand. They wanted to know how we knew the way to Thailand. I said that one of the men we picked up knew the way. He would lead us. I told him we were going to become refugees of war. From there, if we made it that far, we didn't know where we would end up.

"The men were happy with our plan. We finished the eating at dusk. Replenished, we let the men lead us on the open road toward the village. We waited, those two reminding us of the schedule of the village casually, until the firelight dimmed across the houses. They told us the soldiers no longer even guarded the village seeing as how everyone was so helpless. It had been a long and quiet several months. The soldiers had gotten lazy and only came by to do checks at predictable times, once around midnight, once in the dawn, and then around noon.

"When the fire in the family hut was tempered for the night, one of the men was assigned the task of coming to the hut to get your at-tention. It didn't work. That's when Eev decided he himself was going to come to the hut. After he left, we realized that there were too many children to carry, so we followed suit."

Each time the big brother told the story, he ended it always with, "I was ready to shoot those individuals, make them pay for everything that had been taken away. My finger was on the trigger. My heart was ready to squeeze it. I don't know what held me back. It must be the ancestors."

I felt the warmth of Npis's presence at my side, listening to the story. I had promised myself in our time apart that if we met again, I was going to love him so much more, so much better. In those months apart, I learned a desperate truth, that I missed him even more than I missed my own mother. But as life would have it, as life would teach me, and perhaps Npis, too, we could only love each other the same. We were young, we were already at our full capacity, only neither of us knew it, so we kept thinking that there was more goodness, more tenderness, more sweetness to love, something waiting around the corner, a truth that would come out, and somehow all our mistakes, our decisions, our indecisions, the blind trust, the emotions that singed us, all of it would finally be justified.

– Part II –

IF YOU
WOKE UP ONE
MORNING

CHAPTER 12

The Mekong River

Each morning, with the rise of the sun through the dense jungle leaves in the far eastern sky, I watched as my baby grew thinner and lighter in my arms. Dawb was born chubby. In the first month of her life, she'd grown well for me, healthy and strong, suckling at my breast with a hunger that felt primal and true. On the run toward the Mekong River, my baby and I struggled to keep pace with the family.

The other sisters-in-law were made stronger than me. They were for the most part taller and had started with more meat and muscle to cushion their bones. Between feeding the baby and barely eating myself, I became a version of me I had never known.

In the surface of the still pools of water along the trek to Thailand, I saw a woman I didn't recognize grow before me. She was thin and gaunt. Her hair, pulled back from her face, had lost its luster. Her eyes and cheeks were sunken. She could feel her hip bones against her hands. At night, her back bones ached against the hard earth. The worst part was that her baby mirrored this version of herself. Both of us, tired and haggard from morning until dusk, some gray version of who we had been.

I thought things couldn't get any harder for us, but I was wrong. My

right breast became infected. It was my dominant breast, Dawb's preferred breast. The other side had an inverted nipple so the baby could
not latch on. It barely produced. At first, I thought it was a simple block-
age. At night, I tried to massage the breast and expunge the milk. I massaged and massaged until my fingers ached. Out of desperation, I asked
Npis's mother to help. Her medicinal bag had grown light in tending to
the cuts and the sprains of the journey. She could only offer me herbs
to put against the breast, cooling greens to temper its bulging heat. The
herbs did little for the infection. It grew so bad that the only thing that
ran when I tried to express milk for the baby in a pot was a line of thick,
bleeding pus. The heat in my breast spread throughout my body.

I started stumbling on the wild terrain. I had trouble breathing. My
hands braced against others to keep me up. One day, Dawb, unable to
eat, stopped crying. At different points, Npis asked if he could carry
the baby for me. It didn't make sense. He was better off carrying one
of the bigger children. I would carry my baby myself. I grew so dizzy
all the time, so much so that I couldn't walk straight anymore. In those
moments, I rested beneath tall trees, leaning into their trunks, trying
to absorb from the environment the things I needed to survive: cooling moisture, the humid jungle air, the bits of sky between the green
overhead, the hold of the earth itself, earth that reached out to me
with its dampness, its promise of stability. There were many moments,
when urged to walk on, when all I wanted was to set my pack down,
untie my baby, rest my head, close my eyes, and die with my child in
my arms. In those moments, I didn't think about Npis. Just like the
communist movies we had been shown on a projector in the enemy
camp, he would make it out of Laos, he would find someone new, have
another wife and another baby, and me and Dawb would be just one
more casualty of the war. In these dizzying dreams of his life beyond
us, I would feel justified in my decision to die. In those moments, the
scent of wet jungle disappeared, and I was surrounded by the cool,
citrusy smells of my father's orchard calling me home to that place
where the rivers met. My throat, dry, could taste the sweet and sour
juices of the tangerines, their skin thin and glossy. But then, my baby

would call out to me with her light breath. She was still breathing, and her breath pulled at something inside me and forced my eyes open, forced my hands to brace the earth, to get up again and take one heavy step and then one more.

My baby was a skin sack holding bird bones. Her eyes barely opened. She looked up at me unseeing. Her wisp of hair sat unmoving on her round forehead. Close to my chest, she stopped burrowing for milk. Her small hands felt cool to the touch.

I drank rainwater. I prayed to the ancestors for the rainwater to go down my parched throat, to enter into my milk ducts, to free them, to heal me, so that I could feed my baby. My prayers went unanswered hour by hour, day after day. Time stretched endlessly before me, the jungle a haze of unrelenting green, me feeling like I was pulling a boulder heavier than my child and myself. The rainwater did nothing to strengthen me or quicken my steps. I felt the pulse of my heart only in the heated solid thing that had once been my right breast.

One night, Npis's mother came to us and offered a gift: her last can of sweetened condensed milk. It was the most essential gift anyone has ever given me, in the neediest moment of my life. That can did not have the power to return the sound of my baby's cries, but it saved her. Npis boiled water. He mixed in the milk. With my fingertips I dripped the sweetened water bit by bit into her mouth. It gave her enough sustenance to hang on. I could see the light pulse on her thin neck.

Knowing that my baby was holding on gave me enough energy to keep walking, following Npis's bent back in front of me, heavy with a pack and a niece, the girl's tangled hair swaying to one side then the other. The breast infection resolved itself slowly and painfully. The feeling like my breast was about to explode subsided a little one day, and then more the next. By the time we could hear the rush of the Mekong River, the fever had left my body and the pain in my breast had become a dull ache.

The whole group was tense and nervous and defeated. A strange and heavy air had come upon us. We were suddenly anxious not only about the enemy but each other and the momentous situation. With each step

we took toward the Mekong River, we edged closer to severing the life
we knew from the life we might eventually have. Who we had been to
each other in this jungle, we knew that we might no longer be. Every
moment in the heat of the jungle, we had depended on each other to
survive. By crossing the wide expanse of the muddy river, risen high
because it was the rainy season, we would be severing the threads of
our dependence; our lives would no longer be in each other's hands.
Instead, they would be in the hands of strangers from faraway places,
people who had no idea who we were or what we had been through.

For all that we had been in the jungle for nearly five years, I still
knew Laos as the place where the orange blossoms unleashed their
scent and their fruits filled the mouth with sweetness. Laos was home
to that house of my beautiful memories, where my mother and her
garden waited, where my father stood by the open door, anticipating
harvests of fruit from the orchard, fish from the rivers. The rivers of my
childhood were not this one. If I crossed this river, I might never see the
other two again.

From my beautiful Lao teacher, I had learned that the Mekong River
is one of the world's mightiest rivers. She had taught us that it flowed
from the Tibetan Plateau in China all the way down, through six different countries: China, Myanmar, Thailand, Cambodia, Vietnam, and Laos.
Her fingers had traced its journey on a map in a thick book. The drawn
rivers were like the veins underneath the skin of my mother's hands.
Laos was home to my father's dead body and my mother's living one.

I knew little about Thailand. The men said that we would be depending on the mercy of the Thai people for our lives to continue. They said
that there were refugee camps set up by a group of powerful countries.
We would be subjected to their decisions, these foreign nations, though
this fact did not feel like new information. Hadn't we been all along?
Even in Laos, we were at the mercy of the countries who had sent
planes across our skies, dropped rice and bombs for our people to eat
and to die. All I knew was that the Thai people were people, too, and
they were not the ones who had been chasing us or killing us.

We could hear the rush of the Mekong River when our bodies gave out. We had pushed them to their very ends. All we had left were emotions. They boiled over in painful ways.

Along an outcropping of river rocks, one of Npis's brothers threatened to kill him. There were two brothers with inflatable rafts. One had a hole in his; everyone knew this because each time that brother crossed with his family, he had to be in the water, holding the hole closed with his hands. Before the big and final crossing, both brothers stopped to check their rafts. To their surprise, both rafts had holes in them. It could have happened easily along the trek, a sharp branch, a jagged rock edge, an errant bullet. Still, there was a great deal of anger and frustration. The brother with the newly discovered hole decided that it was Npis's fault. He said it must be Npis, because Npis had always been a burden on the family as the youngest; he'd been a brooding boy and now had become a despairing man with a gaunt wife and a dying child. He said that Npis had decided to sabotage him. In a fit of rage, this older brother threatened to kill my husband.

Npis proclaimed his innocence. He hadn't gone anywhere near the raft. He had no reasons to create holes where there were none. Their collective survival was what this whole journey was about. Now that everyone was at the river, why make this unnecessary accusation? The angry brother would hear none of it. My husband then dropped the load he'd been carrying and straightened up, and I watched as he ripped the remaining buttons off his ragged shirt. His bare chest showed ribs rising high, a hollow belly. He said, eyes unblinking, no sign of tears or spark of anger, "Kill me. You want one more person to die here in Laos. You've chosen me. Shoot."

The barrel of a gun pointed at Npis.

Npis stood defiantly, his chin, angled toward the sky, showing the white of his neck.

The other brothers shouted and got up, moved fast to step in between the two men. Npis's mother screamed and tried to wrestle the gun from her older son's hands. But in the end, it was the brother's wife who stepped forward. She walked in front of Npis, faced her husband, and said, in an exhausted voice, "If you want to kill Npis, kill me first."

The gun wavered. It lowered. The angry older brother turned away, shoulders high and tight.

I went to my husband then, the baby strapped to my front, and placed a hand to his chest, felt the panic he would not show. I kept my hand on his frantic heart until the air he'd held inside came out, our child, eyes closed, head weighed heavily on one side, breathing in between us.

The Mekong River didn't just separate Thailand from Laos at the point of our crossing; I could see into the cracks of the family I had married into, a brotherhood strained for too long by the death of a father and the pressures of a war, falling apart bit by bit. The river was separating us from Thailand, but we were also separated from each other; everyone was a keeper of their own truths about what had happened, who the bad and the good were, the actual cost of our collective survival, our shared losses.

Afraid to look too closely, the other adults in the family comforted Npis as they knew how, pats on the shoulder, a helping hand to pull up the pack he had dropped on the rocks of the river, tired words ushering us all toward the sound of fast-running water. The niece he had been carrying for most of the journey offered on the palm of her little hand the two buttons she'd picked up from the ground. For all that we had been through, the hardest part of the journey was still before us.

The Mekong River was wider than any river I had ever seen. I imagined all the rivers of my youth coming together to form the brown powerful thing in front of me. It was a dragon of a river, the most fearsome thing I had ever encountered. Though I had been a child who had lived a life close to two rivers, I had only walked along the shallow edges, bathed on the smooth rocks. I knew the legends about the spirits that haunted rivers, how lonely they were, how hungry they could become when they were challenged. I had never learned how to swim. Were we challenging the dragons of the Mekong River with our crossing, defying the government that had come into power in Laos, looking to cross over into Thailand in the hopes of life? The other bank was little more than a line, trees rising from the other side.

The family decided to make the crossing at midnight, as there would be fewer chances of soldiers spotting us along the bank. All the older brothers invited their mother to cross with their families, but Npis's mother made the decision to cross with us. The two with the rafts would use them, blowing air into the holes as best they could in the river. The rest of us would make do by cutting stretches of bamboo to use as floats.

Like me, Npis's mother did not know how to swim. He would have to pull us both across the river. Though the baby in my arms did not cry, had not cried for days, I rocked her from side to side. I kissed her head every few minutes, whispering, "We are so close, Little One. Hold on. Your mother is not going to let you go no matter what happens in the cold water."

Npis spent our last hour in Laos preparing to leave it. He and the rest of the men snuck into a thicket of bamboo. They felled the long stalks one by one silently, holding each trunk as it fell. They cut it into lengths. The plan was to tie us to the bamboo and then to Npis so that he could pull us in the water.

As he worked, I walked to a nearby patch. I placed my hand at its base. The fallen leaves had created a mat atop the moist earth. I could feel their damp weight beneath my fingers. By the light of the moon, I dug a hole big enough to bury the photographs I had kept with me of my mother, my father, myself, my sisters, and my brothers. I wished I had a plastic bag to keep the photographs in. One day, I wanted to return for the photographs, black-and-white images that blossomed and bloomed with color in my memories of what we had shared.

Npis's voice called out to me in the night. I could tell he was annoyed. I looked at the shadows of Npis and his mother, standing just a few feet away from me. I couldn't see their faces, but I knew the impatient air that came from them both. Who was this person, in this dangerous moment, dallying in the dirt? The sound of water splashed as rough whispers broke into the night. I knew the family groups were leaving one by one. I hurried. I filled the bottom of the dirt pit I had made with fresh bamboo leaves, hoping they would shelter my pictures. I placed the photographs gently on top of the small pile. I covered it up with more leaves before shoveling in the dirt. I stumbled toward the darkened figures of Npis and his mother.

I said, "I'm ready."

Npis tied us with a stretch of rope, his mother and me. I was tied already to my baby with the child-carrying cloth. Whatever we had, we had to leave behind. I could not part with the heavy silver necklace my mother had given me on my wedding day, so I placed it around my neck, tucking it inside my shirt so that the cloth would cushion my baby's head from the metal meant to signify the worth of a Hmong woman. The few pieces of embroidery my mother had given me so that when I died, I would be able to find my way to her, I placed between my baby's belly and my own. If anything should happen to us, to me or to her, then I wanted us both to have a pathway to my mother. I wore all three rings that my brother Looj had given me on my wedding day. The edges of the cut bamboo sliced into my armpits on both sides, but I did not complain. Npis's mother stood still as a statue in the process. She was taking only one bag with her that she'd secured to her back with a piece of tarp, her shaman's tools and a thin bag holding the remains of medicinal herbs. Npis did not look at either of our faces; his own was unreadable in the pitch-black of night.

He took off his clothes—all except his underwear. He walked slowly toward the bank of the river, looking left and right. We were among the last of the families at its edge. He walked into the water, and we followed. I held tight to my baby's body with one hand. When the current was at my thigh, I lost my footing. Cold, muddy water entered my throat. I choked coming back to the surface, my bare feet digging into the mud of the riverbed. With my free hand, I tried to push at the water the way I had seen the boys in our village do in what seemed lifetimes ago. The moment I could no longer touch the bottom of the river, all I felt was its current. When I could keep my eyes open, I trained them on the bobbing head of my husband.

The hand holding my baby's back shifted to supporting her bottom. I knew that if my baby went under the water, she would die. Between the coldness of the water and the coldness of the sky looking down on us, I felt myself fall in and out of consciousness, caught somewhere between living and dying, gasping for air and holding my breath. However long it took to cross that river, the only thing that mattered to me, even in the moment when I lost the necklace at my neck, was the baby at my chest.

In a dream, we made it to the other side of the river in the gray morning. In that same dream, my baby was alive and sound asleep against my chest. I saw how Npis's mother looked, her clothes wet around her, her chest heaving up and down, and the pale ribbons of flesh flowing from my husband's armpits; he was staring in disbelief at the shreds of skin, not knowing what to do. The edges of our bamboo tubes had sliced through his sides and his arms, and it looked like torn fabric away from the blood of his body. In a dream state, I clutched my baby, pale and blue, close to my body and offered a length of my torn shirt toward Npis, to wipe at the rivulets of red down his sides. I felt light as air. My feet were on the ground, but I felt I was floating above it, dirt, rocks, grass, bushes, and trees—all of it was far from me. I could walk the air, climb it like a ladder, to the tops of the trees on Thailand's side, beyond them, travel the stretch between the earth and sky, walk my way to the moon where my father waited for me on clouds like citrus blossoms. I felt I could do it. I reached for her, this sky climber, with my hands.

Npis's mother's rough voice woke me from myself: "What are you doing? Is your baby okay?"

I dropped from my climb into the sky. I blinked and shook myself awake. My baby was not okay. My baby looked dead. My baby was cold as the water we'd come from. My chest heaved. I felt my stomach turning. If anything had been inside, it would have come up, but my stomach was empty, so I felt a wave from within, then a breaking inside. My mouth opened. Cries came forth.

Npis and his mother untied the baby from me. They placed her small body on the soft riverbank. They raised her chin up. Her head fell to the side the moment they let go. I reached for her. I didn't want them to be rough. I reached for her, and I pulled her limp body close to my own, on my heels, kneeling on the dirt, rocking, rocking, rocking until I felt a puff of air. Her chest moved. I held her up, her pale lids fluttered in the early morning. Her mouth opened and a stream of water came out.

Npis and his mother embraced.

As the sun came up that day, Dawb opened her eyes and I saw the bit of brown reflecting the light of the world, and I knew the strength of my baby's spirit, her hold on life, and felt in my own a stirring response. Mothering, I learned on the banks of the Mekong River, was a gift given and accepted. Like Npis's mother, I pulled my child close to me with gratitude in my heart.

CHAPTER 13

Papaya Salad

My mouth puckered with a hit of sour and spicy. Saliva ran down the walls of my mouth. I looked at the woman eating the papaya salad by the side of the road, her thin shoulders hunched protectively over the salad in a folded banana leaf segment, one hand holding it close, beneath her chin, the other, the index finger and thumb, picking up bits of the juicy strands of shredded papaya and placing it in her hungry mouth. I wanted it so much my hand went to my throat. The muscles in my neck, the bit of cartilage at the front and the whole of it, moved again and again as if I were swallowing something more than my own yearning. I looked away, but its pungent smell reeled me in nevertheless, the fish sauce and the fermented shrimp paste, the thin slices of lime and tomatoes and eggplants, the familiar scent of garlic and pounded chili. I knew I had no money, but my hunger was such that the words escaped from me; in a dizzying world, I whispered because I had no ability left to keep the words captive, "I want papaya salad." The craving was not in my stomach; it was the whole of my being.

Npis's hand cupped my left elbow to quicken my steps. Dawb was in a child-carrying cloth in front of him. I had no more strength to carry myself, let alone a baby, now holding her own head up by her scrawny neck, her eyes darker than either Npis's or my own. I'd been hungry for a long time. In truth, I hadn't eaten my fill since I left my family for marriage in the jungle. All along the trek to Thailand, I had felt self-conscious, even when I was pregnant; I was afraid of being judged for eating too much in a time of so little.

We were newcomers in the camp. When we had entered, I'd traded each of the rings that Looj had given me for the basic necessities of our lives: a sleeping mat, a blanket, and a pot. It had been long years since there had been vendors in our lives. We had nothing valuable left to trade. The Thai woman, her hair so dark it looked deep blue in the shade of her umbrella, who sold the papaya salad knew these facts. She called after us, "Som tum! Som tum!" My head turned toward her voice but my body could not follow it. Instead, I followed my husband's back, saw the rise of his shoulder blades through the thin white T-shirt he had been given by Thai villagers after we'd walked away from the banks of the Mekong River.

Given is too soft a word. Npis's skin was peeling off his armpits. All he had on was the pair of underwear he had crossed the river in. When we had gathered with the bigger family and made our way into Thailand, groups of villagers stood by the road looking at us. At some point, the clothes had come flying. The voices calling for "Decency, decency!" ringing loud. We had no trouble understanding the language. Though the dialect was slightly different, this far north in Thailand, many of the people were ethnic Lao. Npis knelt to pick up the crumpled T-shirt and a pair of shorts. We were so ashamed we couldn't look to see who had thrown the clothes. I will never forget the sight of him pulling the shirt down, tugging the fabric as low as it could go.

Now, I stumbled in my flip-flops behind that T-shirt, promising myself that as soon as we could afford it, I would buy Npis a T-shirt, a new one. I would give it to him as a token of my love and understanding. I wanted him to know that I saw the courage it took for him to bend down and pick up the shirt on that dirt road. I had learned many things about my new husband in the year and a half since we'd been married. I had tied myself to a human being who did not have much by way of physical things and, unlike me, did not seem to care about the things money could buy. Npis was used to pretending he didn't want the things other people had. I was not like him. My yearning showed all over my face, my figure, invisible hands reaching for my heart's desires.

Back in our section of the camp, away from the eyes and ears of the people at the market, I felt embarrassed for the words that had escaped my mouth. I knew Npis was hungry, too. I lowered my gaze to our feet; both of our pairs of flip-flops had been donated by a refugee couple who was leaving for America. Even our toes were thin and dusty, curled in, trying to take up less space in this foreign land.

Dawb cried suddenly, and I moved to get her out of the child-carrying cloth. I was thankful for the ways in which our daughter had given me purpose, allowed me cause to escape from the uncomfortable circumstances that had emerged in the camp. Npis helped me untangle her small limbs from the cloth, its once bright red and green colors now muddied permanently by the days in the jungle and the waters of the Mekong River. Dawb was thin and small but far more healthy now that my breasts were working again, her face perpetually tired but also alert in the way of poor children. I worried that she was not getting enough nutrition because much of her milk consisted of little more than the water I drank. Still, in my arms, at my breast, she sucked greedily, and contentedly, one of her hands holding firmly to my little finger.

With Dawb in my arms, I sank to the ground, fumbled about, and found a flat rock by the edge of the path. I sat with my back facing a small fence of sugarcane grass, too young to be sweet, the stalks no bigger than my thumb, but already it was gifting the air with its sugary promise. I swallowed with my child's eager gulps of the cloudy fluid from my right breast—which for everything it had endured somehow had returned to a close semblance of itself.

Hunger now had been a presence in my life for a long time. In fact, I could no longer remember what it was like to be full, or even just comfortable in my body. My body felt more liquid than solid, but my bones felt hollow and jagged at the same time. Each breath made my whole body rise and fall against the weight of the air sitting on top of and around me. The skin over my ribs was as thin as the skin above my hands.

I looked up at Npis. He was doing better than me. He nudged at the dirt with the toe of his flip-flop. He started whistling. Some melody I had never heard. He swayed a little at the music he made.

I studied the man I had married, perhaps not unlike the way my mother had once long ago studied my father. I studied Npis with an impartiality that bordered on harsh. It unsettled him. He stopped his whistling, though he did not look away or try to hide his vulnerability. I saw the question in his gaze: "Tswb, why are you looking at me like this?"

I had married a poor man. He has been marked by poverty in ways I had not. He does not talk of the things we might one day do together, the places we might visit, the houses we might live in. He is a man who has been trained to live for one day hoping for the next. He is not used to the idea of dreams, the logistics of planning a future. In our talk and in our life, the only thing he has offered is the one thing he has, himself. In this way, in this strange and peculiar way, Npis was free in a way that I knew many men were not. He was not chasing a position in the world, running toward notions of education or class or power. He does not know how to pretend to be anything but what he is: a poor man standing by the side of a dusty path, waiting for his thin wife to feed his fragile child.

I felt an overwhelming need to protect him. His shirt, some other person's remnant, was threadbare. His cheekbones were high, and they rose like hills on the plane of his face, hollowed grooves on either side of his full lips. I looked away now, nervous that he might read the expression in my eyes.

Npis started whistling again, a song unfamiliar to me, a tune meeting the world for the first time. His hands clasped and unclasped in front of him. He surveyed the world around us. I looked at it, too.

The dominant color of both our lives had been green in Laos. Our beloved mountains were green, our villages were green, the trees of our youth were green, the grass, too. Now, everywhere we looked, we saw the orange-brown dirt of earth that had been cleared of its green. We saw tan bamboo structures rising in disarray for refugees to hide underneath. We saw the dull aluminum roofs of the more official buildings built by the Thai government. We saw that the only river in our camp was an open sewage canal of brown muck dividing it into two halves of the same whole. We had been told that the camp had overflowed. There were refugees escaping the border by the hour. We saw the people, our people, holding each other up because there was little else to do with our hands on this small bit of earth where we had no farms or fields to tend to. Old grandmothers with their grandchildren on their backs— wrinkled women who had survived somehow when their husbands, sons, and daughters had not. There were groups of children, hanging onto each other, now orphans. There were young widows everywhere, each with mouths to feed, each looking at the world with eyes drowning in liquid. All around us we saw red. Red like the blood that spilled once the bullets had found their home. Red like the fires that exploded when the bombs fell from the skies. There were Hmong people from parts of Laos we had never known, people whose dialects differed from our own. Npis and I were both children of Xieng Khouang, home of the high mountains of Laos. Now, home to more fallen bombs than any other place on earth—but we didn't know this then. All we knew was that we were now refugees of war and we were able to be here on this cleared earth because of the generosity of the Thai government, because of the funding of a thing called the United Nations High Commissioner for Refugees. We saw these things in every piece of paper we were asked to sign, every bit of paper given for us to keep.

On that dirt path, feeding Dawb, I felt gratitude. I was grateful to be alive, to be holding my child, to be feeding her before my husband. I said goodbye to the green of the past.

I could not say goodbye to the fact that I had lost my mother's precious dowry gift, the heavy silver necklace, in the Mekong. It hadn't occurred to me until we were registered as refugees of war that I'd lost the necklace. When asked if I had any paperwork, I began searching for the embroidery my mother had given me, and that's when I remembered the necklace. It was gone. All that remained was the knowledge that my mother had given it to me on my way into marriage.

I looked down at the child in my arms. Her hair was light and brown. Her hairline was a sharp V across the front of her round forehead. I swiped at the V trying to get it to curve into a soft C. It was slightly damp and obeyed. Her eyes were open, nearly black eyes, clear eyes, small eyes, eyes that glittered at me. She smiled around the nipple, a curve of lips. A thin line of milk oozed. I wiped it clean.

Whatever I had lost, at least I had her, my precious human being.

A cool breeze blew, and I let out the air in my lungs slowly. I said to no one in particular, "I've never been so poor. I don't know how to be this poor in a place where people have goods to sell, in a regular world where we aren't running all the time."

No one answered me. A rooster crowed from somewhere in the camp. A dog barked. I breathed again and again trying to assuage the hunger in my belly jostling with the welling of gratitude in my heart. Npis's whistling song continued, growing quieter and quieter. Dawb fell asleep and her small mouth opened, freed my nipple, so I carefully tucked myself back in under the buttons of my shirt. Npis reached for the baby but I shook my head no. I wanted to feel her soft warmth against my chilled body.

When we got home to one of the long, wooden communal houses built for the incoming refugees, I handed Npis the baby so I could help the other sisters-in-law prepare our simple dinner. He nuzzled the sleeping child in his arms and walked to join the circle of his brothers gathered outside on the bamboo sala attached to the front of the house. The men talked every day. They never tired of talking. Often, I made out their laughter. They chose not to talk of the bad times, only the extreme good fortune and the protection of the ancestors that had kept them together, the fact that we were all here now in the refugee camp.

We women did not talk in the same way. We attended to our children quietly. When we talked, it was of simple things: the rations, the crumbling concrete around the two wells we shared on this side of the camp, its pieces deceptively slippery, the wanderings of hungry dogs, the unending stench of the shared toilets, the heat, the unbelievable heat of the Thai sun, how it caused rashes underneath the chins of the little ones and the armpits of the bigger ones. All our voices could become one and no one would notice because our lives were that small and that tied and that fixated on the details. We all existed in a picture of need.

Npis, his mother, one of his older brothers, his wife, their child, me, and our child all shared familial rations and one sleeping room. We had three bamboo platform beds. We set them along different walls, the brother-in-law and his wife close to the wall that led to the shared kitchen, Npis's mother in the middle, and us close to the door that led to the sala. In between each bed, we tied a long sheet of fabric. Our regular rations consisted of rice, Thai mackerel that came to us in frozen blocks, and the occasional vegetable, mainly cabbage. The sister-in-law had steamed the rice already, her little boy on her back. The boy, who had remained healthy in our desperate run through the jungles, was sturdy, hands and feet waving in the air. The thawed fish waited for me in a plastic bowl filled with water.

I said to no one in particular, "I am going to go to the garden patch and gather herbs before cleaning the fish."

I held my breath as I walked by the toilet sheds, the stench of human waste crawling its way down my throat. The square of yellow earth behind was hard and dry. It contained uneven rows of chili peppers, cilantro, and green onion. I gathered the fabric of the sarong between my knees and crouched down. I picked a handful of chili peppers, not yet red but what was available, careful to pinch at the base of their stems. I pulled out a bunch of green onions with wilted dry tips, white roots and all. The bits of dirt that clung to the root ends reminded me of snot. The thought tickled me. I picked only the tips of the cilantro plants, using my nails to cut them off their stems. I worked as quickly as I could. My flip-flops slapped the ground as I walked back to the house, making a wide berth around the line of wooden toilet sheds, each containing a hole in the ground surrounded by buzzing flies with big eyes, emerald bodies, and shimmering wings.

By the doorless entryway into the kitchen area, I rinsed my little harvest with water from the large clay jar. Every morning Npis carried buckets of water from the communal well to fill the kitchen water supply. Each time I thought of the water, I couldn't help but think of the Mekong River we had crossed, the rivers of my youth, all these bodies of water I might never see again. Tears heated the backs of my eyes at the thought. I worked slowly, carefully, my hands in the cool water. I made sure to clean off all the dirt on the roots of the green onion and in between each leaf of cilantro. Although the chili peppers were not dirty, I washed them anyway, feeling the plump firmness of each pale green fruit in between my fingers.

The sister-in-law called, "I've cleaned the fish and it is in the pot already. Bring the herbs when they are ready."

I was filled with guilt. I hadn't taken that long, had I? The speed with which the men and women in Npis's family worked astounded me. I thought everyone was so fast in the jungle because of the war. In the refugee camp, I was learning that they all worked so fast because they just did.

I said, "I will."

I stopped myself from apologizing. I hadn't been dawdling. I had tried my best to make decent time.

Npis's mother said from behind me, "Nyab Npis, you are so meticulous. You work so slowly."

Her words were true. All of her other daughters-in-law were far faster than me. A few of them didn't mind a bit of dirt on their greens, either. But I minded. I thought of my fastidious father, who did everything to the highest standards. I thought about my own mother, who moved with respectable speed but approached each task with attention, with care, with time to spare. Suddenly, I could barely see the greens I was rinsing in the water bowl. The heated tears had bubbled over. My hands swirled in the cool water, feeling blindly for anything at all.

I was not an orphan. Somewhere I had a mother. A mother who saw my meticulousness as an inherited asset, no matter that it was her way to tell me to hurry, to prepare me for the expectations of other people. I knew I was being too sensitive. I tried to blink the tears away. I sniffed quietly, once, twice, three times. I didn't want anyone to see me crying, especially Npis's mother, who had turned back into the kitchen. I didn't want to go back inside until I felt less injured. With the birth of the baby, my emotions had started spilling over. At various times throughout the course of a day, I became like a piece of soaked laundry, liquid dripping down. I wiped my eyes against the sleeve on my shoulder. I grabbed the green onions and peeled the dry outer leaves away from the green stalks, spent more time than I would have otherwise so I could wait for my eyes to dry.

I walked slowly back in. I grabbed the cutting board, a three-inch disk from a tree trunk, from its place along the wall. The wood was heavy and nearly slipped out of my hands. My other hand shook around the handle of the big Hmong knife. I bit my lip and got to the task of slicing the green onion and cilantro into inch-long lengths.

The sister-in-law said, "Don't slice the chili peppers. Throw them in whole. Whoever wants spicy can take them if they want. Children will be eating the broth with rice."

She added, "I'm ready for the herbs."

I brought them to her like a child following the orders of a parent, everything cupped in my palms.

Once dinner was served on the long wooden table, two planks of wood fastened together, legs underneath, I went to Npis to hold my child.

Dawb started crying. Her mouth opened wide. Her eyes squinted closed as she raised her fists to either side.

The family ate while I nursed the hungry baby, drinking a cup of water to control the saliva in my mouth. Once Dawb had fallen asleep in my arms, once Npis took her from me, there was little left at the table. He couldn't set aside food for me. That would look horrible to everyone else. What other husbands in the family saved food for their wives? It was not personal. And yet, I thought if the situation was different, I would have set aside a bit of fish for him. The tears were welling again. I shook my head to clear my eyes. The knowledge that my mother would have set aside a bit of fish for me steadied me and gave me the strength to control my emotions.

On the table, there was a chunk of rice left in the rice bowl. It was enough. There was milky broth left with bits of fish flesh, the wilted cilantro and green onion floating beside the now wrinkled whole chilies.

In those early days, we did not have enough plates for everyone. We each had a spoon. I used the clean spoon left at the table to eat bites of soft rice and sipped spoonfuls of broth. The hot, salty broth ran down my throat. I broke a chili with my spoon on the side of the bowl. The broth tasted better.

I ate as slowly as I worked. In the relative empty of the kitchen now, I allowed my body to relax onto the bench below me. As I chewed the rice, I thought of all the meals I'd loved from the past. When I was a child, my mother used to feed me fish. In our village where two rivers met, fish was plentiful, especially during the rainy season. The fish were small and full of bones. My mother would debone the fish, squeeze its flesh between her index finger and her thumb to make sure that it was boneless before feeding it to me. She followed each bite with a spoonful of rice and water. When I got older and could sit and eat by myself, she still offered me the chunk closest to the head of a cut fish. She said, "There's less bone and more meat closer to a fish's head. There are more bones and less meat near a fish's tail. Remember this when you have children."

One day, I'll feed Dawb fish. I'll squeeze its white flesh between my index finger and my thumb. I'll feed it to her then follow it with a spoonful of rice with water. When she grows older, I'll save the parts of the fish with the least amount of bone for her, the tenderest, safest part, the chunk near the head.

While most children loved drumsticks, my favorite part of a chicken has always been the breast. I liked it when Father boiled it whole and then slowly peeled the cooked chicken breast into strands. He used to serve it to me also with rice and water.

I wonder if one day Dawb will like the drumstick or the breast. When the time comes for her to eat meat, will I be able to buy chicken? What could I do to earn money in the camp? How do I make sure that my daughter has the sweetness of memories to feed her across the tables of her life?

These questions eased the longing in my heart. It turned on a part of my brain I hadn't used in a very long time. When I was a girl and I wanted spending money, I could always harvest from my father's citrus orchard and sell the fruits to passersby. Everyone knew then that our village had the best oranges. People came from surrounding villages to buy our fruits. When I got older, I helped my mother harvest pineapples, which we also grew a distance away from our village, alongside the steep incline of a tall hill, where sunlight drenched the plants and produced the sweetest, most succulent fruits. There was nowhere to grow citrus or pineapples in the camp. Even if there were, I wouldn't know how. I had only ever harvested. I knew that some of the women in the camp made embroidery and craft items and sent them to communities of Hmong people resettled now around the world to sell for money.

The sister-in-law came to help me clear the table. Her son was off her chest. She moved quickly and efficiently around me and said, "Dawb cries each day at dinnertime. You don't get enough to eat."

I told her, "Yes, she does. It's all right. I'm okay."

She said sadly, "If only the family rations were bigger."

I shook my head and told her, "It's okay. I'm okay."

Her words combined with the rice I had eaten and the fish broth I had drunk quieted the emptiness in my belly. I savored a last taste of the herbs, the softened green onion and cilantro, and pushed myself up from the bench. The yearning for papaya salad had dissipated for the day. I knew the craving would consume me again by morning, but I had made it through one more day.

After the dinner dishes were done, I told Npis to heat up water for me to bathe the baby. My mother had told me that a child who is bathed frequently grows better. I am not sure that this is a fact, but I've seen how gardens that are tended do better.

Npis boiled the water in the large, dented teakettle his mother had inherited from another grandmother who had left the camp behind for a life in Canada. None of us knew where Canada was, but the toothless grandmother had told Npis's mother, "You will need this kettle more here than I will need it in Canada."

Npis tempered the hot water with cold water from the jar by the door in a large, red plastic bowl we all reserved for bathing children. He set the bowl by the fire ring, now reduced to hot charcoal in the pool of blackened ash. He placed a short wooden stool beside the bowl of warm water.

I unwrapped my baby like a gift from her swaddle. In the dusk, Dawb looked more yellow and gray than white, her namesake. Her little belly was round. I tapped lightly with the tips of my fingers. It felt hollow. I wiped my hand along her arms and legs, noting how small and thin they were, how very soft she felt, the fuzz on her skin. Dawb delighted in the warmth of the fire's remains and my touch. She turned her head slowly from one contented side to the other, opened her hands to try to catch my fingers. Her legs kicked at the air. I soaked a washing cloth and squeezed most of the water out. I made just enough lather with a thin bar of soap. I wiped at her hair, creating swirls of white suds. The soap smelled like bouquets of flowers. She smiled and I saw that it was a crooked smile, like my sister Xis's childhood smile. Her baby's scent reached out to me, soft and mysteriously appetizing. I made sure to stop and breathe it in deep.

After the bath, I held Dawb for a long time, warming her near the glowing embers of the day's fire. The communal kitchen was quiet. Some of the families had gone to their sleeping rooms for the night, many of them as full as ours. Others had gathered around the shared wells to clean themselves for bed. Those with older children gathered around the elder storytellers in different parts of the camp to listen to the tales they wove with their words, stories they had heard as children, stories they had created themselves in the richness of their imagination. Our lives were packed full of people from sunup until sundown. The near-empty kitchen was the calmest part of the day.

I called to Npis in a hushed voice, "Please bring me the clean swaddle."

We had two. I used them interchangeably, washing and drying them in between uses. Peeing was not so hard. All I needed to do was to fold in the wet parts of the cloth, so it didn't touch the baby's skin. Pooping was more difficult. The baby's poop was getting more solid by the day, thicker and harder to rinse out in sections, which meant I had to wash the whole thing each time and wait for it to dry completely before it was usable again. My hands were rough and red from the washing of the baby swaddles.

When we had first entered the camp, I was greeted by a family from my clan. They said that my mother had sent news of our separation across the family network. She was hoping I would make it out of Laos and into Thailand. The family gave me an address of a nephew who had recently left the camp for America. The nephew and I had been childhood friends. We were the best students in our class. That very first week in the camp, I'd asked the camp workers for a sheet of paper and a pen. I had written to the nephew at the address telling him that I was alive and that I had a baby now. I didn't ask for money. But a month after our arrival, a letter came from him, this childhood friend and relative of mine. In this envelope, along with a letter saying he was happy I was alive and that his family had resettled in a place called St. Paul, Minnesota, he sent a single hundred-dollar bill. My hands shook holding it, the letter and the bill. I studied the money, a rectangle with 100 on each corner, a green seal and a man with a receding hairline on the bill. There were letters across the green, but I couldn't read any of it. It was in English, a language I had only started hearing in the refugee camp from the officials and relief agencies. I had studied a limited amount of French as a girl, but I had little grasp of the language. This bill came from an entirely different world. I exchanged the American bill for Thai baht with a vendor at the market. With the money, I bought two brand-new swaddles for the baby. I bought a can of baby powder so that she wouldn't get heat rash. I bought soap, toothpaste, a toothbrush, and shampoo. I bought needles and thread, and cross-stitching cloth thinking that I might also spend time making embroidery. That day, when I passed the papaya salad vendor, I almost stopped, but did not. Instead, I purchased a can of sweetened condensed milk for Npis's mother, not a replacement for the can that saved my baby in Laos but a daughterly token of my love for her now that we were in Thailand.

I thought of buying one more swaddle with the leftover money, but I knew I couldn't in good conscience. In fact, I couldn't even buy Npis a shirt that day. I needed that money to be able to send my embroidery abroad to my nephew so that he could sell it. I needed some way of keeping my baby healthy, a way of trying to build a life beyond the day.

In bed, with the baby by the wall so Npis wouldn't accidentally roll over her in his sleep, I laid in the middle beside the man I had married and the child we had made. We slept with a single folded blanket as a pillow. We slept without a blanket. Even at night, the air was hot and humid, unlike the cool mountain nights of our childhood in Laos. Npis coughed in the night. The other baby in the room let out a few whimpers before his mother pulled him to her breast. All around us the night was alive.

I breathed into the thick dark, letting the air in my body out, feeling my body sink into the woven bamboo platform holding me from the ground.

Npis did the same.

He whispered into the dark, "You still have a bit of money from your nephew. You could buy yourself some papaya salad if you want."

If I want. I could buy it for myself. If I want. I wanted it so badly. But I had learned that this life is not going to be about what I want. I had to think of my child.

The baby at my side exhaled a breath into the night and turned her head in sleep. I patted her chest lightly with my hands, just enough to let her know that her mother was close to her, looking over her, taking care of her.

CHAPTER 14

Monsoon Storm

I have two daughters. No sons. Npis is a poor man but he is a good-looking one, a young one whose shoulders are still straight and strong.

There are scared widows across the camp who have lost their husbands. There are orphaned young women who are looking to find committed companions so they can leave this place with someone else for the new countries willing to accept Hmong refugees: France, Germany, Canada, and the United States of America.

Many women see Npis as eligible. His family sees me as a wife who has failed to give him a son. The community notices these things. Npis is an easy target for these women. They are far too easy as targets themselves for any man willing and able to do the simple work of spending some time with them.

One particularly humid day when the gnats and black flies fly in layers around the toilet sheds and hover over the sewage canal, the clouds fall low over the camp. By evening, a high wind blows. The elders, who usually set up in the open spaces between the houses to tell stories to the young, say that they do not feel good. They say that when their bodies hurt, when the old war wounds start giving them grief, it means that the heavens have been tested and that bad storms are coming. Npis's mother even says, "The yellow and black winds are upon us."

Our communal house is at the base of a round hill. We are in a segment of the camp consisting only of long, rectangular wooden houses with shared kitchens, sleeping quarters for each unit. The aluminum roof provides little protection from the rising wind; the corners lift a little each time a gust blows at a certain angle. I have never experienced anything like what is going to happen. I know this before it comes but I do not know what to do to up our odds of survival. There is nowhere to hide and nowhere to run. Hmong refugees cannot leave the camp without appropriate documents, approvals for resettlement. There are no emergency plans for weather events, the sky unleashing.

My daughters are young. Dawb is not quite three and Kablia is not yet one.

That night, before we fall asleep, with the girls in between us, I ask Npis, "We'll be okay, right?"

He says, "I don't know."

Npis does not like to say "I don't know."

I am not sure if I am asking him about the storm or our marriage. He, like me, is equally uncertain.

But my husband usually thinks about the worst possible outcomes for any given situation. He lives his life in accordance with what the worst thing can be. In the war, I never asked how things were going to go. He knew as much as I did. Now, here we were, a family of four. I didn't just have one small child to run with. I had a child who was not yet walking because Dawb had contracted polio and one of her legs was now shorter and smaller, weaker than the other. Kablia was only beginning to stand, holding on to chairs and railings for support. Both my girls would need to be carried. Npis would carry Dawb. I would carry Kablia. Where would we go? What if we were separated in the process? How might we survive a life without each other, in real terms?

I fall asleep uneasy. Npis, beside me, keeps watch. Usually Npis falls into a deep slumber long before I do. He snores a little, breathes deep, and these sounds fill our segment of the room. Npis's mother does not make a sound from where she sleeps. His brother, his wife, and their children are even quieter. No sounds of mating frogs, scrambling crickets, or dogs.

In the dark, our roof is blown off. I wake to a sky that is filled to the brim and spilling over on us. We are in a cascade of water. My children are awake, and they are crying and afraid. Rain and wind collect around me, and I know other houses are being demolished, families torn asunder. Npis's mother is gone. So is his brother, his wife, and their children.

Npis and I have grown further apart in the camp, those youthful promises I'd made to myself when we were separated in the jungle now feel naive. But in this moment of danger, I know that we must find a way to work together to escape the storm if our children are to survive.

I am trying to come up with a plan in my head when Npis grabs both girls.

He yells, "Follow me."

Outside, it is too windy, too loud and stormy, for us to see anything. I grab his shirt and I follow as the force of the storm whips me around. I fall every few steps in the slippery mud and each time I nearly drag Npis and the girls down. Instinctively I had put on my shoes, flimsy plastic things. Debris hits us from all sides. A solid thing slams into my back. I'm thankful it does not hit my head.

The open sewage canal that separates our side of the camp from the more permanent structures that house the hospital and the market and the first waves of refugees has reincarnated into something else. The once-small, murky, stagnant stream has realized a potential none of us saw; it is now a fiercely hungry river, its banks caved in. It slices the camp in half, eager to accept all that fall within.

The big trees crack and split around us. The little ones bend and break in their wake.

Npis lunges into the angry water.

He yells, "Everything on this side is going to get destroyed!"

As I had done in the war along the Mekong River, I follow him into the murky water that is the color of melted dirt, its currents carrying what appear to be pieces of buildings.

Wet on wet. My shoes give way immediately in the current. I suck my breath in and raise my neck high. The sewage canal could not have been higher than my thigh in normal conditions but tonight it is nearly up to my face.

In the middle of the crossing, I suddenly can no longer move. Npis has both girls in his arms still. He is yelling at me, but I can no longer hear him. In fact, I can no longer see him. The rain and the wind are so strong I cannot keep my eyes open.

In the Hmong tradition, women and girls are warned not to go near bodies of water when they are on their menstrual cycles. If we do, we chance the dragon spirits, lurking in the water, waiting for the unwary. I am not on my period but my system is still unstable. My younger daughter is not yet one. In the wet of the water, I feel hands wrapping around me. Big hands, strong hands, hands like shackles. They hold fast to my ankles. The only thing I can hear now is the rush of the water.

The hands jerk. I fall. The water hits me in the face, a slap so hard my neck swings away from my body. My hands grasp at the water but there is nothing to hold.

Water is around me. It is drowning me. I am dying. After everything, I'm dying here. I'm dying by myself. My mother will learn of this through the family networks. My husband will marry one of the many young women who are eager for his affections. My young daughters will be raised by a woman who is not me. Let her be kind. Let her be gentle. Let her love them for me. I am not thinking about Npis's love for the girls. I'm hoping that, whoever he chooses to be with after me, she, like my mother had my father's children from his previous marriages, will love mine. Water is going inside me. I'm filling up with water. I am going to be one with the storm on this night. Of all the rivers of my life, this is the one that will claim me.

I wake up coughing on slippery ground. The rain is in my face. Npis is peering down at me. A strange man has my children, is holding them. Npis pulls me up. He throws me over his back. My hands fall on either side.

I wake up in a stranger's bed. My whole body is cold. I can't stop shivering. The sound I hear is the chattering of my teeth. I see Npis sitting with the girls by someone's fire ring ablaze with flames. The world, beyond my chattering teeth, is the sound of wind in a tunnel. I want to blink, but the moment my eyelids close, they refuse to open again.

Npis is nudging me awake. The sunlight from the open doorway that greets my eyes is fierce after the monsoon storm. He says, "The baby is hungry. We have to go back to our side of the camp and see what's left. We have to make sure everyone is okay."

The baby needs to feed, so despite the chills and the pressing weight of exhaustion on top of me, I get up. There is a family around us, the faces of distant relatives. We are in their house. They have concrete walls. I look up. The aluminum roof of their house is intact. There is breakfast on a round table.

The older woman with a blue cloth tied around her hair comes and tells me, "Eat. You suffered through the storm. I was so afraid you had died."

I'm too weak to eat. But I gesture for my youngest. I reach for a familiar button that is not there. I look down. I'm wearing a red polyester shirt. Instead of buttons, there are clips. I unclip the stranger's shirt on my body. I feed Kablia. Dawb is scared. She looks at me with her round eyes from the dirt floor. The lines on her face, creased in concern, the furrows across her forehead give me a look into the far future, a future in which I may no longer be here, and my heart physically hurts. Ever since I became a mother, these thoughts about death have visited me often. I push them aside. I gesture for Npis to carry her up on the bed, too, to settle her close to me. Dawb snuggles and hides her face in my side as the baby in my arms sucks desperately from my right breast, the working one. My father's quivering voice comes to me. Whenever there was a hungry child at the table, he'd say, "This child is in a hurry to grow." My youngest is in a hurry to grow.

The return of these lost words settles the storm that is still raging inside me. My body softens. My movements feel sluggish. I tell myself: *Feed the baby, feed the toddler, eat a little, drink hot broth, you'll feel better, a future where your children will be without you is far away.*

I do exactly what I tell myself. I manage to thank the older woman for her clothes. I thank the family for their hospitality. I say, "I'll bring the clothes back when I feel better."

I'm still too shaky to carry the children so Npis lifts both girls up, one in each arm, and I follow. I have no shoes on. I feel the prick of the sticks on the ground, the pebbles hard against the sensitive soles of my feet. I walk as a traveler might in the land of the dead on the backs of the spiky caterpillars.

On this side of the camp, there are no dogs to be seen, neither are there chickens pecking at the corners of the houses. The chicken coops, round woven bamboo hoops, are scattered about the yard. Some of the doors to the houses are blown over, hanging on because of a hinge. For the most part, the buildings are intact, and the people seem to be as well. As we walk further toward our side of the camp, the damage appears slowly. A tree is uprooted. A roof is partially lifted. When we get to the old sewage canal, I'm scared. In the bright light, it is a deceptive thing, risen high, murky as ever, the current fast. I see the things being carried: someone else's shoe, a broken umbrella, something heavier and more mysterious just beneath the surface. Every bit of my body wants to flee. But a large tree has fallen across the length of it in the night and there is now a makeshift bridge to cross over.

Npis looks back at me briefly, says, "You'll be okay."

I want to believe him but I'm not so sure because I am already not okay.

I watch him cross with the girls. He stands on the other side, a young man with a head of thick hair in disarray, wavy hair that curls out from the back of his neck. I notice for the first time that he is also wearing borrowed clothing, a pair of pants that are too big, bell-bottom slacks he does not own. A shirt that is tight, buttoned up the front. He looks strange in the clothes, like an actor sent forth from the Thai magazines that float among the younger women in the camp. For a moment, the gushing water in between us, he feels as far from me as the stars in the magazines.

I stare at my husband, chills running through my body still. Here is a man, hopelessly trying to be a man in a place where his manhood means nothing. He is unable to hunt for food or tend a field. He is unable to get educated or get a job. Here is a man who works as an assistant in the camp hospital for three hundred baht a month. It is not enough to buy his wife papaya salad at the market when she hungers for it. It is only enough to keep the children clothed, to keep shoes on their feet. He sings our collective sorrow at festivities in the camp when the elders pull him to their center, ask him to sing so they can cry openly with each other. Here is a poet with a beautiful voice. A poet whose voice cries even when his eyes are dry. Old words, this time from my mother, come back to me: "It takes some men lifetimes before they learn how to cry." Will this young man one day cry? Will I be around to cry with him when some other young person is singing of the shared sadness of our people?

He calls to me, "You can cross the river."

I tell him, "It's not a real river. It is a river of sewage."

He says, "Don't be afraid."

He is a man now rocking on both legs trying to pacify his children, waiting for his shaky skeleton of a wife to cross a river of feces on a fallen tree. Dawb reaches for me with both of her arms, her palms open, fingers curling in. She wants me. I nod to placate her.

In my heart, I make a resolution: the other women in the camp can have Npis if they want. I decide: if he wants me, he will not go to them. If he goes to them, it is the end for us. I refuse to live in fear of him leaving me, of him loving someone else more than me, finding in their arms whatever is missing in my own. I focus on Dawb.

I cross the fallen tree slowly, first one shaking leg and then the other. It is wide enough that in childhood I could cross it in an easy run. But I'm nearly twenty years old, and in the life I inhabit, all I can do is muster one shaky step at a time. The world around me swirls. The sound of the rushing water underneath me reaches up to surround me. I steady myself by pushing my hands hard into my belly. I straighten my lips into that familiar line. I steel myself, and somehow I make it across the fallen tree. I look up to see Npis's back already walking away from me with my children in his arms, Dawb's head turned to me, her mouth in a frown of sadness.

Everything we own is wet. The clothes have flown out of their basket. The square mirror we had on the wall remained on its nail, reflecting the mess that is our lives. The large sheets in between the beds fallen and torn. There is no roof anymore, so I assure myself that our few possessions will dry in the sun. I am still moving slowly, processing one thing at a time, trying to resolve one issue in my mind before the next. I can see Npis's growing annoyance. I tell him, "I have chills." Around us the rest of the family is doing the same thing. They are all okay. I am relieved that Npis's mother is on both feet, supported on both sides by her older grandchildren. We are all surveying the damage. What is taken in that storm will be clear to me in the months and years after.

I have one more miscarriage and then another.

In between the miscarriages, I take care of my daughters and they grow for me. Dawb's legs grow a little stronger and she learns how to stand on her own. She sees other kids running and she wants to follow. The yearning is such that it moves her feet, one at a time, and slowly she manages to walk where they run. Kablia has deep dimples that peek from her plump cheeks. I've beaded a small bracelet for her, and I have included a bell, a reminder of who I am. Each time she hears a step, a voice, a whistle, the bell on her wrist shakes and she laughs.

The pieces of my heart that are full are brimming with love for my girls.

The pieces of my heart that are empty grow more cavernous with each miscarriage, each little boy who was conceived in an effort to fortify our love story slipping forth from my body. Each time I have a miscarriage, the people around us say in fearful voices, "Is this it? Npis's wife is dying. There's too much blood loss." Each time I have a miscarriage there is a piece of me that wants to die with the slippery thing that has come from my body. But I don't and I return to my living girls and the little life we share.

Npis feels responsible for the pregnancies if not the losses. He grows cold beside me. His coldness makes me angry. I despair. My sorrow sends him further from me. It is a predictable cycle. I hear from the other sisters-in-law that there are women he is seeing in the camp, beautiful, young, and healthy. I act disinterested. I don't like the pitying looks. I don't like the knowledge that we are falling apart in front of everyone, that everything is coming undone.

In these tragic years, in the spread of the six miscarriages, I have nightmares of the hands holding my ankles in the water. If I were with my mother, I would tell her. If I told her, she would do something. She would get a pig and chickens. She would have a shaman come over or do a ceremony herself. She would call my sick spirit back. It was clear to me that my spirit had taken flight that dark night, that it was lost somewhere in the flow of that river of sewage. I had seen this happen many times as a child. A boy goes to catch fish. In the water, he encounters something unspeakable. In the days after, he loses his appetite. He loses his energy. He stays in bed through long days, staring into nothing. A concerning cry from a parent calls a shaman. The shaman performs a ceremony. They barter for what is lost. In the end, if the shaman is successful, the boy will slowly gain strength in his body again, gain an appetite for life, and rise forth slowly and surely. If my mother were here in this camp with me, I'd tell her about the hands in the river and she would fight for me, and I'd learn how to fight for myself. As it was: only Npis's mother was present. She saw his unhappiness grow, and she wanted him to be happy again—even if it meant saying goodbye to me. And this reality haunts me like the feeling of the hands beneath the water, how a mother will fight for her child.

CHAPTER 15

Death by a Sugarcane Grove

In the buzzing world of the refugee camp, I feel a quiet emptiness swallowing me. I don't know where to find my departed spirit in the world that we belong to; I don't know where she hides in the life I share with my children and Npis. A slender woman who looks like me and sounds like me gets up early with the dawn each day. She makes rice and fish soup. She feeds her children at the wooden table and wipes their mouths clean with gentle hands. The woman who is me has no sense of purpose; her willingness to live dwindles. She is tired of having to endure the nightmares that keep her from rest and the daytime hunger, always the hunger. The hunger for food. The hunger for love. The hunger for a girlhood across a river, a life beyond this one. This woman tries to kill herself in this hot place where big families gather around the communal well each night to bathe together, where younger siblings will shriek and cry and laugh all at once when their older brother or sister pours the buckets of cold water over their soapy heads, each unit waiting their turn to leave.

The woman who is prepared to die knows that there is an old toothless vendor at the camp market who sells pills that fizz in the water. Relatives with silver to clean will buy the pills to ensure that the necklaces they own continue to shine. This woman does not have any silver. She lost the silver necklace her mother had given her for her wedding in the Mekong River years ago. She has not made enough money to buy a new silver necklace in all the time in the camp. How long has it been? Her youngest is four now. The family has been in the camp for nearly six years. Suicide abounds in this place where the Hmong wait for resettlement. There are whispers after their deaths. It chases their heavy bodies, smelling like rot for days, for weeks—until someone else kills themselves. Many of the people who kill themselves use the fizzing pills. They are inexpensive, and the process, the woman hears, is fast.

The woman who goes through the motions of my life gets up earlier than the dawn. She does not make rice or fish soup in the kitchen this morning. Lights no fires. Instead, she walks on gentle steps in the dark to the big clay water jar by the door of the communal kitchen. There, she borrows Npis's black plastic comb and runs it through her long, thick hair. Npis has not yet gotten the day's water supply. He is still sleeping in bed with his daughters on either arm. The water in the jar is not even halfway full. In the still blue lingering light of night, the trees in the distance are suggestions of themselves. The woman sees a reflection in the water as she looks down into the clay jar; she knows it is a ghost looking at her. She does not need light to know what this ghost looks like. The ghost is thin. Her chin is sharp. Her nose looks particularly big on her small face. Her eyes, too, have grown large like a cartoon. She is harsh, all angles and lines that don't fit, that feel jagged. Her face carries an expression like her stomach is sour. The woman is tired of the ghost; she turns away from the sad mirror of the water and pulls her hair back in a ponytail, then she twists, and folds it until it is a stack against the back of her head. She clips it with her nice clip, the brown plastic one with silver flowers engraved on its surface. She squeezes a bit of white toothpaste onto her red toothbrush. The tube is nearly empty, but she does not have to worry about buying a new one. The bristles on the old brush are hard and stiff. They stab her gums. They bleed. She spits out the blood, made fresh by the toothpaste; it almost makes her smile. The thought that she bleeds brings comfort. She cleanses her mouth with cupped hands full of cold water. She washes her faces. Then, she takes a deep breath and tugs at her shirt. She secures her sarong with the metal belt around her thin waist, no babies pushing it out. Inside the belt, she's stuck a few bills. She'll need them. The woman takes a deep breath, straightens her spine, and then starts walking toward the camp market just as the gray thins and the light of day unfolds.

It rained in the night although the woman hadn't noticed. The earth is slippery. Her plastic shoes stick with each step. A lonesome mother dog approaches her with sad eyes. The dog is quiet. Her breasts are heavy with milk though her frame is thin, flesh sagging off bones. The woman is sorry she has nothing to offer this hungry mother dog. Her inability to help another life urges her toward her dismal mission.

The rushing river of her nightmares is no more. The canal is stagnant and low, a mixture of brown solids and liquids stinking up the whole of the world. A few water bugs dance across its thick surface, creating small ripples. Not even a child could drown in the river of feces now. The top of the fallen tree has been scraped into a solid bridge. The woman crosses quickly just as the early-morning roosters start to crow from this side of the camp. A thin line of pink thickens into a band of peach and slips into orange along the eastern sky.

At the camp market, only the earliest vendors have set up their stalls. The heavy woman butcher is dividing the cuts of pork on a piece of bloody plastic over the roughly made wooden table with her big heavy Hmong knife. The congee woman has just taken the lid off her pot as steam rises from its bubbling contents and blown into the embers glowing in the portable clay stove. The couple who sells live chickens have just unpacked the tired animals from the old rice sacks they used to transport them on their truck and stuffed the metal cages full of white- and brown-feathered creatures. Down the line, the old toothless woman who sells fizzing pills is already set up. Her table is lined with small packets of capsules in little palm-sized zipped see-through plastic bags. She stands behind the table, a bent woman, the size of a child in her heavy morning sweater.

My feet cannot take my body to the table fast enough. My eyes run over the packets of blue pills, the capsules of red and green and blue, the familiar umbrella red of the Decolgen, the paracetamol that I have purchased many times for my girls when they battled colds and other ailments. There are uniform boxes full of oils for the ills of the body, cooling menthol oils that are spicy and bitter to the taste buds but open up airways and soothe away nausea. The table is full of remedies.

My heart is pumping too fast. My breath is short and shallow. Tears I hadn't planned on shedding leak through. I wipe at the corners of my eyes like a child with my open palms. I straighten my lips into the familiar defense line, but it is quivering and unstable. I swallow the thing that is trying to consume me. My throat feels parched and dry.

The old woman looks up at me when I approach her table in my hurry. Her hair is pulled back with the familiar blue cloth common to Hmong women of her generation. My own mother used to wear a wrap just like hers.

The vendor asks, "What can I get you today, young woman?"

I tell her, "I am looking for silver cleaning pills."

She studies me. Her lids are curtains that have fallen low above her eyes. Her pink tongue comes out of her mouth. I tell myself to look only at her mouth. She has no more teeth. Her gums are pink as a baby's. Her tongue, too, is pink and it looks soft and wet. She licks her bottom lip again. I don't see what her eyes see.

Her voice comes from far away, a slight tremble carrying the words: "I don't have any left."

I look down at the world of pills on her table. My gaze is once again so wet I can barely see. I am mad at my tears. At this rate, I will be my own undoing.

I don't even know what the pills look like. I remember them as circular and white, but I'd only ever seen them in the hands of others. I feel a choking sensation at my throat.

I tell her, "Please help me."

The old woman says, "I am sorry, but I will not sell you any silver cleaning pills today."

My right hand skims the surface above the nameless pills. I want my hand to be a magnet. I want the packet of pills to jump up into my hold. Nothing happens. The floating hand starts shaking. I can't control it. It is moving faster and faster.

My hand is caught. The old woman's hold is firm.

Suddenly, I'm a bird.

I'm a girl again. My special nephew in America is a boy again. He hands me a bird he has caught. It is a little blue bird. It squeaks and cries, opens its beaked mouth so I see the triangle of red in its throat. I am gentle as he places the small, warm body in my hands. My fingers encircle its body, full of heart, throbbing in fear.

Both of the old woman's hands are around mine. She engulfs my trembling hand like it is a fragile thing. I am nothing more than a frightened bird, crying now because I've lost my ability to fly.

Her pink tongue licks at her bottom lip again but I don't see it, it is the sound that comes to me. I've met many toothless older people in my time. I try to pull my hand back a little, to see if there's give, room to escape. Her hands refuse my weak attempt.

A small tight voice I don't recognize emerges from me: "What other vendors carry the pills?"

The old woman is speaking very softly now, each word an island connected to the next by wind and water. "I don't know. It is a long line of vendors from here until the end. You walk and you ask them. This old lady does not have any for you today."

All my life I had fought to stay alive. Even before I knew it, I, like my daughters, had sucked at my mother's breasts, hungry to grow. In all my memories of being hurt as a child, I'd run to my mother to let her know, to my brothers to inform them, each time searching for care. In the jungle years, I had somehow kept walking and holding on—in the lonely days as a captive enemy, in the painful delivery of my first child, in the frantic flight after our rescue, even when my infected breast made me believe death was the natural conclusion, a piece of me had held on to life. Now that I was ready for death, this old woman was making it hard.

I pull my hand with more force. Hers offer no resistance this time. To my shame and sadness, I am free.

The old woman tells me, "I don't know whose daughter you are or whose wife or whose mother, but you will not get any silver cleaning pills from me on this day."

Her voice becomes gentle once more. "I will not let anyone sell you the pills today either, kuv tus me ntxhais."

Kuv tus me ntxhais, my daughter. I had heard it years ago from my mother. In the moments when she wasn't addressing me. In the moments when she was in conversation with another and Tswb came up. In fact, I had just uttered the words last night, by the fire, to my own girls, directly, first to Dawb and then to Kablia, identifying them as mine.

I turn away from the old woman.

I say with my back to her, "You can't do that."

I walk away.

The woman who is me walks away, feet crisscrossing, stumbling, no dignity, no grace. The woman does not wipe away her tears. She cries openly, going from one vendor to the next asking, pleading, for silver cleaning pills. Her desperation is immense. Many of the vendors don't even respond with words. They just shake their heads. A few take steps away from the open-mouthed cries of the woman and her proffered hands, pushed together in front of her heart. The woman pleading to die is not Tswb Muas. She is a woman with no name of her own.

By the time I reach the end of the line of vendors, I have three capsules in a little plastic bag in the closed palm of my left hand. A lone vendor, a man, sells me the three pills. He said they were his last three.

The woman, grateful for the pills, stumbles along the path away from the market, in the opposite direction of her daughters, still asleep, in the arms of the man who would raise them with a new woman by his side. This thought quickens the woman's steps.

Beside a grove of mature sugarcane, on the far side of the camp, the woman stops. She sees that there is a flat rock near the side of the dirt path, a good place as any for the act. She is prepared to sit down, to open the packet, to take the pills. But there is a problem.

The woman has never been able to take pills without water to wash them down. She looks around her. No water anywhere. She opens the little plastic bag and takes out the pills. They are bigger than she had expected. She knows she can't dry swallow them. She takes a deep breath. She feels the sides of her face. Her skin is moist and wet. She feels the strands of her hair that have come undone about her neck. She takes the clip off the back of her head. She pulls the heavy strands together again in one hand and twists. She folds her hair like a ribbon and then reclips her hair. She pulls at the skirt and the shirt. She secures the metal belt around her waist, makes sure its buckle is at her belly button. She sees that the sky has lifted itself. A new day has fully dawned. She knows that if she does not hurry, the man on the other side of the camp will wake up, the little girls will whimper and cry and call out for their mother, hands searching the cold place where she had been. The romance of the dark morning is gone. The woman is suddenly very tired. The muddy earth is sticky. She hurries back toward the camp market once again. One of her plastic shoes sticks in the gooey mess of earth. She tries to free herself. She falls forward. She manages to catch herself on her hands. The plastic bag—which she's forgotten to close—lets a pill slip into the mud. It is dirty, disgusting now. She can't put it in her mouth. She is going to die, but not by swallowing the pill now coated with mud that might have been peed on by dogs or pooped on by chickens. She gets up. Her sarong is now wet and caked with dirt at her knees. She has lost patience not only with the world but with herself. This place isn't for her. She yearns for a return to the shade of her father's orchard, the sweet, clean scent of the flowers that bloom and fall to the ground, a time before she lost everything, her mother in that jungle, Npis and the beauty of their friendship even in a war.

At the camp market, she goes directly to the vendor who sells sweet drinks. The colorful sodas in the glass bottles are expensive. She buys the cheapest drink: a sweet syrupy liquid in a plastic bag with a straw hanging out of one side.

On the way back to the sugarcane grove, that resting rock she'd seen, the woman puts the two remaining pills in her mouth, sucks at the straw until the bitterness is gone. In its place: sugary water.

The woman is a girl again in that village where the rivers meet. It is sugarcane harvesting season. Her father is not yet sick. He still has enough strength in his arms to chop at the base of the sugarcane patch he's planted in a corner of the backyard garden. He still has enough control over the sickle in his hands to peel off the hard bark. He hands her a stretch the length of her entire arm. The girl opens her mouth wide. She takes a big bite of the fibrous stalk and chews and chews. Sweet sugarcane juice fills her mouth. She closes her eyes and gives in to the taste, as the smell of orange blossoms welcome her home.

On the rock, the woman sits. She raises both legs in front of her. She wraps her arms around her knees. She lays her tired head to rest.

A child stumbles upon the body, fallen on the ground, fizzing at the mouth. The child screams. People come running. Among them, Npis.

Npis had woken up to find my place in bed empty, the door to the sala slightly ajar. He saw that my shoes were gone. The prints I had made in the muddy earth led him to the market. At the market, he'd lost sight of my steps. Until a child's screams cut through the sounds of the market and stopped the vendors and the early-morning customers in their tracks: "A dead woman, a dead woman here!"

CHAPTER 16

The Ghost

I woke up in the camp hospital. I heard the whirring of the fan over me. For a moment, I thought I had had another miscarriage. I opened my eyes to find Npis sitting where he usually sat, on a stool by the end of the bed. His head was in his hands. His legs, like the fan above me, in continuous motion, up and down, up and down, except he made no sound on the concrete, the heels of both his feet, clad in green flip-flops, never touching the floor. I closed my eyes again. I did not want to talk or be talked to.

I was in my early twenties. I was a woman. I had children. I lived a life. And yet all I wanted was to be someone's child again. I wanted to be young once more. If I were a kid, I could wake up and feel embarrassed and chastised and everything would continue. My parents would call me to the table, they would put a spoon in my hand and tell me to eat—as I did with Dawb when she misbehaved and was ashamed of herself. But I was not a child and both my mother and father were far from my reach, so I pretended to be unconscious for much longer than I was, though I knew I could not pretend forever.

My thoughts went to my girls. If Npis was here. Where were they?

When I had miscarriages, it was usually the sisters-in-law who took them, sometimes dividing them between the women.

I asked, "Where are my girls?"

Npis's head swung up. His legs stilled. Then, nothing was still. The air around us vibrated with his gasping cries. My own rose to meet his. Our ache was so deep and neither of us knew how to fill it. The empty was the miscarriages, the poverty, the fact that I missed my family and he was with his, it was the little family we had made and how we both had a shared responsibility to take care of the children—despite the fact that we both needed care ourselves, care we could not give each other. We cried until we grew self-conscious of those around us and each other. We quieted ourselves. We cried some more until our tears stopped. It was only our hearts heaving at the end, and then Npis was standing beside the hospital bed and his hands were empty by his side. I found myself reaching for his fingers, the warmth of his touch.

He said, "It was all too much. You've gone through too much. If I could give you a better life, I would. I'm sorry, I can't. I have little to offer you."

He freed me from shame with his words.

I was living a life where there was little on offer, and I yearned for more. A part of me wanted a second chance, to return to that jungle in Laos, to that chaotic night, to that grove of trees behind where my family had camped, to say to the young me, "Don't go with Npis. Neither of you can see what is coming."

It was the fact that while we had outrun so much death to get to where we were, where we were was a place we couldn't have imagined, in dreams or nightmares. This holding center, where grief haunted us, lived with us and inside of us, where we were expected to wait patiently, to take care of ourselves and each other, and somehow be okay, be thankful. The future was an unpredictable place, and neither Npis nor I could see individually or together what that future might hold. All we knew were the heartache and the tears.

I nodded to show Npis that I accepted the truth of his words. We were in agreement. He was stating the truth of our lives. The time had

finally come for us to talk, to hear each other, and to decide whether
we believed in ourselves and each other, and I knew that after all the
clamoring, the hurting, what I said next would determine the future of
our lives, together or apart. In the scale of our destiny, our marriage was
the only thing that felt within our range of control. It was clear to me
that Npis would not fight me, whichever way my words traveled.

On that hospital bed, I knew I had a choice to make. All I needed
to do was make a decision and we would be over and I could start re-
claiming the pieces of me that I had lost along the way to us. I did not
need to tell him about the rumors of him and other women or the pain
that their possibilities caused me. I did not need to tell him about how
hard I had worked to take care of our children, his family, and him. I
did not need to ask him to do more for me, to be more patient and kind,
to return to the friend he had been in those early days of our marriage,
the young man I missed. All I needed to do was say, "I cannot continue
in this marriage."

Or I could simply turn my back to him after the tears, in the wake of
his words, and my position would be clear.

On that hospital bed, I thought of all the times I could have said no
to Npis. On the day of our first meeting, I could have walked without
turning back. On his visits later, I could have done what I knew to do
so well, disregarded his presence, turned him down, walked away. He
wouldn't have chased me. He wouldn't have gone searching for me. On
that hospital bed, I realized how each time, I had chosen him—before
without my knowing—but this time if I did choose him, the truth was
in between us, and there could be no excuses, for me or anyone else.

On that hospital bed, I accepted the fact of my unglamorous love
story. I acknowledged that I had chosen it for myself. Npis. A man with
no standing in his family. A man with no standing in the world. A man
who demanded a strength from me I couldn't always give. I saw the
limitations of Npis, not as a young man in the jungles of Laos just struggling to survive, but as a man in a life beyond a war. A man who would
not push the people around him to accommodate his life—let alone his
dreams. On that hospital bed, I knew that I had to become the kind of

woman I never imagined for myself: the kind who also knew her own limitations as a human being, the fact that she was willing to die and leave her children, for a possibility elsewhere, a place free from sorrow, from the great losses, the great yearnings. Npis and I were both weaker than we wanted to be. All we had was ourselves or each other. On that hospital bed, we chose each other, again.

And after the hospital, life resumed. Nothing had changed. It was as it had been. I continued having miscarriages and suffering by myself and sometimes with Npis. The girls grew a little bit bigger and their light extended further from me. With their words, they allowed others to enter their worlds. With their laughter, they invited fun from cousins, aunts, and uncles, their grandma, too. And I returned to my place beneath the overhang of our communal roof, holding pieces of embroidery on my lap, attending to the needle and the thread.

Ours was not the only marriage on the brink of disaster. Many of the couples our age and younger, whether they'd married in the jungle or in the camp, fought. Our proximity to each other was close. It was almost as if the place was haunted by a ghost who wanted love to die.

One day, one of the couples in our communal house had a falling-out. The husband had been gone all day. When he returned, he had no shirt on. He was hungry from wherever he'd been. He helped himself to a bowl of rice and stood in the communal kitchen eating. All day his young wife had sat working on her nails. She'd used a nail clipper to cut each nail to a sharp V. She'd painted them red, a deep red, layers and layers of nail polish. As the man was eating, his wife snuck up behind him. He was unaware of her presence. She scraped his back with both hands, and blood seeped where her carefully manufactured claws sliced through. The man yelped in pain. Npis's mother tried to intervene. The woman said, "I hate men with penises sticking out, wandering freely around the camp, hoping someone will jump on for a ride." Npis's mother backed away. We all did as the man screamed in pain and ran in the direction of his older brother's house.

On yet another occasion, a couple to the right of us in the communal house had a fight. No one knew why. They were mostly a quiet pair. Once in a while, if irritated or annoyed, the wife would swipe her husband with a shirt or bat him away with a hand, and whenever he was unhappy he had a horrible habit of mumbling, "All over this camp, people die every day. There are drums for the dead that beat on and on. Why can't one of them beat for you?" These words were childish and cruel, but they generally were as bad as it got. Except on that one occasion, when out of nowhere we saw the husband turn over their dining table and begin throwing the handmade wooden stools at his wife. Their children cried and screamed. The men tried to go and calm down the raging man, to no avail. The wife, incredibly fleet of foot, scampered away from the thrown objects, her baby in her arms.

In the scale of the arguments and fights among the married couples on our side of Ban Vinai Refugee Camp, even within our communal house, the coldness and despair in my marriage was not unique. Npis and I were never the loudest or the most physical. In fact, we were more controlled than others, and that did not help our situation any. We were waiting for something in our lives to change, unsure and uncertain how we might ourselves be effective agents of our own change.

In the waiting, I heard from a relative that my sister Xis had married and she and her new husband had successfully fled Laos. They had been in a different camp for just a few months, then they had applied for resettlement, and because there were only the two of them, not a big family wanting to travel together, they had been sponsored to go to America by a church. They now lived with a white family in a place called Massachusetts. Xis followed the news with a letter containing her address and an offer to sell my embroidery to the members of the church she was now part of. I sent her my embroidery. She sent me whatever money she could sell the pieces for. The money was enough for me to supplement the rations of the family and buy the occasional dress for the girls.

One day, I passed by a stall selling shirts. There were red T-shirts, white T-shirts, blue T-shirts, yellow T-shirts. All of them were bright and bold. I didn't like any of them for Npis. I asked to see the nicer shirts. The woman showed me polo shirts. Knit-fabric shirts with collars. There was a dark blue one. It had three buttons close to its neck, also in blue. I had enough money with me to buy the shirt. It was my first gift for Npis in our marriage.

I offered it to him that very evening after the girls were asleep, when his brother and his wife and their now many children quieted their talk, after Npis's mother's snores grew steady. He touched the soft fabric of the shirt then he handed it back to me.

He said, "I'll wear it when we take pictures."

The corners of my mouth lifted.

The next day, food at the table tasted better than the day before. Even the boiled water from the dented kettle tasted sweeter than it had previously. Day by day, I grew stronger in my body and my heart.

Each night, our little family gathered on our platform bed. The girls slept between us. Above their heads, Npis and I sometimes stretched our hands and sometimes our fingers clasped. Other times, they did not. Sometimes we spoke of our fears. Other times, we spoke of nothing at all. We just listened to the crickets singing their songs outside, the wind blowing through the slits in the walls.

I whispered to Npis, "I'm afraid of ghosts."

He whispered back, "There's very little room for the living in this camp, let alone the hauntings of the dead."

On a sunny, windswept day, one of Npis's nieces, Nkauj Ib, and I were walking on a path that cut across the hills that surrounded Ban Vinai Refugee Camp. We were on our way home. We had gone to a different segment of the camp to accept a gift. A relative had killed a pig and had sent word for us to go and get a serving of meat for the family. It was not a big pig, but it was generous of them to share and we were thankful.

Even in the camp, some of the old practices from village life survived.

If I pass by a stranger's open door and they are gathered around the dining table, inevitably, they would invite me to join the meal. Of course, a refusal is customary, but the older people practice a tenacious insistence. They would set down their spoons and come to the doorway, compelling me inside to a bite of rice and a sip of broth. They would say, "There's not much to eat, but all our hearts will get fuller if we sit together awhile."

If someone died, no one waited for an invitation to visit. We would all go and gather close to speak of our communal grief and lament the loss as a Hmong family. If there was heavy work to be done, such as butchering an animal, or tedious work such as washing baskets of mustard greens, or complicated work such as helping to move a family from one segment of the camp to the other, then everyone close by would lend a hand. In a difficult moment, we would all help carry the sorrow, the weight of work, and the sadness.

These are beautiful things about my people. The spirit of generosity by the distant relatives and the fresh meat buoyed us up that day. I carried the meat in a plastic bag swinging from my right hand. It was a comfortable weight. The sun was lowering in the west where the grass appeared golden like wheat. Near the setting sun, frothy clouds in shades of pink and orange stretched their arms wide. A cool wind blew so that the waist-high grass along the side of the path danced, recalling the road to and from my childhood. The niece, Nkauj Ib, and I were talking casually.

I happened to look toward the right slope of the hill we were on, cautious because I knew there were burial mounds for the camp's dead on this stretch of our walk. I expected to see the mounds in the dirt, offerings of food and drink, the darkened ashes of burnt joss paper, the shortened ends of incense sticks having done their work. Instead, I saw a man, completely naked, standing over a freshly dug grave mound, his hands on his penis.

I screamed.

I ran.

Nkauj Ib ran with me. Nkauj Ib ran in front of me. She was faster than me. Taller. She had longer legs. I screamed again as I raced to keep up with the back of her white shirt, holding fast to the meat, even in my fright.

By the time we made it home, we were both breathless, sides aching.

She said to everyone who'd come running at our frantic return, "We saw a ghost on the burial hill."

Everyone believed her.

I nearly did as well. My chest squeezing tight.

The younger children wanted to know exactly where the ghost was and what it looked like.

I managed, "A man."

I didn't go into details. What we saw was more dangerous than a ghost. What I saw was a man, completely naked, standing above a grave mound, massaging himself, looking directly at us, at me. What I saw was a violation. I wasn't going to explain this to the kids or the other adults. I heard the buzz of questions that might come my way. What were you looking for up there? How long did you look to see that he was touching himself? Did he look back at you?

All the Hmong women knew not to let our daughters far from our sight. We, the younger Hmong women, knew that the Thai guards and other men in the camp could not be trusted. Beneath the bustle of our lives in the camp, there was a darkness lurking, looking for opportunities to swirl up and pull down the living, particularly women. Stories of rape abounded. Always in a whisper because there were people to protect. Always in a whisper because there were powerful people and less powerful people. We all knew someone who had disappeared. The authorities would say they had left the camp, run back to the old country. That night, I held my girls close to me, speaking quietly into their hair as sleep came to them, "Never play far away from your mother and father's gazes. Never. Never. Never."

Years after we left the camp, in a different room under that same old moon, reflected now on the other side of the world, I told Npis the truth about what we saw on that hill. I said, "Npis, the ghosts I feared most in Ban Vinai Refugee Camp were not the dead ones but the ones who could take those I love from the land of the living, the ones who I knew could take me and you and tear us apart."

CHAPTER 17

Running Away

You are now a refugee in a neighboring country. You will become
a refugee all over again in a new country. These are the truths
that mark the experience, the first leaving, the second, for some—the
third, the fourth, the fifth. Everything becomes a leaving once you've
left home.

I start a business in the refugee camp where I make sweet, slippery
tapioca dessert. One of the older sisters-in-law teaches me how to make
tapioca worms by boiling water and mixing it with tapioca starch. The
hot water cooks the dough, turns the white flour into an opaque color. I
use my hands to knead more tapioca starch into the burning hot dough.
My hands heat up. They burn. I blow at my red hands and keep working
the dough until I have a firm ball, until I can roll it into an elastic sheet
with a glass bottle. I layer the pieces, still steaming hot, and then I cut
them into strips with a big Hmong knife that Npis sharpens religiously
each evening. I prepare a pot of boiling water to cook them on the
flames of the fire. When the cooked strips grow fat and translucent and
float on the surface, they are cooked and ready to soak in cold water.
I make a thick simple syrup by boiling bags of sugar in a bit of water
and mixing it continuously with a wooden paddle Npis has made for

the purpose. I don't take it off the heat until the clear liquid turns into watery coffee and the scent of caramel fills the room. Next, I have to prepare the coconut milk. The work is hard but monotonous.

In the dark of the morning hours, I wake up every day quietly to ensure that the business survives. I blow the air in my chest into the night embers until they glow in the communal kitchen. I feed the red lines in the darkened coals with bits of tinder until there is smoke and flames. My long shadow on the back wall of the kitchen scares me when I pass by the hot flames, arms double my own in length reaching down, so I make it a point not to look at the wall as I boil the water, mix the starch, roll the dough, cut it, and then continue forth until all my ingredients are ready. I work slowly and quietly knowing that this business is temporary. It will not last. Nothing does in this holding place for refugees.

I hate to wake Npis up but I'm not strong enough to crack into the mature coconuts so that I can scrape out the hard meat and make coconut milk. I have no choice. I enter the sleeping quarters. Npis is sleeping on the outer edge of the bamboo platform we share with our children. His arms reach across the bodies of our daughters. In his sleep, I see his exhaustion, the shadows of his cheekbones, not as sharp as they were before but still there, evidence of our situation. He is a heavy sleeper. My gaze alone cannot wake him the way his can wake me. I reach for his shoulder, feel the warmth of his skin, and shake him.

In the gray, we work together. His presence beside me changes the morning. Our shadows from the fire that we cast on the back wall of the kitchen are having more fun than we are. They look like shadow puppets playacting a life for an audience of two, silly and serious at once. Unlike mine alone, the darkened outlines of Npis and me entertain. In the flesh, we talk in murmurs. I know I am a perfectionist. I am as meticulous as ever. Everything must be clean. All the tapioca strings must be cut to the length of my index finger—not Npis's, mine. In truth, we don't work well together, so I tell him what to do and he complies to the best of his ability. I recognize this as a fact of our lives. I think to myself, *Today is going to be another long day.*

All the long days in the refugee camp keep adding up. Years have come and gone. People leave. People enter. People are born. And people die. All of it happens in the same square mile of our lives. The goodbyes and the welcomes, the breakups and the makeups. The fears. All of it happens every day, across the days.

Npis and I are fighting again. I forget what I am mad at Npis about. Kablia is being a brat, crying, crying, crying for something she wants that I cannot give her. I take a rubber band and tell her to turn around. I stretch the rubber band in my hands until it is taut. I let go of my left hand. My younger child screams. She runs away from me. Npis chases after her. He finds her hiding behind a tree. He returns carrying her like she is seriously injured. He is mad at me. I take older Dawb and we leave for the house of a distant relative on the other side of the camp. I pack nothing. I can feel Npis's gaze following me, but he does not call me back or offer me a way to stay, to apologize, to comfort the children, both sobbing now, one in his arms and the other in mine.

That night in the house of the distant relative, on a hard platform bed, beneath an old blanket, frayed at its edges and emanating the musky smells of unfamiliar bodies, I think about my options. We've been in the camp for nearly eight years. My marriage cannot sustain the pressures of this transient life where we get older everywhere, find ways of making a little money so we can grow even older as we wait for our children to grow up. If I had brothers, close family, in the camp, I would divorce Npis. I would take both my daughters. We would leave for America. But everyone I have is also everyone Npis has. We share the same people now. Even these distant relatives whose house I'm in, they are also Npis's relatives; if he had come to them in the dark asking for a place to rest, they'd put him right here in this bed full of odors. Worse, if I leave Npis, who would love our girls the way he does? Who would wake in the dawn to be told what to do, step by step, each morning? Not because he doesn't know but because his wife wants everything to be perfect in an imperfect life. Sleep is impossible, even with my arms around Dawb's body. I nestle my head even deeper into her hair, the warm freshness of the flowery soap I'd wash her with tonight. I weep, thinking: *Who washed Kablia tonight on the other side of the camp? Is she sleeping with the day's sweat and tears drying on her body?*

In the still-dark dawn, I wake Dawb with a touch to her hair and we make our way out of the relative's bed, fold their old blanket at its feet. I feel like a child guiding a child. I feel embarrassed and stupid; these feelings have become friends inside me. I also feel contriteness and a sense of responsibility: to stop myself from doing something I haven't thought carefully through. Dawb's little hand in mine, we take the path back to our side of the camp, me looking both ways for living and dead ghosts. There is no one and nothing. Just the loud chirping of frogs from the river of feces. The crickets beneath the water jars by the darkened doorways of individual and communal houses. The hungry dogs look at us from the patios of neighbors and friends though even they know that we have nothing to offer them, so they don't move toward us, just bow their heads as we pass. Dawb stumbles with the uneven strength in her legs and I am overcome by guilt, so I carry her. With her weight in my arms, my breathing grows raspy. At our communal house, I set her down on the stairs and hold her hand as she guides me past the doorways to our sleeping room. We find that the door has been left untied—something that Npis and I never do.

Npis and Kablia are both asleep in the darkened room. Her face is buried in his chest. His arms circle her body. She is so small beneath the thin blanket that if I didn't know how to look for her, I would have missed her entirely. I am forlorn at this observation. Our space on the bed waits for us. Dawb crawls into her place, pulls the blanket high beneath her chin, and closes her eyes, shifting close to her sister's body. In my place by the wall, I lie straight as the dead, eyes closed, tears leaking down both sides of my face. I know I should wake up to make the sweet tapioca dessert for the day so I can sell it at the market. But my body refuses.

Npis and I are tired of life in Ban Vinai Refugee Camp. In the day, we don't talk to each other but we are swept up in all the stories from Laos that keep flooding in. We can't help ourselves. We are caught up in these stories that could have so easily been ours, that belong to those we care about.

Npis's mother is in a sad state. She has three nephews, belonging to three brothers who are all dead. These nephews are like brothers to each other in a life where they have been orphans together. They are cousin brothers.

The smartest and youngest among the three cousin brothers, Zeb, has chosen to stay behind in Laos, has been reeducated into the new system, and has a minor post in a communist village. The second and most loyal of the three cousin brothers, Tuam, had escaped Laos and been with us for a few weeks in the camp but has chosen to return to the old country to try to rescue his wife and children, all captives in a communist village, the exact one where Zeb has the post. The third and oldest of the cousin brothers, Pheej, has been in the camp for as long as we have and has just received news that his family will leave Thailand within a year or so for a place called Michigan.

Zeb was secretly helping Tuam plan an escape for his family. Their plan did not go as they had hoped. Zeb told Tuam to sneak out of the camp, travel back to the Mekong River, cross it, travel the day to the communist village, and wait there in the dark by the reeds that grew along the low rice fields. Once the villagers were asleep, Zeb would come and retrieve Tuam, and they would go round up his family, and he would help them escape. Zeb told Tuam to carry enough floaties in his backpack for the members of his family. The Mekong River was high and they would need them to cross safely. Tuam did exactly as Zeb instructed. He left the refugee camp one night. Those closest to him knew exactly where he'd gone and why. Pheej knew that he'd traveled back into Laos with a backpack full of floaties.

At the designated meeting place near the communist village, to Tuam's surprise, there was a group of Hmong men crouched low among the tall reeds when he got there. He and they started talking. The men were looking to leave Laos. Like him, they had family members held captive in the enemy village and were hoping to free them. What was he doing there by himself? Tuam said he was waiting for someone to come get him once the commotion in the village died down. He told them he had a backpack full of floaties and was going to try to rescue his family from captivity on that very night. The men nodded their understanding. Then, they began whispering among themselves. Tuam found it peculiar. Before he could do anything about this strange buzzing among the men, several of them pulled out guns. They killed him on the spot. They ravaged his backpack and took his floaties.

When Zeb came to get Tuam around midnight, he found his cousin brother's bullet-ridden body lying in a pool of blood. He saw the empty backpack, floaties all gone. He didn't know who had murdered his cousin brother but he realized what had happened.

Zeb could not bear the thought of leaving Tuam's body unburied. He knew he could not stay the night, burying the body. He knew it would be found, this close to the rice fields and the village. Zeb decided to go to the leader of the communist village that very night, a Lao man named Bountong. He went to Bountong's house, knocked on his door; when the man opened it, he said, "I have killed my cousin brother by the edge of the low rice fields. He'd snuck back into Laos to try to rescue his family. I now ask your permission to bury his body."

Bountong was surprised by these words, having heard Zeb talk on other occasions about his strong bond with his cousin brothers, Tuam and Pheej. Bountong led a contingent of men to go and survey the low rice fields, to see if indeed this was true. To his surprise and delight, he found Tuam's body just as Zeb had described it, bullet-ridden in a pool of blood. Bountong graciously granted permission for Zeb to bury Tuam. In the morning, the burial was conducted, even with help from Bountong's own men. Bountong celebrated Zeb as a loyal and committed comrade of the communist party.

News of Zeb's valiant patriotism traveled quickly—even to us in the refugee camp. In a heat of despair and anger, Pheej snuck out of the camp to go and meet Zeb for the last time across the Mekong River.

There, away from the eyes and ears of everyone, Pheej, the oldest of the cousin brothers, told Zeb, the youngest, "We are no longer brothers, you and me. I am here to ask the heavens above to crack your neck because you don't deserve to live. What the countries do to us, what politics demands of us, does not absolve us from the things we do to those who love us, who've grown up with us. You are no good for the living now. You belong in the realm of dead men."

Zeb offered no excuses or explanations. He kept his head low as Pheej walked away from him in disgust. Pheej made it back safely to the camp. On his way to Michigan with his family, he came to visit Npis's mother, their only remaining aunt. He told her that the brotherhood among Zeb, Tuam, and himself was no more.

Pheej left Ban Vinai Refugee Camp heavy with hurt. One of the men who had been party to Tuam's murder had made it safely across the Mekong River and was now in the camp and had visited Npis's older brothers and told them what had transpired that dark night in the high reeds near the rice fields of that communist village, how he and a group of men desperate to leave the country with their families had killed Tuam and stolen his floaties, and how to their immense surprise Zeb, his own cousin brother, had taken responsibility for the murder. Npis's mother is inconsolable, her heart breaking for each of her nephews.

These stories keep coming out of the old country, keep reminding us that the war we had escaped continues for those who had been left behind, those who had returned, and how it might never end, just the Mekong River in between. Npis's mother's sorrow over the situation is difficult to witness. She walks around the communal houses, she laments and cries for Zeb, Tuam, and Pheej and their brotherhood to herself. She feels that she has failed them as their aunt, unable to help them reconcile the sordid facts of this war. It is clear she is also full of fear for her own sons in this place that is still haunted by the horrors of the war; brotherhoods are fragile things.

In the night, Npis and I start to discuss a plan to leave the camp or divorce. The girls are awake, aware of the tension between us. We ask them who they will choose to stay with or go with in the eventuality of our divorce. Whatever commitments we've made previously, we've forgotten. We are still both in our twenties. The girls start crying. We know we are being immature and we've hurt them with our sad questions. We know this is bad parenting. Why do we need them to choose us? Why do we want to know that we are loved in these ways? Why do we do this to them and ourselves? Our immaturity is immense. We start crying with the children, pulling them close, whispering, "We are just kidding, we are just kidding. We would never make you choose."

The next day, the joke we've levied on the children falls on us. My mother-in-law cries for our whole family, all her remaining children to stay in the camp. Her eldest son has left already with his family. She will not survive if her youngest follows suit. She holds Npis's arms against her bosom. Witnessing this, I wish I had a mother to cry like that for me. But I don't, and I know that our staying would mean more than just her broken heart. Npis's and mine are also on the line. But even more than that, our girls. My girls. What will happen to them if we never leave this place where no one can stay forever? Still, I feel like a horrible daughter-in-law and Npis's face is as heavy as my heart feels.

There's an announcement that the camp is closing. These announcements have happened before, but the authorities say that this time it is serious. Npis and I know that sooner or later we will have to leave. But he cannot break his mother's heart. He cannot go against the wishes of one of his elder brothers, the one who wants to stay because he is afraid of life in America. Npis is afraid to choose, not only between America and an uncertain life in Thailand but between his mother's wishes and mine.

I cannot help but remember that horrid ambush in Laos, when the bullet grazed Npis's shin, and how in the bloody aftermath it was his mother who was not afraid to clean up the broken parts of him. A thought crossed my mind to tell Npis, "Stay with your mother. She loves you most. Even more than me," but I see my girls. They stand in my arms. They are looking at their grandmother, the only grandmother they know, gripping their father's arm, so I say nothing. This is between Npis and his mother, not me or the girls.

One night, as the crickets chirp outside and an infant cries from one of the nearby sleeping rooms, in the dark of ours, with the girls sleeping, I make the decision for myself. I tell Npis that I am leaving with the girls. I expect him to fight me, but he has no more energy for fights. After a long moment of silence, after the 3:00 a.m. dogs' howl to the moon, he tells me in a quiet voice that he'll follow me anywhere.

I say to him, "Then the decision is ours. Not mine. It is ours. It is for our children. It is for our future. It isn't against your mother or your brothers or even the wishes of our individual hearts. It is the only feasible way forward."

These are the most certain words I've ever spoken to my husband.

Before this moment, we were still realizing that we were alive, that the war in Laos had not killed us, and that while we had left the country, the war within it raged within us, its ghosts haunted us.

Before this moment, we were still waiting for our elders to make decisions about our future. We were waiting for them to say, "This is what is going to happen next."

In this moment, I am asking Npis in certain terms to do the thing that he had asked of me in that war-torn jungle in Laos: to walk with me toward the future. His hesitance is my own. His decision also mine.

Together, we take the steps one by one. Npis and I talk to people who have undergone the resettlement process. We go and we do our paperwork to once again talk about the story of how we became refugees. We answer the questions of the Thai man doing the interview as best we can. There's a Hmong interpreter to help us understand what we need to do and how uncertain governments can be. He tells us that we will have to check the board outside the office to see if and when we can do a resettlement interview. We are to report with all family members to the appointment or else we forfeit our chances for resettlement. We are given a case number. Npis checks the board every day. When Npis sees our names on the board one afternoon, we report to the interview with our girls a week later. We see that this time, not only is our family a number but each member of our family has been issued their own number, a T-number. The interview is more than two hours long. The person conducting this interview is now a different person. They say that they are both workers for the same organization, the United Nations High Commissioner for Refugees. The girls are quiet in our arms, eyes wide open, looking at everything. The person behind the desk tells us their job is to review our "claim." Npis and I are both confused. Our story of how we became refugees as a claim, something that we are saying is true but can be untrue, baffles both of us. I'm quiet, but Npis says, "Why would I want to make my story this way, if I could create a story of my wanting? Do you really think that our imaginations cannot produce kinder truths for our lives?" The person nods and tells Npis, "I understand you, but this is the protocol we must follow. You have to understand that there is a very long process for refugee resettlement. There are a lot of refugees and not a lot of places willing to accept them. To get successfully resettled, you have to go through the whole thing one step at a time. My job is to make sure that we can convince whole countries who do not know what you have lived through that you are worth a chance, that you might be worthwhile citizens of these nations one day." When Npis hears these words, his chest falls and he goes through the details one by one again, how he was just a boy when the war started, but how when the Americans left, he had to become a man to help defend his family—his elderly mother, who is not register-ing to come to America with us; his young wife, me; our older daughter; and now the younger one. They want biographical information on each person on the case. Npis begins with Kablia because hers is the easiest; she was born in the camp, this life is all she knows; Dawb was born in an enemy village in Laos, at the time of the crossing, she was just over a month old, yes, she has a medical condition because she had polio in the camp, and now she walks with a slight limp; Npis does not know how to tell my story, so I speak for my own story, separate from his or the girls'. I say, "I am Tswb Muas, and I was born in a village called Dej Tshuam, a place where two rivers meet." I tell them I am literate, but Lao and Hmong may not be useful for me in a life abroad, I tell them that I had not imagined this life for myself, and yet here it is and here I am hoping to continue it—elsewhere. I make my story short and direct, the way I am. Plus, I think they've heard thousands of stories like ours before. By now, it should make sense. Except, their face does not reg-ister any deeper comprehension. Their pen moves quickly on a piece of paper. My version of my story is too short. They look to Npis. He needs to do a better job. Npis takes a deep breath and begins his story. When he tells it, it is so sad I weep; his fatherlessness, his inability to protect or defend in a war where he was too young to have a say in its trajectory, too powerless, his letting go and holding on—because of his mother and then his wife and now most especially because of his children, his beautiful daughters whom he yearns to see educated. As he talks, the person is writing, writing, writing. Their final question is, "What have you done to support the Americans?" We tell the truth: We have kept their secrets. We have not hurt or harmed any Americans who have lived and worked and traveled through our villages. The truth isn't enough. Npis has to memorize the names of American generals and official fighting places and he has to agree to have fought with the Americans—despite the fact that he was only a boy and while he would have, his mother prevented him from doing so. Finally, they tell us they are preparing and will be submitting a Resettlement Registration Form. Their team will decide if we have given them enough "determination for each adult on the case" and "a substantiated explanation of the need for resettlement." Once their decision is made and if everything goes through, we will hear about medical screenings and other requirements for resettlement. The whole process takes nearly two years. By the time we have a date for resettlement, Kablia has turned six and Dawb is eight; I've turned twenty-six and Npis is nearly twenty-nine.

When we have a departure date, Npis's mother falls apart. I watch her trying to hold all the fears inside. We all see the fears bubbling out of her. Her hands shake and clutch at her chest, trying to burrow into her heart. She unleashes the cries that she has been harboring for what feels like decades. She tries to sway Npis with words. She has none for me. She tries to hold him back by pulling on his arms. He lets her hold his arms because they both know it isn't enough. I weep for her silently. I hold the girls close, and I wonder if one day my arms and my fears will also not be enough to hold my children back, to keep them close. I cannot help but think about my own departure from my mother, how I was not there to see her despair at my leaving. In the end, she says, "Npis, nothing I say will keep you here. Where you go, my heart will follow."

The night of our departure the dogs clamor and cry throughout the camp. Refugees cannot take pets when they are resettled. We are part of the biggest movement of Hmong people out of Ban Vinai Refugee Camp in January of 1980. The new year has just happened. Npis's mother had stood in front of the door of our sleeping quarters, calling all of our spirits in from the old year with chicken eggs in a bowl of rice grains, incense sticks sending her words into the dark night. Come the morning, the camp will fill with homeless dogs. After each wave of refugees leaves for a world beyond, the forsaken animals wander in groups, eyes glinting, bellies sunken, heads low to the ground. At night, they cry and cry for the families they used to have. Npis has two dogs. He will leave them behind in the morning.

I cannot sleep that night. I am a light sleeper. With the dogs restlessly howling, I am up at all hours of the night. I am afraid of the shadows. They hold the spirits of all who will be left behind, who have been left behind in this dry wait for resettlement. I stay in our sleeping quarters but I twist and turn looking for comfort, palms against my ears, heart hammering in my chest.

I cry with the dogs.

I miss my mother in Laos. I miss my life as a girl. I miss my family like the dogs miss theirs. There is little I or they can do. We are now divided not only by men with guns, the force of a raging river, but time, so much time and distance. My mother does not know I am leaving. When I get to America, I will send her a cassette tape. I will tell her about this new country where I must survive or I will be forced to watch my children suffer away from me. I've heard some of the women mention that they've heard that in America, if parents can't provide for their children, the government will take them and give them to others or raise them as children of the state.

The morning rooster crow comes to me from far away. When I open my eyes, the girls are up, sitting on the bed. Npis is no longer in the room. When I sit up to join them, Dawb's hands fall on the wet place where my head had been. She wants to know why my head rest is wet. I tell my children the truth. In my telling, the tears that had halted fall again.

I don't want the girls to cry with me. For them, I wipe away my tears. I pull them close and we lie back down. I cushion their heads with my arms, a pillow for them to dream on. They snuggle close to me and take deep breaths against my beating heart. I ease them back into sleep. They will need all the rest they can get for the long journey ahead of us.

When they awake in the late morning, we will finish our packing. Our two suitcases will be filled with the change of clothes the UNHCR people have given us, a Hmong knife, a pot, a rice steamer, my traditional Hmong clothes, the pieces of embroidery from my mother that survived the Mekong River crossing, and a photo album of the pictures we've taken in the refugee camp. There's the one of me standing on the hill, with the red umbrella, looking at Npis. Npis who has borrowed the camera. Npis who will count to three and take the photo—even though my face won't change when the camera clicks because I have little to smile about. There's the photo of Npis in the blue shirt with the buttons at its neck that I had given him, and other photographs of Npis and me and our girls. There are others, photos with Npis's mother, and some with the children playing in the dirt. When the girls wake up, Npis will wash their faces with a wet towel from the clay jar by the door for the last time. He will help them brush their teeth. He is not as gentle and slow as I am on this last morning. Then, he will lead his girls and they will say goodbye to the dogs, our pets. He will whistle and the dogs will come running from beneath the patio. The girls will play with the dogs under his watch. Npis knows that when he leaves the camp, he'll have to leave his two dogs behind like all the others before him.

When the hour comes for us to depart the camp, I wonder if my mother's heart from faraway Laos will be able to follow me to America. My family, like so many others who had remained in Laos, were reeducated and resettled close to the Lao capital of Vientiane so that they can be more closely supervised. When Npis's mother comes to say goodbye, when the orange bus roars its diesel breath, I feel out of breath myself. All the words I want to say to Npis's mother, who has also been my mother for the last decade of my life, won't leave my throat. My throat quivers and it shakes. My words would come out trembling and wet, I know it. I want to tell her, in many ways, thank you and I'll see you on the other side of the world. But the words I want to say . . . never come out, and instead I weep, and I hold her close, and I say, "Mother, I'll miss you."

Like the other leaving in my life, I don't have to look back to know what Ban Vinai Refugee Camp looks like. I don't have to see through the cloud of dust and smoke to know what is behind the moving bus and its fog of pollution: all those communal houses with their aluminum roofs baking in the hot sun, the wells with the broken concrete around them, that river of feces that sits unleashing its stench, inviting the flies to lay their eggs. I don't say goodbye to the six little boys who came from me but could not share in my life. I don't make promises of a future where I will return. Still, my heart cries, and I cannot help but put my hand to the glass of the window, to try to hold something of this place; it is nearly a decade of my life I am leaving here.

As the bus takes us away, the chorus of cries in the crowded bus grow quiet with each mile that passes. My girls are both looking out the window and ahead. I recognize this is their first sight of a world beyond the refugee camp and its guards with their guns. This is their first time in a vehicle traveling at these speeds. Their bottoms rise up each time the bus hits a bump in the road and they look at each other, light in their eyes. My own heart, a mother's heart now, points to the trees separating the green fields, how the road diverges at a sign and becomes two, and in the far distance: the smoke of a city rising. I point to the road signs, which I can slowly read because they are virtually the same characters in Lao, only less curvy, and I tell them, "We are heading toward the capital of Thailand, Krung Thep."

Many years later, when Pheej is an old man, he will return to Laos from Michigan. He'll wear a watch on his left hand, a hat atop his head, and feel his round stomach pushing against the leather of his belt beneath the sweltering heat of the sun. Outside a bustling airport, on a street with clouds of yellow dust, the scent of diesel coming in waves, he'll stand waiting. The first person who runs to him will be Zeb. Zeb, too, has become an old man. He'll wear a button-up shirt that has been washed many times over; his frail body, leathery skin and bones, is lost in the fabric that hangs on him. Zeb will not look Pheej in the face, but instead count his toes and fingers. Zeb will say to Pheej, again and again, "It was these toes that led Tuam and me toward brotherhood after our fathers died. It was these hands that held fast to ours and showed us the way to each other when we were lost as boys by ourselves. Although our bodies have parted in this life, my heart has never wandered from your side."

Part III

HEAVEN AND EARTH ARE SHAKEN

On the plane, all the white people are preoccupied with books and magazines. Some of them are sleeping. Npis looks out the window, a captive of the sky. Dawb sleeps her usual sleep, deep breaths that make her thin chest rise high and then sink low. She's tired on our way to America. Kablia, like her father, has her head turned to the window on the other side of the aisle. We tell the girls that Hmong babies live in the sky before they are born, where they fly with the clouds. My youngest is looking for the babies. I put my hand on my empty womb. With each hour that passes, I feel those wet hands holding my ankles grow weaker and weaker. I kick my legs beneath the high chair of the airplane and I move them in a motion like running. I am pushing myself through the sky, trying to leave all the ghosts in the past.

CHAPTER 18

My Name Is
Tswb Muas

In the car, the children breathe against the windows and fog up the glass. On the coldest nights, the girls will do addition and subtraction problems with their fingers, streaks of wet, racing each other to the correct answers, fighting when they are unsure who is correct. Npis will leave the car running. He will tap the steering wheel with his fingers. He has become impatient in America. It is as if the waiting in the refugee camp has taken every bit of patience he had and now there is none left. Everywhere he is, he is tapping away. Steering wheels. Walls. When there is no support, his right hand taps inside the left.

I'm used to shivering because of the condition of my body; now in Minnesota I shake because of the conditions outside of it. When winter comes, it feels like a big truck is speeding toward me. Where once my days were long, they have become slippery as tapioca strands, falling through my hands. There is a clock in every building I walk into: downtown where the welfare office is, on the wall of the waiting room at the clinic, and even in the church basements where we get our clothes and furniture. In fact, we have even picked a clock at the thrift store for our house. Tick, tick, tick, tick, all the time. Npis and I talk about how it feels like everyone is in the future, and we are coming from the past. We have been tossed through time. I shiver at the thought, and because it is cold here in a way I have never known.

It is late March. We have been in America for nine months. Since September, evening has been coming early. Already the stars glitter in the sky high above the school building. The grass on either side of the sidewalk is covered beneath a thick mess of frozen snow, now dirty and gray. I am amazed at how the people who are used to this weather are already wearing shorts outside. My little family is waiting for me to come out of evening high school. I am shivering, although the teachers say that spring is nearly here.

I go to Central High School in St. Paul. I'm told it is the oldest high school in Minnesota, built in 1866. This kind of history is hard for me to think about. My father, who has been dead for most of my life now, wasn't even alive then. I struggle to think about how one building could stand for so long, how generations of families have gone to this school, how without war structures made of concrete and steel can hold. I am proud that I go to a regular high school, although I go to the evening school. When I get to Central after the regular class day ends, there are still teenagers wandering the building in groups of two or three, some of them playing sports like soccer and other games I don't know but that intimidate me. Especially the one where the players wear round helmets and padding on their bodies. One of the sisters-in-law hates the game because her son likes it a lot. She says all the time, it looks like they are just trying to "jump each other to death." These athletes walk down the hallway, lined with red lockers, like it is their home. They are younger than us refugee students but bigger and louder; they take up more space. We adult learners, most of us newcomers, try to stay close to the walls, because Central is more their school than ours.

The wind is angry tonight, and the sky is letting down small flakes. In the dark of evening, the wind whips the snow along the streets into shapes like sheet-clad American ghosts in the orange glow of the streetlamps.

Npis will tell the girls that I should have just taken the GED test like he did. Instead, they have to wait for me, night after night, season after season. It's going to take me two years to get a high school diploma, at least. Npis thinks we are too old to go to school like this; he is twenty-nine and I am twenty-seven. We have children to care for. Instead, Monday through Friday, the girls are waiting away precious minutes in a car and we are wasting precious gas we don't have money to buy. He tells the girls that tonight I'll have homework, just like last night.

"Your mother is so stubborn," he will say to them.

Dawb and Kablia won't answer because they don't want to take a side. They don't want to have to choose between him or me in the eventuality of a divorce. They don't want us to argue or disagree. They are older now. We made our mistake that fateful night in Thailand and they remind us in their own way every single day in America of how we have traumatized them.

Npis has been at school all day, too. He's trying to get his machine operating certificate at the community college. He has lots of math homework. He is not good at math. I am better at math than he is, but I can't help him. I don't understand his books. Besides, I also have homework of my own to do.

The family is relieved when the wide doors open at the top of the stairs, and they can see bright fluorescent light entering into the night. Men and women, most of us refugees from the wars in Southeast Asia, walk out. Many of us are shivering in our winter jackets. The American jackets are too big and everybody looks like a child with the books in their hands, most held tightly across their chest. The stairs to the street level are steep at Central High School.

I've witnessed falls, especially in the early days of winter, when things freeze and thaw and ice becomes invisible. A wrong step and a man goes down on his bottom, hard. A small push to hurry from behind and a woman stumbles forward. As she tries to grab the railing, her hands miss, and her mouth ends up hard against the cold metal. All of us are afraid of falling, especially the women, now that we are walking into another season of freezing and thawing.

The family in the car knows that I will be among the last individuals leaving the double doors. I am slow at everything. Walking, talking, cooking, cleaning, making sure my jacket is buttoned up, making sure my boots are tied securely. Making sure that every step I take is the most careful one I can manage. My family knows me well, and I've also come to terms with these elements of who I am now that there are no other eyes on me in America in our little home, no commentaries other than Npis's, and he only makes them when we are on our way somewhere.

Naturally, I am among the last students to come out. My gray jacket reaches to my knees. I carry a bag of books on my arms. My hood is up but the children will know it is me because I hold the rails and take each step slowly. I have not told the girls, but I am pregnant. My stomach is small, so they can't tell, and I won't tell them because I do not want to disappoint them if anything goes wrong. A cold gust of wind blows in my face and I halt my progress so I can turn away from its power. I and my classmates, the Vietnamese and the Cambodians, the Lao and the Hmong, say to one another, "This is the wind that goes through skin and bones."

Npis knows I am pregnant. He is not confident that I will be able to keep the baby inside me alive either. He acts like it is not a big deal, so I act like it is not a big deal.

In the summer, our family will go many times to the doctor, a white woman whom all the wives of the relatives recommend because she is not mean to Hmong people. Her name is Dr. Waxler.

Dr. Waxler works in a clinic on the West Side of St. Paul. When Npis takes me to the clinic, we pass by lots of stores with Spanish words, the windows full of colorful stuffed animals, cartoon figures, and boxcars wearing bright cone heads for parties. I never ask Npis to stop the car so I can go inside the stores but I'm curious. One day, I want to go. I want to go everywhere. Just to "window-shop"—like my sister Xis says.

Xis and her husband and their two children moved from Massachusetts and now live in Minnesota. Nplooj is also here with her children; after escaping with her and the children to Thailand, Nplooj's husband snuck back into Laos, where he was tragically killed. In all the years we were apart, my sisters and I never dreamed we would be together again, but as suddenly as we were torn apart, we have been reunited, and Xis and I love to "window-shop." One time, all three of us window-shopped for so long at a thrift store on Maryland Avenue that Nplooj sat down and tears of exhaustion fell as she said, "I am not going to window-shop with you two again."

Npis and Nplooj share the same feelings about stores. They don't like the fact that there is so much to buy and so little money to spend. I can understand this, but I feel differently. It is good to know what is out there, even if it is beyond our means.

Npis and I never go into the stores on the West Side, nor does he go in to see the doctor with me. Npis always stops in the parking lot of the clinic. He prefers to sit outside beside the crabapple trees with the windows open, with the girls in the backseat chattering away. Occasionally, I ask him if he and the girls want to come inside with me. He always answers, "No, we'll wait out here." The girls ask if I'm sick. I tell them, "No." My response is enough for them; they do not ask anything else, and I do not tell them that I'm pregnant. I always walk into the clinic by myself.

Dr. Waxler's clinic has a Hmong receptionist and a Hmong nurse, and I can speak to them in Hmong. In fact, most of the clinic is full of Spanish- and Hmong-speaking patients who all have healthcare through the state. Even some of the signs are in Hmong and Spanish.

The doctor will tell me that the baby is small but healthy. I will decide not to find out if the baby is a boy or a girl. It will be too sad to know and to lose the baby now that we're in America. I will be afraid. The Hmong nurse will take my blood pressure and my temperature and will ask me to stand on a scale. On the examining table, the doctor will say, "You are healthy, too."

I am healthier than I have been in a very long time. The scale says I weigh 130 pounds. When I look at my face in the bathroom mirror I see that it is full and my cheeks are pink—usually with cold in the winter and humid heat in the summer. I am not a strong woman, but my body feels full and collected in America.

But summer is still far away from the cold of our late March evening. My pregnancy is a quiet secret between Npis and me. I breath the cold air in slowly.

When I finally reach the car, from my slow walk down the Central High School steps, before I open its door, I make a point to look back at the building, knowing that in the morning it will be filled with regular high school kids, many born right here in America, whose English comes as easily to them as spit. When I turn back to the car, I hold my breath. There is a cloud of dark smoke billowing from the brown Subaru. The scent of gasoline and smoke sting my eyes and tickle my throat. I worry about the girls breathing in the chemicals that cause the smell and form a cloud around the car. I hear the familiar click of the car door opening. Npis keeps it locked at all times when the girls are in the vehicle.

The car holding my family is warm—though the stench of burnt gasoline from the exhaust has seeped into everything. The air-conditioning stopped working long before the car became ours on payments. But the heat works, and I'm thankful on this cold night when my body shivers and shivers. The girls are loud in their greeting.

The girls are busy in America in a way I don't remember them being in Thailand. They go to school. They come home. At home, though it is just the two of them, they play games, do puzzles, watch television, and speak to each other for hours without exhaustion. Dawb is fluent in English already. The next fall, she will win the school-wide spelling bee competition by studying the heavy Webster's dictionary Npis has taped all over so that it will last the girls their whole education through. Kablia though does not speak English at school despite the fact that her English is fine; I know this because she and Dawb can both argue in English and Hmong at the same time, at the same speed. They say, "Hi, Mommy." They don't call me Niam anymore except when they speak of me to other Hmong people, their aunts, uncles, or cousins. As a way of greeting the girls, I say, "Zaum zoo zoo." Sit nicely. Npis is quiet. I grow quiet with him in the car home, a billowing storm of exhaust in our wake. Our car embarrasses me. Other drivers look at us with curiosity and annoyance on their faces. We are polluting the streets with our old car. We have no money to fix it or change it out, so I let my face carry my apology. It is a new look on my face in America.

We live in the McDonough Homes, a government housing project. The parking lots are usually full by the time we get home. Lots of the cars that do on-street parking end up getting stolen or broken into. Many mornings, we wake to small cubes of glass glinting where cars had been. It is tricky to find a parking space, but Npis is lucky tonight and there's an empty space in the corner of the lot big enough for our small car. The smell of its exhaust makes my stomach unstable. Npis is concerned that it won't pass the exhaust test and we'll have no car to take us anywhere. I put my hand on my small belly and try to breathe through the nausea. The child inside me is so small, but already I feel I am not alone in my body anymore. The good thing about being pregnant in Minnesota is that the moment you open the car door, the world outside flows in—unlike all my pregnancies in the camp where the scent of the outside and the inside are the same, where there were no windows to open or close, cars to get in and out of.

The girls race in front of us, unafraid of possible falls. Their knees and shins are continually bruised, but unless there is blood, they don't seem to mind. Their jackets are both unzipped and I want to call out to them, but I don't. I let it go this time. It has been a long enough day. Npis offers his hand nonchalantly. Now that we are in America and we live by ourselves, these little gestures have become natural to us. There are no eyes to look, others to whisper or comment about. I take his hand. I hand him my books. We walk slowly on the sidewalk, careful of the broken liquor bottles close to the edges of the sidewalks. All around is the familiar brown of the town houses, all symmetrical, standing solid against the night, a night when the sky is dark, stars shining down, but the ground is white with snow. Lights are on in the different living rooms. A few windows are open to ventilate. Music I don't know drifts through the screens and across the dark to us. The warmth of Npis's hand is exaggerated in this cold. We've never danced together and may never dance together, but I already know what dancing with Npis will feel like because of the moment we are in, our girls ahead of us, only the night surrounding us. Npis's head moves a little in tune with the beats of the song. It is a nice thing, to hold hands with Npis in winter-

time in America. By the time we make it to the door, the girls have the
screen door open, and they are wedged inside.

Kablia wants to know, "Will we survive through the night if we have
to hide behind a screen door?"

Dawb is a good sister: "If it is both of us and I wedged you in first
and then I stand in the back and try to cover you, you might survive."

Kablia: "But you won't?"

Npis: "No one will need to survive a winter's night standing outside
hiding in a screen door."

He holds the screen door, takes the keys from his jacket pocket,
inserts the house key, jiggles the round silvery knob on the brown
door, and lets us into the town house. The black-and-white television
sits in its place. Beside it, a Styrofoam cooler where I am growing a
Hmong herb women eat after giving birth. Beside that, the vacuum
cleaner I found at the church basement, its cord wrapped neatly in its
clips. In front of the television, there are two sofas, one opposite the
set, the other against the adjacent wall. The wall with the front door
has a line of windows, four of them, tall and narrow, each with a metal
screen on the outside. I take off my coat, make sure I don't step on the
girls' shoes, and I put on my flip-flops. Like my father from long ago,
the soles of my feet are sensitive; I don't walk barefoot anywhere in
the house. I hang the gray coat in the closet and make a straight line
down the small hallway that leads to the kitchen. I have to prepare our
evening meal. I want to get the food on the table before Kablia starts
talking about how hungry she is.

I turn on the light in the little kitchen. I go to the sink by the far
wall and turn on the hot water so that I can wash my hands with the
thick blue dish soap beside it. I open the refrigerator to the right of
the sink and I see the metal bowl full of the fish I've thawed out, cut
into chunks, and marinated with salt and MSG, mixed with whole chili
peppers, pounded lemongrass stalks, and a handful of herbs: green
onion, cilantro, mint, and then tomatoes for a touch of tartness. I set the
steamer I've brought from Thailand on the stove. I put the fish in the
metal bowl in the steamer. I open the refrigerator again. I see the bunch

of asparagus. I take it and go to the sink and I wash each spear individually. I use a paring knife and I cut off each of the scaled leaves and shave around the tip. I will blanch it and we can eat it with the simple chili paste I've pounded this morning—Thai chilies, MSG, and salt—the way Npis likes it. The way my mother taught me when I was young.

In that old wooden house in that village where the rivers met, I learned how to make the simple chili paste so that I could eat it with the lemons my father grew along the edge of his citrus orchard. As a child, I loved sour. I couldn't get enough of it. I'd harvest the lemons before they turned yellow when their rinds were green as the limes, only thicker. I'd slice off the skin of the unripe fruit and then cut them into slices and mix them with chili paste and eat whole bowls until my mouth lost all feeling, until tears fell from my eyes from the sour and the spicy. My mother marveled watching me eat and weep by the spoonful. She used to say, "One day, your stomach will not be able to tolerate that amount of acid, Tswb."

My mouth salivates at the memory of lemons from long ago. Pregnancy has given me a strong craving for sour but the limes we get in Minnesota are harder, not as fragrant or juicy. They seem to have been harvested before they were ready, and then of course they had to travel further to get here, this cold place where the only fruits that grow happily seem to be apples. I can't eat the lemons here without hurting for my mother and father.

Now that I'm in America, I don't send cassette tape recordings to my mother like I used to in Thailand. In her old age, it seems she has less to say to me. She hardly sends recordings to me anymore, either. When she does, her voice, though full of the familiar quivers, is no longer as clear. It sounds hoarse and strained at the same time. I ask myself if we have perhaps gotten used to missing each other. I write letters to Soob, the brother with the rooster from the war, the one who had been to school with me and could read and write. This is how we check in with each other, by writing letters several times each year. I write in Hmong. He writes back in Hmong. Although we both can write in Lao, Hmong feels more intimate even though we both only ever write of the things floating on the surface of our lives. Our lives are so far apart that a letter cannot speak to the hardships we have endured, the particulars of our circumstances. I am afraid that if we go any deeper, we will both fall apart. I also understand that we can't talk about the past in our letters to each other; the communist government in power is not afraid to hurt the Hmong who remain in their country with ties to those abroad. Soob and I ask after each other's health and that of family. I ask about my mother's health and he tells me, in each letter, the same thing, not addressing me by name but as Npis's wife:

> Niam Npis,
>
> I've received your recent letter. We are fine here. Please don't worry. Mother is getting older. She suffers from a loss of appetite. Her hair is full of white. She misses you as ever. She wants me to tell you that you shouldn't worry about her. The years pass and they wear on her. Please let Npis and the children know that we miss them and wonder if there will ever be a day when you might perhaps return to Laos for a visit. The little store we tend at the 52 Market is going well. Your sister-in-law spends all her days there. I tend to the few heads of cows I continue to keep. Life is what it can be.
>
> Signed,
> Your brother, Soob Muas

Our letters don't say very much but they linger with me for days. I have no satisfactory idea of how my family is, what their living circumstances are, the kinds of beds they sleep in, the houses they hide under. I know that the life they now live is different from the life we shared. I know that Kilometer 52, where they live, is a small city located fifty-two kilometers from the capital city of Vientiane, close to the government in power, easy to monitor. In the photographs that Soob occasionally sends, I see my mother dressed in a shirt tucked into a floral skirt, her legs brown and thin, feet clad in flip-flops. My mother, whose cheeks are sunken because her teeth are gone, whose eyes are deep set and dark, who stands with her long arms dangling at her side. In the photographs, I see Maiv standing beside her, dressed also in a shirt but instead of a skirt, she wears a sarong, tied at the waist. Maiv looking nearly as old as Mother, a head shorter and messier. I run my hands over the glossy images, again and again.

Npis does not ask what Soob says in the letters we exchange. I don't have much to share with him after I read them. Even after all these years, my family remain strangers to Npis. He only cares for them because he cares for me. This is different than my relationship to his family. I know each person individually, have shared moments, good and bad, daily experiences that have forged their own bonds separate from my relationship to Npis or his to them. This disparate situation is yet one more travesty from the war. I cannot blame him for the opportunities that were not present in his life any more than I can blame myself, and yet it is not a situation without injury.

When dinner is ready, I call Npis and the girls to the table. For a moment, I miss Npis's mother. She's in California with one of Npis's older brothers. In the end, the whole of the family had to leave the camp and Thailand. Our small unit was just among the first. Now, four of his brothers are in California, learning how to farm on American soil, and two of them are here in Minnesota with us. Npis's mother will visit in the summer. The girls will cry when they see her. She will cry when she sees them. In the monthlong visit, she will sit at our table and the past and the present will be equally strong. But for now, the past is all that we have left behind, and tonight, it is just the four of us and the baby inside me.

Every detail of the dinner table is important to me. The big melamine rice bowl with the blue flowers twirling on the outside is in the center of the square table. The steamed fish in its metal bowl is on one side. The plate of asparagus spears is on the other. The little bowl of chili is in front of the rice. Around the laminated square table, peeling at its edge, pushed against the wall and the narrow window in the kitchen, I set out two plates on the left for Dawb and Kalia, I set a space for myself in the middle, and to my right I put a plate for Npis. I put a silvery soup spoon on the belly of each plate, the handle touching at the place where 1:00 p.m. should be, face down.

I wonder, in my most optimistic heart, if this setup will be temporary: just the four of us. What if this baby I carry inside survives? What if it is a boy? What if our whole life changes when this one comes? The what-ifs make my body stiff with anticipation.

Just a month ago, I had started bleeding. In fear, I'd woken Npis up in the night. We knew the routines from Thailand. But here in America, things were different. There were no sisters-in-law waiting in the wings to take the girls for the night. No water wagon waiting for me or camp hospital with its swirling fan above. As it was, Npis got up and turned on the light in our room. The light revealed the small stain in the place where I slept, a smear of red across the brown floral sheets I'd gotten from the church basement, but it was not enough to be a baby, even an early one.

He asked, "Are you miscarrying?"

I put my hand to my belly. I was not cramping.

I shook my head no.

Together, we changed the sheets. We moved from the brown floral flat sheet to the blue floral one. Other than the difference in color and design, the fabric of each sheet washed and rewashed so many times that some parts were threadbare, they were the same. Npis did the tugging around the corners of the mattress. He didn't want me to exert force. We slept on an old mattress on top of an older box spring, set on top of hard plastic crates that we got for free from the Hmong men who drove a truck delivering government food once a week to the housing project.

We settle into bed again. I pull the top sheet and blanket on top of me. I am the only woman in the family who has taken to this American practice of using a top sheet underneath a cover. Within minutes, Npis is snoring lightly. I can't sleep. In the freshly made bed, I lie as straight as I can, legs pressed tight, as if the force of my thighs could hold the baby inside me safe.

In the morning, I called my sisters Nplooj and Xis. Both of them picked up the phone immediately. They listened to what was happening. They tried to reassure me, each saying, "The pregnancy is early. The baby should be fine." Both of them told me to tell Npis to call a shaman.

Nyiaj Lauj Lis was a respected shaman who worked across the Hmong community. He and his family lived in the same housing project as us, just further down the hill where there were housing units with more bedrooms. He was an elder, wrinkled and thin, tall for his generation. In fact, his leanness reminded me of my own father. Upon our first meeting, I felt a kinship with him immediately.

Nyiaj Lauj agreed to come to the house to do a ceremony to safeguard the baby inside me. Npis's two older brothers who had also been resettled in Minnesota came with their families. A small pig was sacrificed. From the animal, we boiled chunks of meat with pounded lemongrass stalks, and tore in pieces of Hmong mustard greens at the end, seasoned with salt and a touch of MSG. We stir-fried the belly with ginger and green onions and cilantro, seasoned with soy sauce, salt, and a hint of MSG. We steamed rice and made a chili sauce. As a treat for the children, we bought sodas from the store to accompany the meal. It was simple and fortifying.

The shaman's ritual was specific: the child and I were different beings; we were each destined to live different fates. The ceremony itself was a safety precaution. If anything should happen to the child, let me live. If anything should happen to me, let the child live. Negotiations were made with the ancestral spirits.

After the ceremony, Nyiaj Lauj gathered the baby's spirit into a bowl of water and covered it with a plate. He turned the bowl upside down, capturing the water inside. It did not leak. He told Npis and me, "Keep this under your bed. Do not move it. Do not take it out until the baby is born. Once the baby is born and safely home, you can remove the bowl and clean it up."

I've checked the bowl every day for the last month. I won't touch a thing, afraid to even sweep the dust bunnies that have gathered around it. I make sure that it looks the same as when Npis and I had crouched low and placed the bowl underneath our bed. The bowl is fine, untampered. Each time I kneel on the tiled floor and crouch below, I feel that my stomach has grown tighter, that the life inside me has gotten stronger. The girls have not noticed the bowl at all. They have not asked any questions. Even during the ceremony, they were not curious about the reasons why relatives had come. They were more interested in playing with their cousins.

Now, we gather around the table, our little laminated table with the peeling sides, on a regular evening after a normal day of going to school. Npis, Dawb, Kablia, and me. I pick out two chunks of fish, one for each girl. I choose the two chunks closest to the head—as my mother had done for me. I will help Kablia pick through her chunk to ensure that all the bones are removed. I will feel the soft flakes of fish between my thumb and index finger to make sure that there are no bones before she eats it. Dawb assures me she is now old enough to pick out her own fish bones. Only after the girls get their fish do I tell Npis to break the whole chilies into the steamed fish. I serve my daughters each a spoon-ful of rice and a little bit more. The elders used to say it was bad luck to serve anyone only a single scoop. The old superstitions remain despite the oceans in between the present and the past. The girls eat dutifully. Npis eats with gusto. I know his waist is thickening here in America.

My husband likes my cooking. He never complains. Even at the be-ginning of the pregnancy when I was tired and often sick, when I made the simplest dishes, he'd eat with gratitude. I made rice every day, of course. But there were days when we ate slices of peeled ginger dipped in salt while the girls ate boiled beef hot dogs with rice and water.

Sitting with my family, I think to myself: our life is so quiet. I think to myself: in the camp, I never knew this kind of quiet. Even in the depths of the jungle, always there was the sound of wild animals, of rockets and bullets, of children's whimpers and cries. I think: it has been nearly a decade since I've held a baby to my breast.

Cleaning up for four people is easy when the youngest will turn nine by year's end. It takes me little time to clear the table and do the dishes. Our white teachers in high school tell us to dry them and put them away but I have purchased a dish drain from the thrift store. I let the dishes air dry on the drain by the sink. I can hear Npis tell the girls stories in the front room.

I settle at the dining table again. After the girls go to bed, Npis sits opposite me. He opens up his backpack. He takes out his books. We will do our homework together. Npis's book is open to a graphed sheet of paper. There are careful drawings of angles. Beside each, he writes small numbers and letters in an equation. Although he is writing in English, from where I sit, his script could easily be Lao. And yet I know we are as far as we've ever been from the country of our birth. The walls around us are thick. No light coming through slits, no scent of rain or sound of wind. The quiet from upstairs tells me the girls are asleep or on their way toward it. The silence between us now was different from all of the ones we had shared in the past; there was no anger or second-guessing, no thinking, *What will I do next?*

Inside my book, there are many worksheets tucked in between the pages of carefully written notes in blue pen. I get to today's worksheet. It says: Name. In the empty line by that word, I write: Tswb Muas, in careful letters with the same blue pen.

I had been Npis's wife, Nyab Npis or Niam Npis. Then, I had become Dawb's mom, Dawb Niam. Each time I do my homework, I am asked what my name is. I write the right one, the one that I had been given all those many years ago, in that small village where two rivers meet, in that wooden house that no longer exists, in that place of memory where my mother waits in the garden, where my father stands by the door.

CHAPTER 19

At the Gate
Between Life and Death

I n Hmong we say that to welcome life, one must travel to the gate of death. This is what I did for you, Txuj.

I worried that you would die inside me as all the other boys had in Ban Vinai Refugee Camp. Even though we were in America, I could not stop the old fears. I worried that I would never get to meet you. In thinking of you, I could only conjure what I had known from my years of sadness and grief: a baby the width of a soda can, one the length of a cob of corn, feet the size of thumbs, fingers frail as blades of grass, each too small to join me in life.

With the shaman's bowl of water tucked underneath our bed, the fresh blood that had trickled from me halted. Every day that I waited for you became a meditation on the quiet in our lives but for the summer breezes blowing the debris, paper napkins and empty snack bags, outside our window, or gusts growing stronger with autumn on its way, sending the trash can lids banging against each other in the backyard. I thought of the yearning I had carried all those years for a son who might find me a stronger footing in my marriage and the culture I had been born into, the wide world of men. I could not tell anyone of my secret hope. Npis was afraid to believe after the experiences in Thailand. The girls were too young to grasp the chasm of my fear and I didn't want them to feel diminished by my heart's desire for a boy. Born and raised a woman, now living far from the place of my birth, I knew how hard it was to find a respectable place in a world dominated by men's ideas and their actions.

On the black-and-white television, the American president from when we had come into the country, Ronald Reagan, talked on and on. Npis and his brothers, when they watched, remarked on his incredible hair though he was an old man already, running fingers through their own thinning hair. In the war, many of the people who held guns in the air, pointed at others, were men. In the camp, it was mostly the men in uniforms who gave orders while everyone else followed. In class, my white teachers made jokes about the Hmong men even as I see the ways in which the white men and women were unequal in the ways they talked and moved. Already, I had two girls whose journeys would be hard because they were not born as men.

The cramps started in the night.

I was in that old timeless dream.

Npis and I are back in the jungle. We are visiting my family. A strong wind blows and the wide leaves of the banana grove slap against each other. There is a large regiment of soldiers coming, and Npis and I must decide what to do. Do we return to his family group so we can run with them? Do we stay with my family, have dinner first, and then leave? When will we be able to visit again? I want to stay. Npis wants to go. My mother is on her way to a stream to get water for the evening meal. I don't go and say goodbye. My mother stands in the clearing, the water pail in her hand, staring at me, waiting. I tell myself I am no longer a girl. I am a woman now. I will fight my husband forever if I must. This moment, this last meal with my mother, is worth everything. The heat in my chest grows hot but before the lava of my words flows, before I am able to jerk my hand free from Npis's and run to my mother, I wake.

The mound of my belly felt particularly warm to my touch. The first cramps came like small waves to the shore of my being. What began as a pulsing grew in power. A sound like the ocean entered my ears, an ocean I'd only ever heard from a shell at a garage sale. The rush of liquid, layers of it. I curled my legs and turned to the edge of the bed on my left. The discomfort grew as the pulsing turned into waves of pain. My skin grew damp. I pushed the blanket aside. I sat up.

Your father's breathing was deep. He slept with his back to me. The light in the room was watery and gray. It came from the one metal and glass window that looked toward another building just like ours, an identical window across the little yard. The tiles beneath my bare feet were cold. Immediately, I felt for and found my slippers.

The morning outside our bedroom window was muted. A line of pink sat at the edge of the sky. I saw the outline of trees in the spaces between the housing units. In the dawn as in the daytime, the buildings cut into the hillside, each a small fortress of concrete and steel rising out of the earth. I couldn't help but think: *How would these homes in America hold up to bombs from the sky? Metal on concrete. Fire on steel.* I shook myself from the thought. We'd all die the same beneath that hot blaze of hate, of anger, the flames of power. Why does the war visit me here?

I didn't turn on the light. I grabbed the canvas bag where I'd hidden the blue baby blanket I'd bought from Kmart, the three pairs of small white socks, "0–3 months" written on the soles of each in plastic letters, and the set of six baby gloves. Underneath these little items, I'd folded a change of clothes for me, underwear, a bra, and further down, I felt for and found the cotton swaddles I'd sewn—just in case. Next, I went to the alcove with a rod where I hung Npis's and my clothes. In a folded laundry basket, I found clean underwear, a bra, my favorite maternity dress, the blue one that I'd gotten from a garage sale with flowers and a wide white collar.

In the bathroom, I turned on the light. It was so bright I shirked away from my own reflection in the rectangle mirror. The hungry woman from Thailand was no more. I had cut off my hair and permed it. Where once my face was angled and pinched, it was full, carrying the strain of late pregnancy. I breathed deeply, to calm myself and the living baby inside me. We were full term. Nine months. I brushed my teeth. I made a note to pack my toothbrush and toothpaste. I washed my face with Dove soap. I pulled the cloud of hair around my face back and clipped it on the side. The thought that the child inside me might die was weighted by another thought: my own possible demise.

Txuj, the sound of your sisters' alarm clock broke me from my reverie. I grabbed my toothbrush and toothpaste, stuck them in the canvas bag, changed quickly into the maternity dress, and the morning routine commenced. I headed downstairs to the kitchen and made the girls Wai Wai instant noodles for breakfast. I broke in an egg to add more nutrition to their preferred breakfast. I did not add in the chili packet because I didn't want either of them to have stomach issues at school. I split the broth and noodles evenly between the girls. When the waves of pain washed over me, I breathed deeply. Your sisters finished their noodles, put on their autumn sweaters, and walked to the school bus with no concerns about me. As we did each morning, I watched from the doorway until the yellow school bus came and picked them up in the bright light of morning. The air that greeted me was fresh and clean, cooling. Npis got up on his own soon after and prepared for the day.

Npis came downstairs and found me tucking the peach bedsheet we'd placed on top of one of the sofas into the cushions. The cushions had pet hair from the couch's previous owners and we couldn't get the fibers out so we covered it for the girls' sake. He saw the canvas bag by the front door. He had a workbook from class in his hands, but he placed it on the television set and said, "It's time to go to the hospital."

I said, "Yes."

Outside, the sun was bright. The wind was gentle. Thin layers of clouds scattered across the blue of the sky. The leaves of the big trees had turned away from the green of summer. There were trees that were orange. Others that were yellow. Some that contained bits of green, orange, and yellow. Still, there were other trees bursting with reds and pinks. The trees in Minnesota bloomed on the day of your arrival, Txuj.

Your father asked, "Do you need help getting to the car?"

I said, "I can make it on my own, but let's stop by the neighbor auntie and tell her where we are going. Tell her to get the girls after school. To keep them at her house until your brother can pick them up."

I stood on the main sidewalk and watched as Npis walked quickly, the canvas bag in his hand, to the brown door of the neighboring auntie. He knocked loudly with his knuckles against the screen door. In seconds, the door opened. I heard their conversation. The auntie, a kind woman with a bad perm similar to mine but even more untamed, had a perpetual red face. She lived with her two sons. One was grown and in high school. The other was just a year older than Dawb. She was a second wife. Her husband stayed with his first wife and children in the Mount Airy Homes, another housing project closer to downtown St. Paul. She called out to me, "Dawb Niam, I had no idea you were even pregnant! Oh, this is wonderful news! Don't worry. I'll take care of the girls. They will be fine with me and the boys."

I waved and thanked her, catching my breath as I lowered my hand.

Npis walked in front of me toward the car in the small lot, the canvas bag swinging in his hands. His shoulders were straight and stiff. I could feel his tension as I followed, making sure each step was on firm ground, feeling suddenly detached from my body, even afraid of it.

I saw myself: a woman with a small belly in a maternity dress she'd bought from a garage sale, wearing tan sandals, walking with a hand to her waist, the other on her belly, beneath a bright sun. Her perm is pushed to the side of her face with a plastic hair clip. She carries a brown leather purse she bought from a thrift store. Inside that purse, she has a wallet. Inside the wallet, she has twenty-three dollars in cash and a piece of paper with phone numbers of family. She has her medical card and those of her whole family. Hidden in the small pocket of the purse, there was still an emergency pad. She keeps a black plastic comb tucked to the side of the wallet. At the bottom of her purse, there's sample dental floss from the dentist. Also at the bottom, there's a round Carmex lip moisturizer tin. The last item in her purse is the most unnecessary, a tube of darkish pink lipstick she'd gotten from Kmart and wears only on special occasions like the Hmong New Year's celebration or for family photographs. The purse dangles from her elbow, nearly to the ground because the woman is short.

I had always taken a measure of pride in the way I looked. My mother cared about these things. It had transferred naturally to me. In Laos as a young woman, I knew myself to be pretty. There were people to tell me this. In Thailand, despite everything, I knew myself to still be a good-looking woman. I could feel the gazes of men whenever I walked past on a road. In America, my good looks, like all that had transpired in Laos and Thailand, became a secret that only your father and I shared. Men and women shuffle by me without a glance. What they saw first when they needed to see me was that I was a refugee, a woman who spoke little English, a newcomer to the country. And yet, I knew that in your father's eyes I remained an attractive woman. He does not say this and will never say it. He does not need to. Just as I don't tell him I think he's handsome, we know how we feel about each other where it matters, deep in our bellies, beneath our beating hearts. For him and myself, I hold a standard.

I knew that standard would have no place in a hospital room. When I had delivered Dawb and Kablia years ago, people didn't look inside me. I wore a skirt. I knelt. My babies slipped out of me. The umbilical cord was cut. The placenta fell out. I cleaned myself when I was able. No one touched me there. No one peeked at me there. No one saw me there. I had heard from relatives who had given birth in America that in this country women give birth lying on their backs, with their legs wide open, and that the doctors and nurses look and touch and clean you right there after the baby is born. They've assured me, "But you won't even be embarrassed because you'll be in so much pain." They also warned, "American women like to scream when they give birth. It can get very loud."

The closer I got to the car, the more apprehensive I felt about the process of delivering a child in America. My doctor was a woman, but I had no idea who the nurses would be. There would be a team. This means: a lot of people will see me in a most vulnerable state, see me in my most vulnerable place.

The only reason I didn't turn back was the cramps that continued to roll across my lower half, each time with more urgency. I stopped, and waited them through. Npis stopped each time I stopped, although he didn't turn toward me. A thread of anger grew inside me; why does he allow his feelings to get in the way of the situation? I'm the pregnant one, the one about to deliver a baby. It was my body that was going to break open, and yet there he was, submitting to his fears. I could feel my emotions working up to meet the contractions.

The parking lot was nearly empty. Most of our neighbors who can drive were enrolled in job training programs or already working in the factories. Many of them had left for the day.

At the car, Npis opened my door. This is something only white men do on television. I got in the car. He placed the canvas bag at my feet. He closed the door. He walked around to the driver's side.

When the ignition started and the car beeped, I asked through clenched teeth, "Will you stay in the delivery room with me?"

Npis had been far away when Dawb was born in the enemy camp. When Kablia was born, he had not been in our sleeping quarters during the birth. For the deliveries of both my girls, I was surrounded by the women in the family. His mother had presided. The sisters-in-law had helped. With Kablia, he had waited until I was lying down with the baby sound asleep beside me to come and see us. My husband is afraid of sickness and death. I knew this despite the fact that we had never talked about it. As I waited for your father to answer, I thought for the first time: *He will not be by my side when I die one day because his fear of death is bigger than everything else.*

To my surprise, your father said, without looking at me, "Yes, I'll be by your side."

The scent of exhaust from the car triggered nausea. I kept swallowing down the rising of bile in my throat, feeling the flow of saliva on the walls of my mouth. I hadn't eaten anything since the night before. For breakfast, I had half a cup of warm water. I was so uncomfortable that I didn't even notice how other drivers gestured and sneered at the smoke cloud accompanying us on the highway.

On the way to St. Joseph's Hospital in downtown St. Paul, I twisted and turned on the passenger seat, trying to ease the nausea and balance the growing cramps. I didn't want my water to break, to wet the contents of the canvas bag at my feet or the seat of the car. That would be a tricky mess. I told your father unnecessarily, "Just go to the emergency room entrance."

His fingers tapped on the steering wheel the whole drive to the hospital. The rhythm was erratic and fast.

At the hospital, things happened quickly at first. I was rushed into the delivery ward in a wheelchair. People walked around me. The lights were bright. There were lots of machines. They beeped and buzzed. The nurses took off my clothes and placed a gown on me. I was on a bed. The nurses and doctors poked my arm and set up an IV. They placed their hands on my belly. They looked in between my legs. They checked for dilation. To my surprise I was not embarrassed at all.

The nurses asked me, "How are you feeling?"

I answered, "Okay"—all the way until things were not okay.

Your father stood by my side. I pushed and pushed. I pushed and pushed. Dr. Waxler arrived at some point in the pushing. She told me to rest. She told me to push. This went on for an hour, and then two. I grew tired. I couldn't keep my eyes open anymore. I couldn't talk anymore. Your father stood stiffly by my side, telling me in Hmong what the doctor and nurses said in English. I didn't need the interpretation, but he just needed something to do with himself. The nurses and doctor tried to be calm.

I lost consciousness.

At some point, your father will tell me later, nothing was calm anymore. Dr. Waxler called in other doctors. The nurses raced around getting things ready. Your father was scared that I would have to undergo a C-section. He was convinced that I was dying.

In the motion of the room, your father asked his father's spirit to hold me to life, to keep me and the baby safe, to help me deliver this child into the world. He held my limp hand—until the doctors asked him to step to the side.

They wheeled in a machine. It was a vacuum. They placed the vacuum over my vagina. They turned it on. The vacuum sucked you out of me.

I came to when they placed you on my chest, face down, head to my left breast. I shifted until you were at my right breast, the one with the noninverted nipple. You were so small and naked, hands reaching on either side. You didn't cry. Your head was long, strangely long because you'd been sucked out of me. Fine black hair. A bluish head. You were alive.

Your father said, "He is alive. We have a son."

I said, "I'm alive, too."

Your father left the room to call relatives, to let people know that I had safely delivered a boy into the world. The first person he called was his mother in California. He told her that he now had a son. He told her that he already had a name for the little boy, Txuj. Knowledge. Txuj. Ability. Txuj. The one who had the skills to make it successfully to us. He had been thinking of a name for you for years, afraid to tell anyone, until you came.

The noises dimmed around you and me. Your eyes were closed. But you were alive. Your weight, barely six pounds, settled the trembling in my heart. Still, my hands shook holding you close to my right breast as you struggled to latch. I couldn't believe it. Bones so fragile. Skin so soft. Then, you cried, and dispelled the quiet with your voice.

The nurses and the doctors laughed. At long last, you'd arrived, and you were safe. I had never been a particularly spiritual person, but I knew that for the rest of my life I owed a debt of gratitude I would never be able to pay to Nyiaj Lauj Lis, the shaman who safeguarded your spirit and kept you whole inside me. The spirit in the sky on our way to America who had shaken me free from the ghostly hands of Ban Vinai Refugee Camp, the storm that had raged within all of us in that place where we waited hopelessly for a future to begin.

I made a promise to myself: no matter what happens in your life, how disobedient you might grow to be, how unruly, I would always temper my anger and response with the knowledge of how much I had wanted you, dreamed of you, how desperately I waited for the reality of you. I would know that whatever our life together turned out to be, my life was better for having you in it.

Your older sisters came when I was much younger, before I knew that I wanted to be a mother. They came at a time of great uncertainty. They came before the miscarriages, before I knew how hard it would be to deliver living children into this world.

I look at photographs of you as an infant and then a toddler. You with your little arms and legs, lines of flesh along the short stretch of bone. Your smile, slightly lopsided, your eyes round and direct. Your hair, when you were a baby, spiked from your head. Your father, with you in his arms and you on his shoulders when you were big enough to hold what remained of his hair. Your sisters, one on each side, holding you up by the arms like a patient in a hospital, too weak to stand on your own.

In the backyard of our town house in the project, you learned how to stand and how to walk. You wore sandals that I bought new. You wore a fake leather jacket, a hand-me-down from a relative, until the brown plastic flaked off like old scabs. When your teeth grew, the two front ones were straight, the canines sharp as knives. I fed you bits of rice massaged with flakes of white fish that I picked off the bones and squeezed between my index finger and my thumb to ensure they were safe for your mouth. There are pictures of you, tired and sick, moving from one ear infection to the other, from one pink bottle of amoxicillin to the next. How you hated the medicine. How you used to scrunch up your face, push your tongue against the thick pink liquid until it oozed out of your mouth. In those moments, your father's temper grew short.

Always he said, the words tight, "I'm just trying to help you feel better."

Always I told him, "Don't be mad at the child. He's come a long way to be here with us."

The words I spoke to your father about you recalled my own mother's words to me growing up. She thought always of the fact that I had disappeared that day in Little Cucumber's jacket. She always said that the fact that my brother had found me and returned me to her was a miracle. I belonged to a woman who believed in miracles. Txuj, you made a believer out of me.

Txuj, if I could give you the life I wanted, your heart would never break. Know this. Know that each time your heart is broken, mine aches.

CHAPTER 20

The Hmong
Word for *Love*

The Mall of America has been open for more than a year. Many of the relatives have visited the mall. At family gatherings and picnics, the women talk about how big the shopping center is. I am excited by the wonder in their voices. I want to go and see it, just to see it, but I'm too old to ask Npis. I have my driving permit. I can't seem to pass the driving test. Every time there is a person with a piece of paper on a tablet judging me, I get too nervous. It is too much like work, where the supervisor walks around, writing notes on us, and deciding who gets a raise and who does not. Npis hates shopping. He hates seeing the children want things and being unable to buy it for them. He thinks that window-shopping is stupid. The bags of gummy worms and little boxes of Tic Tacs that he gets for the children each time we go into a store aren't enough. He feels inadequate at all the shopping places in our lives. Everywhere, whenever there is anything about Hmong people, white people say that in America, Hmong women are doing well but Hmong men are not. I don't know if this is true, but I think about it in our everyday life.

At the grocery store, I'm the one who stands in the checkout lines because we must use the WIC vouchers to pay for the milk and eggs and the process is slow. The people behind us let us know that we are taking too long because they sigh, they tap the tiles on the floor with their feet. Sometimes, they'll say, "Let's go to the other line. This is going to take forever." I have to pretend not to hear or see. The people behind the cash register hate it, too, because everything on the belt has to be in a specific order. They, too, sigh when a WIC customer makes their way into the line. I try my best to help them by sorting the food items in the order of the vouchers but sometimes this makes them even madder. Many times, they've said, "Stop it. I've got it!"—and I feel like a child who has done something wrong. But I am a mother, a small one. The little table along the cash register where tall white people sign their checks is at my chin. My children stand around me with big eyes looking up. I am still taller than my children, the adult here with them. I stand with my chin up. I flatten my lip into the familiar line from my younger days.

Npis usually waits for us by the sliding doors. If the children are willing, he takes them with him, and they stand looking at the free magazines for cars and houses for sale. I know Npis is embarrassed of the WIC shopping trips so I do it, I pay with the vouchers and I feel judged but I try not to let it show. I tell my children, "I don't care what other people think."

I don't tell them the other part, that the thoughts of strangers are not as important to me as the danger of hunger. I don't tell them that I've seen enough and known enough of hunger to do anything to keep it away from them, the gnawing in the belly, the processing of air and water. The hunger even for something so simple as the smell of papaya salad.

Every Thanksgiving, a man comes to our door. He drives a truck. It reads: Meals on Wheels. He walks quickly to the brown door with his black jacket zipped to the neck, his cap pulled low. He will come with a warm grocery bag or a cardboard box. Inside it, there will be meals. Turkey slices, mashed potatoes, corn, green beans, and cranberry sauce from the can. On top of everything, there will be thick brown gravy. We will eat these meals together around the table and we will call it Thanksgiving. Npis and I don't enjoy the too-dry turkey slices and the mashed potatoes with no bite, but we don't say anything because the children do. They especially like mixing the red jellied cranberry sauce with their meat, dessert and dinner in one. When the children go back to school the following week, they will know that they have had turkey, too. But Npis, he does not open the door when the man comes. I do. The children will clamor to the window. They will say, "The man is coming. The Thanksgiving Man is coming, Mom"—and wherever I am in the house, I will walk to the door, I will pass Npis, and I will open the door to the cold of late November. The man will be polite.

He will say, "Happy Thanksgiving, folks."

I'll say, "Thank you. Thank you so much."

I'll stand at the door, the food in my hands, until the man gets back to his truck and drives to the next poor family waiting for a Thanksgiving meal. I will look upon the grass, curled close to the ground, yellowing, preparing for the winter or else already hidden below the inches of fallen snow, and I will feel like the ground: hard. I will miss the warmth of my youth, of being a normal person in the world, not depending on others though those memories grow further every year.

I will miss when I was girl. I will miss the New Year's celebrations. The feasting. The ritual bathing by the river in that little village of my youth, Dej Tshuam, the place of my beginning. I will miss the eggs that my parents saved for weeks in advance of the celebration. My father standing by the door of our house, calling into the dark for our spirits to come home for the harvest, from the cold, from the wanderings of the year past. If I close my eyes and quiet my ears, I can hear his voice calling out, among the other names of my family, "Tswb aws los tsev"—Tswb, come home. The grain sheds full to the top with unshelled corn, with grain, with rice. Our house full of brothers and sisters-in-law, nieces and nephews. The scent of incense sticks rising from my father's altar. Tables full of boiled chickens and steamed rice, garden greens boiled in broth, bowls full of pounded chili with salt. I could taste it all with each bite of mashed potatoes that goes down my throat. Nostalgia flavors the food I eat here.

In America, in my marriage, I've had to become stronger with the addition of each child. These stronger versions of myself are not celebratory in nature. It does not feel like something to be proud of. I feel like a person who is what Dawb and Kablia call "a poseur." I am pretending to be something I'm not. I am pretending that I can't hear or see judgment because I cannot afford to respond in a useful or thoughtful or articulate manner; it would just be tears and heartache spilling out in places and before people who wouldn't know what to do. At the same time, I know the person I have become is less desperate than the person I was in Thailand, the one who was willing to die. Here, at least, I'm fighting, and I feel the cost of this fight in the tightness of my muscles, the stiffness of my limbs, in the body that I hold up despite the fact that all I want to do is sag, melt into it. Npis knows this. I know that he has also become a different version of himself. The one who stands to the side, admits deep inside there's too much he cannot do for the woman he loves, or more painfully: that he cannot be the kind of father who can give his children the things they clamor for and dream out loud. The life we share demands a kind of generosity. He will not comment on the stiffness of my body, even at night, even with him, and I keep standing in line with WIC vouchers and opening the door for the Thanksgiving man. In America, we have become versions of ourselves that we do not love but need. Somehow in Thailand, in the waiting years, rubbed raw by the war, we could not be anything but the remnants of flesh and bone trying to find shelter in our bodies. I will not observe out loud to Npis the fact that I have to do most of the hard things to make our lives in America possible, only to my children.

So although I want to go to the Mall of America, I don't say anything to Npis.

It isn't until Dawb and Kablia clamor and clamor and clamor that the talk starts to buzz about our house. We are no longer in the housing project. Our application to Section 8 government-subsidized housing has been approved. We are living in a house that the girls tell us is haunted by the spirit of a little boy that grows big in anger. Npis and I are both now working at a company half an hour outside St. Paul. We are assemblers alongside a conveyer belt. We put together cooling parts for cars, Npis and I and a few other Hmong relatives, with a mean woman named Stacy, and a supervisor who acts important all the time. We work on the night shift. I make a friend, a Cambodian woman whose name is Bich and every time she tells someone her name, the white people around us look uncomfortable because it sounds like a bad word in English. She talks a lot, my friend, and she makes the night go faster. She speaks in broken English but so do I, so we have no trouble understanding each other. She's older than me. She has two grown daughters. She gives me the clothes they've outgrown for my girls. The biggest change in our life though isn't the move to a house in a neighborhood full of older white people on a quiet intersection in St. Paul or the new job, and it isn't just the addition of Txuj, our son; it is also the fact that we have a new daughter in our lives. Our newest addition's name is Hlub.

Hlub has turned two. Npis cuts her hair in a perfect bowl of thick brown. She has straight bangs across her forehead and then straight hair along the length of her chin. She has round eyes and the skin underneath her brows is continually pink. She has pouty lips and a little button nose, round cheeks. She doesn't talk much but she's not a difficult child. She's born in the run of everything. She will be my true middle child, the fourth in a line of seven surviving children. Her birth is easy and after the hardship of Txuj's, I'm grateful to her from birth. Hlub is stubborn. She likes gentleness and softness. If Npis or I raise our voices at her, she will balk and she is impossible to wrangle in. I've learned this lesson. I will not yell at or raise my hand to her. I know that I do not want to measure my will against hers, that this is not the kind of mother I will be to this child of mine. I remember the time before Dawb and I think about how little I knew, thinking that I could just be one kind of mother, not realizing that to each child I needed to be a different version of myself. So, one day, after hearing Dawb and Kablia talk about visiting the Mall of America, Hlub says to her father and me, "I want to go to the Mall of America. I want to see it."

Npis starts shaking his head immediately, but I stop him by saying, "Let's take the kids to the Mall of America this weekend. People from other states and countries come just to see it here in Minnesota. We live here. Let's take the kids."

Npis is not happy.

He says, "What if the children get hurt?"

I say, "We'll make sure they don't."

He says, "We can't guarantee their safety at the mall."

I tell him, "We can't guarantee it here, either."

He says, "We don't have money."

I tell him, "We won't spend any money. Tell me something I don't know."

He is scowling.

I tell him, "Besides, I really want to go and see the Mall of America, too."

He sighs.

I sigh with him.

Later, I hear him tell the children, "Fine. This weekend, because your mother really wants me to take you all, we'll go to the Mall of America."

The Subaru is long dead. It died one cold winter's night and could not be awakened. We call Teev, the Hmong mechanic we all use in the family. He used to work at a Toyota dealership but found it hard with the white men who asked him to not only be a mechanic but an interpreter and janitor, so he quit. He now fixes cars for people in the community for cash in the old uniform shirt and matching pants he still keeps from the shop. He smokes nonstop when he fixes cars. His hands are dirty because he doesn't wash them, he only wipes them on the dirty blue pants smeared with oil and other car fluids. He is very thin, a skeleton of a man. His hair, too, is thin and unruly. He doesn't shave completely but has no beard, only scraggly hair growing from his chin like a character from a Chinese movie. His eyes are always slightly squinting, like he is measuring something in the air, or on your face or form. I try not to talk to him, and keep the children away when we need his services. When Npis calls Teev for his services, Npis knows that he has to help him. They run around in Teev's once-black pickup truck with the rust eating it from below, the metal above his tires so worn that sunlight pokes into it and makes it look crispy and edible like a cookie, across the junkyards of St. Paul looking for used batteries and car parts. After nearly seven hundred dollars spent and a week of driving around, Teev tells Npis, "Your Subaru can't be fixed."

We have to get another car. A different relative tells Npis that there are car auctions and agrees to take Npis to an auction in Iowa. Npis is excited to go on a trip, to see an America beyond the Twin Cities. On a bright morning, without clouds in the sky, they make their way across state lines in the relative's gray Toyota Corolla.

They return the next day late in the afternoon with Npis driving a used Toyota 4Runner. The car has lines of black and red on its side. It costs nearly $10,000. We'd managed to save $2,500. Npis's mother has given us $2,000 of her savings to get the car. The rest we've borrowed from one of Npis's brothers. Npis's mother says to him over the telephone, "I've seen car accidents and the smaller car always has more damage than the big car. Please get a big car with this money." She feels that this Toyota 4Runner will keep her son safe. On the day the car arrives, the children run to the single-car garage with its peeling white paint and crowd at the little rectangle window to peek at the new car. Dawb and Kalia oooh and aaah while Txuj and Hlub jump and raise their hands in the air like some of the tall basketball players in their sweaty jerseys do after they make a basket on television. We don't know it yet, but the car has been in a bad accident, and it will not be a good vehicle for us. All we know is that it is nicer than anything we've ever owned.

On a Saturday, the kids and Npis and I pack ourselves into the Toyota 4Runner for the big Mall of America trip. While the new car does not feel significantly wider, it is much higher than the old car had been. The kids like a cartoon where there is a family who uses their feet to move their car. In the Subaru, when all six of us were packed in, I always wanted to move my feet to help the poor engine out. In this new car, I feel no need to do that. In fact, I use my left hand to brace against the door because I feel so far off the ground. Npis and I sit up front. The kids settle in the back. They have to share seat belts because there aren't enough. The two youngest sit in the center, sharing the belt. Dawb and Kablia sit on either side, staring out the window. The children are jittery with anticipation. They are excited but they keep it contained because they know their father is on edge. He is frustrated at the exit off the highway and the multiple entries into the Mall of America parking ramps. There are a lot of cars and even more people going to the mall. A driver honks at us and Npis winces at the sound. I'm in awe when we see the sign for the Mall of America with the red, white, and blue ribbon and star above it. I'm like a kid going somewhere I've never been.

I'm nine years old again. My mother is taking me to Long Tieng, the CIA headquarters in Phou Bia. We have citrus fruits, pomelos the size of heads, to sell. There's an airstrip in the middle of a valley. The makeshift town stretches on either side, with dirt paths leading in circular directions. I get to eat from a noodle vendor, a Lao woman who sells bowls of rice noodles with pork broth, finely sliced green onion and cilantro on top. There is a bowl full of sliced limes. Customers can take as much as they want. I squeeze two whole slices in my bowl. From the small plastic bottle full of crushed chilies, I help myself to a heaping spoon. Closer to the airstrip, there are official-looking buildings. I see nurses dressed in white walking in heels from building to building. I peek into an open doorway, and I see desks lined up and nurses typing fast. I say to myself: one day I am going to learn how to type and I'm going to wear a white nurse's outfit. It is my mother's voice that calls out to me, "Tswb, come here. We have to get to the market now." We are at the market for half a day, just my mother and me. We are there only long enough for the pomelos to sell out. When the basket is empty, my mother counts the coins and bills, and tells me, "I want to get back to Dej Tshuam before dark."

I decide right there in the Toyota 4Runner and in front of the big sign for the shopping complex that I want to make our excursion to the Mall of America an unforgettable experience for my children. I don't even pretend to hide my excitement anymore. Npis notices and his shoulders relax, his body gives in to the force of mine. We find parking safely and we tell the girls to memorize our parking place. Inside the Mall of America, the air smells new and manufactured. The lights are dazzling. There is music playing on speakers overhead. There are people everywhere, all ages, all kinds of families and friends walking in big and small groups. The children and I are struck by the activity of shoppers around us. There are so many parents at the mall. They are walking around, pushing strollers and holding the hands of young children. We find ourselves following the families walking with some confidence, and we end up at the indoor amusement park, the heart of the action. There are glass ceilings above us letting in real sunlight. There are trees and they feel real against my palm, cool and alive. There are rides. The children on the rides are screaming and screaming. My children look wide-eyed at one ride and then another. The tickets are too expensive. We decide to buy tickets for the youngest to go on a ride together. Dawb and Kablia are both old enough to understand that we don't have money to spend for fun. We all cheer as Txuj and Hlub get on a small train and go around in circles, too self-conscious to scream but their smiles are louder than all the other screams to this beaming mother. We walk around the first floor of the mall and Npis and I hold the little kids' hands while Dawb and Kablia walk in front. We work in tandem to point to all the things the younger kids have not seen before, things we ourselves are also experiencing for the first time, a world built for families to laugh and play together. There's a ride where people seem to be sitting in a hollow log and they are going up and down like the log is falling. There's another ride where kids and adults sit on what appears to be a giant swing and they are twirled beneath the spread of a mushroom umbrella. Npis, in his fashion when the children want things we cannot afford, buys them sugary treats, a bag of little donuts to share, a syrupy red drink that is semifrozen. The children are happy, and we walk around and around in a dizzying bubble of sound, light, and people, our steps bouncing a little despite the hardness of the floor underneath our feet and the fact that both Npis and I suffer from painful soles because of the hard factory floors at work.

I know I am smiling and stretching my face with joy. I see us for a moment the way I see other people: Npis and I, with our beautiful children, just a regular family walking in a place designed to bring people together and let them enjoy life for a time. Dawb with her long, thick hair growing out and tied back in a ponytail is observing everything, ever conscious of how we navigate new spaces in a country whose fences are sometimes invisible. Kablia, also wanting long hair, but unable to tame the tangles in her ponytail, letting her arms swing wide at her side, carefree like a child whose movements have never been limited. Txuj, walking with his hands raised high in the hold of his father's, moves with curious amazement. Hlub walking on her own now and me following behind her because even though this is her first time at the Mall of America and she is only two, she seems to know where she wants to go.

For many of the families around us, it is a fun day. For us, it is a life-changing day. My older girls look into the glimmery windows of the stores, see the mannequins with their hips jutting out and hats pulled low over their white molded faces, hands at their sides, pointed down. They don't have to say anything, I know they want the jackets and the shoes, they want the handbags and the scarves. They don't ask to go into the stores or indicate their yearning, but I tell myself: one day my girls will be able to go into any of these stores and look around. The other two, Txuj and Hlub, are high on sugar and people. My belly protrudes. Inside it, the baby kicks, already part of our adventure.

After two hours of saying no to more rides, Npis is done. We are seated on a curved bench beside huge pots full of flowers. Kablia inches close. She pinches the leaves of the plants between her fingers. She whispers to me with wonder, "Mom, these are real."

I nod like I know.

I tell her, "Don't pinch the leaves."

Npis says, "Okay. Let's go home."

The children, caught in the gleam of the lights and the volume of the voices around us and the songs coming from above, are not ready. They plead. I hate it when they resort to begging. Npis hates it even more.

He says, "It's enough. We'll come back next time."

Kablia says, "No, we won't."

Npis looks at Kablia. She grows quiet.

I always feel a need to mediate.

I tell the children, "Let's go home. We'll come back next time. We know what the Mall of America looks like now."

The older children are not happy but they nod.

Hlub looks up at her father from the straight line of her bangs; she says to him, "You want to go home. You go. I don't want to go home yet."

Npis is too shocked to say anything.

Hlub jumps down from the bench, her sandaled feet round and plump, her toddler legs beneath the knit dress full of sunflowers steady and strong. At her neck, she wears a strand of clear beads I've made for her, small and glimmery. Her eyes are round as grapes, and she focuses both on her father's face.

She tells him, in English, "I go by myself."

Npis laughs. He doesn't know what else to do. This is the first time I hear this laugh from Npis. There are moments when the children delight him and his eyes widen into joy, then crease at the corners. There are moments when a relative or a stranger has said something he finds amusing and his teeth show in an open and easy laugh. There are moments when he laughs at me because of the things I've said and it has sparked some idea of fun. This laugh though is different. It is startled laughter. It is amazement and uncertainty. Hlub has puzzled her father.

Our youngest turns from us and walks away, the straight line of brown hair at her nape swinging with her steps.

I continue sitting with the other children as Npis follows Hlub into the crowd. She does not look back. She keeps walking. He walks behind her. To my surprise, he does not rush to grab her arm. They disappear into the crowd of people moving as if they are in a trance beneath the shiny lights.

Fifteen minutes later, Npis walks back toward us with wiggling Hlub in his arms. He wanted to see how far she would go. She went too far for his comfort. She is mad but she's not crying. She's fighting to "go by herself." Npis is now clearly embarrassed. He's saying to her in low tones, "If you keep on fighting, people will think I'm stealing you." His words mean nothing to her.

In the Toyota 4Runner on the way home, Hlub is angry. Her little arms are crossed in front of her. Txuj sleeps by her side, head on Dawb's shoulder. I look at my third daughter in the backseat. Her eyes clear and large, flashing anger at her father still. She's only two, our born-in-America daughter, our daughter who is pushing to show us something new about ourselves as her parents in this country.

Npis chose Hlub's name. Hlub is the Hmong word for *love*. In the hospital, unable to choose a satisfactory name, we'd written down "Kab Npauj" to recall "Kablia." But we knew it was not the right name for our fourth child. Kab Npauj, a little moth, drawn to flames. Even when we named her, I thought: what if she is the fire? From the baby's earliest days in her father's arms, he referred to her as, "Me Hlub." Little love. She was our little love.

Strong and resolute. More stubborn than either of us.

We knew she would go her own way. If we didn't want to lose sight of her, one of us had to follow while the other waited. If we dared wrestle her back, she would have to contend with her unhappiness. In this moment and the many after it, Npis will follow her until his comfort gives and then he will try to force her back and it will not work, but I will always wait for her. I will get scared. I will lose my patience and grow angry. I will despair, and then I will find in me a well of hope, enough of it to keep going, because I love her and I believe in her.

In raising this child, I will learn something fundamental about motherhood, that our children will make decisions across the trajectories of their lives and that sometimes these decisions will take them far from us.

In raising this child, I will learn a truth about my own situation as a daughter.

The spirit of my mother will wait for me in that jungle. She will stand in that clearing, the water pail close by, and look in the direction I have walked. All I have to do is find my way back. Her arms will be waiting for me. Despite the fear and the anger, none of it would equal the relief of my return, her knowing that for all that the world has to offer, for all the things that I yearn for, there is no more comforting place for me to be seen and loved than beside her.

CHAPTER 21

Inheritance

I have a miscarriage in America before and after you, Zuabli. The one before you happened in the early months of pregnancy. That grief I could carry in the light of the losses I've known, but the one after is the most painful one I will endure.

In an old home video, your teenage cousins are visiting the moldy house. You are not yet two years old. You have the traditional bowl cut that your father has now mastered. Your cousins are young men. They have their hands in the pockets of their blue jeans. They are talking among themselves, laughing. You are rolling on the carpeted floor. One of them has shoelaces. You untie them. He kneels and ties them back up. You want to play. He's preoccupied with the more exciting talk of his age group. He rises. He checks himself out in the old gold-painted mirror we inherited with the house. Your brother Txuj comes by. He is seven years old and he wears athletic shorts that go past his knees, a T-shirt nearly to the hem of the shorts. He has the round belly of a child who needs to run outside but can't because of the long Minnesota winters, the dangers of the streets on the East Side of St. Paul's crumbling neighborhoods, streets filled with potholes that cut into the tires of cars, rusty nails that can puncture rubber along the sidewalks. You jump on your brother's back, a small ball of muscles. His face reddens because your hands are tight around his neck and he did not anticipate the jump. He pries your hands apart. You slide down his back slowly.

You run to me. You have on a pair of Txuj's baby joggers, the two-colored ones, blue and purple, and then one of Hlub's old knit dresses, this one of daisies in bloom. Your father has dressed you again. He now works the first shift at a different company. I'm still on the night shift at the old one. We have to take turns taking care of you all. The neighborhood we live in is unsafe. Across the street, a woman was shot through her walls before we moved in. Some of the neighbors say they see her still figure looking out the top window of the house on the darkest of nights. We have agreed that one of us must be home with the children. We know too well how bullets slice through flesh and make ghosts of both the living and the dead.

You are short and stout. Built solid. You started walking at seven months and talking at the same time. You with your head of thick hair, straight and glossy. Your pupils so large your eyes appear black. You with the tiny beauty mark on the right corner of your top lip. Your grandmother used to say that such a mark meant that you'd earn your keep with the strength of your mouth, the power of your words. You with the husky, breathless voice, the wheezing when you run fast or play hard.

You say, "Mommy, I just want to hold Txuj but he won't let me. Make him let me."

You don't know that I've just had a miscarriage, another little boy; I carried him well into the sixth month of pregnancy, this one who shouldn't have died inside me but did. I had a summer rash. Each time I felt the warmth of the sun, I'd start itching. I'd gone to the doctor. The doctor, no longer Dr. Waxler because we had new insurance through work, had prescribed a cream. It hadn't worked. I returned to the doctor again. That same doctor prescribed pills. I'd taken the pills, just two doses of them, across the spread of two days, when the baby inside me stopped moving. Your father and I had scheduled a visit to the doctor once again, now afraid not of the skin rash but the quiet I felt in my core. The doctor couldn't find a pulse on the baby. By then,

I didn't trust her. By then, I wasn't sure whether I could trust myself. I made an appointment with a different doctor. Same conclusion: the baby inside no longer had a pulse. Without other recourse, we scheduled an induction. A baby boy, bigger than all the ones in Thailand, a baby with fingers and toes, fuzz on his head. A dead baby whose head tilted to the side. The scars I stitched up in America, the ones inside my heart, came undone one by one. If this baby boy was alive, I would now be at the ninth month of pregnancy. He would soon be coming. You didn't know any of this. You were two years old. You understood you were my baby.

You repeat yourself, "Mommy, I just want to hold Txuj but he won't let me. Make him let me."

I couldn't hear you. I didn't respond to you.

In the video, I'm sitting on the sofa staring at the dark screen on the television, playing out a movie in my head, something to salvage my aching heart. In the movie, the baby boy is alive inside me and about to be born. In the movie, I've taken out and cleaned the electric heater we bought for Txuj and all the swaddles I've sewn for my American babies. In the movie, I'm thinking about adding one to our family, no longer a little family, a family soon to receive its sixth child. But no one sees this movie. Only I know it is there. My hair is cut short to accommodate the work in the factory. The perms of our early American days are gone. Long hair is dangerous by the big machines. Untamed curls are also dangerous by the machines. I'm caught in my feelings, but you believe you are my baby and you refuse to let me drown in the hole that has opened up in my heart.

You place both your hands on my face. I feel their weight, their fleshiness, their strength. You pull my face right to yours. You smile, the corners of your eyes crinkling. You kiss me, right on the lips, you kiss me again, and then you wrap your pudgy arms around my neck and pull tight and squeeze with every bit of strength you have. You squeeze the broken out of me for a moment, and in the video a startled laugh escapes me as my arms encircle your small body and lift you up.

Away from the video, in the first years of your life, not only does your father dress you more often than me, but he is more present in ways that I could not be because I was still nursing this last dead baby I will deliver.

You will write in your Stanford essay many years later about how it was in your father's arms that you learned how to dream. You'll write about the mornings when you'd force him awake by peeling his eyelids up and pushing your eyeball right up to his. You'll write about how once he was up, once he had dressed you in the pale morning light and fed you, how you would spend the day following him from one task to the other while your siblings were in school, and I was at the factory now working the day shift so your father could work at night. This is the brief period in our lives when your father will do the laundry because we've bought a used washing machine and a used dryer and settled the unmatched pair into the little alcove by the kitchen, right up beside the plastic utility sink. This is the brief period in our lives when your father will cook many of the meals for his children, dishes all of you will love forever and remember as singular: his khao pad (Thai fried rice with tomatoes, eggs, cilantro, green onion, minced pork, bits of chicken, and cuts of thick-stemmed Chinese broccoli, which he'll call by the Thai name *pak kana*) and his beef curry (which I have no memories of tasting but you will tell me is the best). This is the brief period in our lives when your father will do the work I've always done because my heart is hurting for the loss of a baby boy whose death I believed was preventable. In your personal statement, you will write about your father as the man who told you the story about the mouse who fell in love with the sun, one of the most foundational stories of your life. You will write about the story your father told you of a future in which his daughter, little Zuabli, will drive not only a red car but the reddest car in the world, and travel not only on a regular street but the fastest of highways. You will write about how, through his stories and his devotion, your father has built a bridge of words for you to journey toward your future.

In the first two years of your life, I remember you as a newborn. I remember how you had a seizure three days after your birth. I remember the fear choking my throat in the ambulance with you on our way to the hospital, the feeling like all the muscles in my legs had melted away, leaving me to stand on bones as soft as tofu. I remember my helplessness as the nurse with the rough hands pulled at your newborn arms and legs, then poked you three times to secure an IV. I remember how you did not wince or register the pain of the long needle. When the hospital room grew quiet, I knelt beside your little crib, and I held your small hands in my own. I whispered in your ears, "Please be okay. Please let my little daughter be okay. Your mother loves you so much, wants you so bad. Please." I prayed to the ancestors, to your long-dead grandfather, to my own father, to all the forces in the world, all the gods that might heed the worry of a mother unable to help her child, unable to keep her safe, uncertain of her fate. And I remember the relief that filled me when your eyes opened, and hours later when the scans showed that your brain was undamaged by the seizure.

Your beautiful, perfect brain. You were born smart. Your father and I understood that our only job was to keep you so. Your father did the work when I couldn't. But then, the day came again when I could and I did, Zuabli.

I wasn't ready to let you go to school, but you insisted. At the age of four, you told your father and me, "I want to know what happens at school." By the time you came along, Hlub had taught me enough about the power of a child's will. But your father was reluctant. He said, "You will spend much of your life in school. Play at home for another year." He pleaded, "Be with your daddy for another year." You refused. We gave in.

Your father shoveled the walkway from our house to the end of the block after each snowfall because your legs were too short to clear the snowbanks. Every morning, before I left for work, I made sure to put your clothes for the day along the electric heater at the base of the walls so that they'd be warm and inviting for you. On the days that I could, I combed your thick hair, which you insisted on growing long despite your father's desire that you hold on to the bowl cut. You were never happy unless the clothes and the hair were perfect.

You inherited my hair. My mother and brothers and sisters used to talk often about how thick my hair was and how heavy. They talked of its incredible blackness, so smooth and shiny it looked like satin. Your hair reminds me of the hair of my childhood. Not the fine strands I now have on my head, the occasional white poking through, always shorter than the rest, more interested in sticking up than lying down, bothering me. Your ideas of perfection, too, reminded me of my own. The flat line of my mouth. The beads I used to put in my hair and around my neck. You are more like me in your wants than all the rest of my children.

Your idea of perfect because you were still wearing 3T and 4T clothing was that they were a matching set. Your favorite clothes were a navy-blue outfit with big floral collars around the neck and pants made from the same print as the collars. After I tied your hair back in a ponytail, you would use your little hands to slide along the edges of your scalp. If it was not perfectly smooth, you'd ask me to do it again. In the moments when I was rushing because the dishes had to be done or the pot of hot water on the stove was boiling over, or simply because we were running late for the school bus, I'd tell you, "It is fine. We'll do a better job tomorrow." You'd cry until you were late for the long yellow bus carrying Hlub and Txuj off, both their little faces pressed against the dirty glass looking for you, and your father would have to drop you off at school, tired as he was from the night shift. You'd cry until I gave in.

I knew a pattern was emerging in my parenting. I was giving in to all my children. Each time they wanted something, I wanted them to have it. While your father abstained from stores and sites of fun, I found myself trying to make up for it. I found myself spending more than I had carefully budgeted each time we went to the grocery store. I knew this pattern was happening because I grew afraid that I'd run out of opportunities to do more. My oldest girls were getting older, closer to the age I was when your father and I chanced upon each other in that jungle, to that moment when I walked away from my mother toward marriage in the dark of night, my blinding youth. A fear was growing inside me that I wouldn't have enough time to give each of you the things that I wanted you to have, more than anything the memories of joy and happiness in our old house beneath the American elm.

I had never been a talker. I was a listener. But suddenly words filled me, memories of my life with my mother assailed me. My father, who I had always adored, started feeling like a dream. I had somehow woken up with the loss of the babies in America, the birth of you, the fact that your older sisters were now teenagers.

The way my mother ate her pho. She never seasoned it. She always had it with a side of white rice. She drank the broth and ate the rice. She would leave the noodles behind in the bowl.

The way my mother talked. She was not a soft-spoken woman. She did not yell, either. There were words other mothers said to their children in moments of anger that she refused to say to us, like "Tsov tom." Tiger bite. Worthy of a tiger's bite. Someone doomed for failure and pain unless they heeded the immediate warnings of the person speaking to them. She refused and now I refuse. The way she told us never to say "peb pluav." We are without. We may be poor, we may be struggling and suffering in the moment. I've lived a life of poverty and I have gone without many things, but I have never been completely without—myself, others, memories of being loved, knowledge of worth. My mother's approach to language and meaning was plainspoken, far from the poetry of my father or yours.

I wanted my children to know my mother. I didn't know how to impart her but through my own mothering, my own decisions as a parent.

When you insisted, no matter how late the time, no matter how many other things I had to do, I made the time to redo your hair. I wanted it to be good enough for you. So, we'd sit, me on the edge of the sagging corduroy sofa, you in between my knees on the woven bamboo stool, and I'd comb your thick hair until it was perfectly smooth with the red plastic comb with big teeth then pull the heavy strands together gently into a ponytail and secure it, always with a black hair tie because that was your preference.

In those years, I ran on my love for you alone. I gave up on sleep. I spaced my precious showers every other night. I had given up on the perms of our early American years, but I allowed the months in between my haircuts to grow long because your father and I could not find the fifteen minutes we needed for him to set up his trimmer in the bathroom for my cut. I stopped going to and buying dollar items like little coin purses and little glass cups at the garage sales I adored (though your father hated it because he didn't know when a seller would mistreat us or where we'd put anything). In those years, the days were long but the nights were short, the weeks flashed by on the free calendars from Asian stores in the blinking of eyes, dates crossed out in big Xs by your small hands.

Though they were modest, your father and I had goals. We wanted to save money and pay back his brother and sister-in-law for the car loan to buy the Toyota 4Runner, which was now falling apart. Its back doors had stopped working. The children had to crawl in through the two front ones. The mechanic man who worked for the community, Teev, came by and told us that a new transmission would be necessary soon because the car had a burning smell and made noises each time it was turned toward neutral. We knew another car purchase was imminent. We knew the only way to make any extra dollars was to work overtime, so we did. Both of us, whenever overtime was necessary, at our different jobs. I was still at the old car coolant factory thirty minutes away from home. Your father was now working in the cities for a small company that made plaques and trophies just a mile down the hill from our house. Finally, he was making use of his education, all those nights doing math homework, machine operating. The overtime hours meant that we hardly saw each other.

I missed your father, but even before him, what I needed to function was sleep. I worked the day shift. I woke up each day at 4:30 a.m. so I could make rice and prepare a lunch. I was picked up by 5:30 by a relative who worked at the same company. I helped her pay for the gas in her car. We drove through the early-morning traffic across the seasons to stand at our places along the assembly lines and start work by 6:00. I worked ten-hour days. I came home by 5:00 in the evening. Your father would be gone already. He'd leave right before Dawb and Kablia came home from the high school where one boy had shot another in the parking lot and then requested a song be played the next morning, a song Dawb and Kablia both loved called "Please Forgive Me." Your father worked from 3:00 p.m. until midnight. Like me, he was sleep deprived. We had our shared goals, and none of them were each other.

For our first decade in America, the days raced by. The years, though, were like the boats on the horizons of the oceans where we've never been, impossible to see clearly. All we have left from those years are the photographs that Dawb took of all of you children.

There's a photograph of both Dawb and Kablia with horrible haircuts they'd given each other, sitting on a sofa in a small apartment we lived in for six months, a transition between the haunted Section 8 house and the little house beneath the American elm. Both sulking because the other had done a bad job.

There's another photo with all of you in the cramped kitchen of the moldy house with its dirty carpeted floor that I had hoped we would be able to change when we first moved in but were unable to. There's a cake on the rickety table. It is someone's birthday. You and your cousins are gathered around the cake with huge smiles—never mind that there are no presents.

There's another photograph of a kiddie pool in the front yard, set up in the small space of sunlight in front of the sagging porch, before the reach of the shade of the American elm at the yard's right corner. You and Hlub are sitting inside it. Txuj is standing by its side, the hose in his hands, drops of water floating down like diamonds in the sunlight.

There's another photograph of a sleepover with the cousins. Npis has taken Dawb and Kablia to the movie rental place on University Avenue where the Hmong stores are. They must have done well in school and gotten good grades. They've rented scary movies from Thailand, a Chinese drama starring their favorite actor, Leon Lai, and their cousins have come over. The children are sprawled on woven plastic mats across the living room, all their eyes on the television screen in the corner, bowls of potato chips in front of them along with cups of soda.

In the photographs from these years, you all look happy and healthy, and although I was not present for each of these events happening, they are precious to me. They tell me that while I was not able to be with my children, they were not alone. It is what I had hoped the cassettes in

Thailand had offered my mother, that the letters I exchange with Soob offer to my family.

There is a particular photograph of you, Zuabli, that I look at often. You are eight years old. Your long hair is parted at the side, pulled back from your face except for the strands of baby hair that stick to your damp forehead because it is hot outside. It is Dawb's graduation from college. There are many group photographs of Dawb standing in between your father and me, with your grandmother, photographs of the whole family gathered on the green grass of Hamline University, but the only portrait from that day is of you. I've put Dawb's graduation gown on you, the cap on your head, the cords at your neck. Everything is much too large and too long. You are standing before a flower bed in bloom, yellow and pink petals cupping the sky. Your smile is shy, but you are proud of your sister, and I can see your dreams in your eyes.

In that photograph, I see everything good that can happen for my little girl. I don't see any of the bad things. Any of the hardships. Any of the struggles. I don't see how you will have to fight to find a way to the highway of the future, build for yourself a vehicle that is strong enough to ensure you can carry all you love with you.

Even in our worst moments in the jungle, when we talked of the future, my mother spoke of it as a bright place. She told me the war couldn't last forever. She told me that one day I could return to school, and that we might even return to Dej Tshuam, our village where the two rivers meet. I've never blamed her for not seeing the conditions or circumstances of my life. I've always held close her belief in me. Although she did not know anything about being a nurse or typing on a machine, she knew it was my dream, and even though I do not get to be a nurse or type with quick fingers in this lifetime, I know what it is like to dream—and now you, Zuabli, are the keeper of many dreams, your father's and mine, but most importantly your own. These dreams are riches that money cannot buy, a way of waking up the heart when it is weary, calling on the spirit when the body is weak.

CHAPTER 23

When My Mother Dies

On the day that my mother died, Npis and I were at the garden. It was a hot summer and the plants were thirsty. We'd leased a little plot of land along a highway for fifty dollars that year. Many other Hmong families had done the same. Each plot was marked by sticks in the ground, tied with old T-shirt remnants. The gardens supplemented our earnings and allowed us to eat the vegetables we were familiar with: Hmong cilantro, which grew into thick stalks like dill and sprouted clusters of small white flowers whose scent was strong and heady, its flavor more pungent than the store-bought variety; Hmong mustard greens with golden flowers, crunchy stalks, and tender leaves; Hmong mustard greens without flowers, thick-stemmed and slightly bitter, which tasted best when boiled with pork and lemongrass; and different varieties of Hmong pumpkins, big and misshapen, their outside full of warts, but the flesh inside sweet and nutty. Each plant was born from a seed carried in some pocket from the old world. Its seeds shared and reproduced here in America. Npis and I, like all the other Hmong farmers, drove to the plot with our car trunks filled with old milk gallons full of water from our sinks for the thirsty plants struggling valiantly in the heat.

I wore a hat that day. On top of my hat, I'd tied a long-sleeved shirt to protect my neck from the sun's fierce rays. Neither Npis nor I had much experience gardening because we were younger children in our families and never had a chance to live the farming life as adults, but we'd both picked up enough from observing our mothers in their gardens and the fields. Still, ours was far from the lushest of the gardens near the highway because our work schedules prohibited regular watering and I refused to use fertilizers, afraid they would cause cancer. Already, cancer had entered our lives. People around us were beginning to contend with it, this mysterious disease that came to many parts of the body in many forms, that resulted so often in death across our community.

I stood in the center of the garden and surveyed our plants. Our greens were puny, lots of their outer leaves wilting. Our cucumbers were small, their surface prickly, the length and size of children's fingers beneath the fuzzy leaves holding fast to the sprawling stalks. Our peppers were short and thin, their fruits no bigger than the bodies of Tylenol capsules. Still, I felt proud looking at our work. Npis and I had teamed up and we tilled the earth and there were growing things where seeds had been buried. In fact, we would have a harvest of our own. The cherry tomatoes were already red on the vine. The cilantro was growing tall. The green onions grew in fat bunches, their small bulbs rising from the earth. We could store them in the basement for seasons beyond this one.

We got to work. Npis picked the tender tips of pumpkin vines while I gathered the sawtooth herbs that grew like dandelions on the hard surface of the earth. My hat nearly blew off my head many times as trucks sped by on the highway. Each time, I pulled it back on my head and secured the knot I'd tied with the arms of the shirt beneath my neck despite the heat. In the thin shade of my hat, I felt I understood what my mother and Npis's mother must have felt tilling their gardens to feed their children with the burning sun at their backs.

On the drive back to the house that morning, I turned on the radio in the maroon Cadillac that Npis had purchased, a used police car long repurposed for regular life. We listened to country songs, our favor-

ites because at the factories they were always played. We didn't always
know the meaning of the words but Npis could sing them as I hummed
along. The hot rush of the air into my opened window was strong and
competed with the song on the radio, Tanya Tucker's song about spar-
rows in a hurricane. The part where she sings "a stack of bills they can't
pay" always makes me think of Npis and me. I rarely sweat but my neck
and forehead were sticky to the touch, my body sinking into the seat
holding me, my breathing growing heavy with exhaustion.

When Npis parked the car, he got out to unload the five-gallon buckets we'd filled at the garden, the plastic bags of pumpkin tips. I was
hungry, sleepy from the sun's rays and the morning's work.

Unlike Npis and the children, I didn't mind a life without meat. A favorite summer meal of mine: fresh cucumbers peeled and sliced, dipped
in salt and chili flakes, eaten with fresh rice. I was disappointed that the
cucumbers were too young to pick, but figured some peeled and sliced
ginger would do. I had told Dawb and Kablia to make rice that morning. I knew Npis would want an actual meal with meat and broth but I
would attend to that after I'd eaten a bit of food. I was thirsty, too.

We helped each other carry the summer harvest into the house. The
youngest of the children reached for us, eager for embraces. Dawb and
Kablia ran to the car to help finish unloading the vegetables.

Although I was hungry and thirsty, I felt even more uncomfortable
in my clothing. The humidity of the morning had penetrated into my
skin and clothes. I went into the bedroom to change into a pair of knit
shorts and a T-shirt. Npis's mother did not approve when I wore shorts
but she was at one of Npis's brother's houses and the day was simply
too hot that even if she were at our house, I'd wear it anyway and ig-
nore the disapproval. How nice it would be to go window-shop with
Xis and Nplooj, to take the children along so they could enjoy the air-
conditioning in a store.

When I was in the dim bedroom, its shades pulled down to keep the
house cooler, taking off the sticky clothes and putting on fresh ones,
Dawb told her father that my sister Xis had called. Our mother had died
in Laos. The girls didn't know how to tell me.

I was pulling on a shirt when Npis entered the room we shared with our youngest children. I looked at him and asked if he wanted me to pull out a pair of shorts and a T-shirt for him, too. He waved aside my offer.

He said, "I need to tell you."

He said, "Your mother is dead."

The room stilled, and then it reeled.

I called him a liar.

I walked out of the bedroom, past Npis still standing in the same place beside the open door to our room, thinking, *I'll call Xis myself and talk to her, clarify the situation*. I passed by the entryway into the living room, where Kablia was now playing with the younger children. It wasn't until I was in the kitchen where Dawb sat with Txuj at the dining table, at the phone hanging on the white wall, holding the receiver in my right hand, now suddenly unsure of Xis's phone number, that my mouth opened, wet with saliva, and a cry emerged from deep inside me.

Dawb and Txuj were startled and scared by the keening that was coming from me. Npis had followed and gathered them out of the kitchen. I cried by myself. I had no idea how much feeling I had stored inside me, believing one day I would see my mother again, and all the hurts and the hopes would come out in the stories we would share. I'd thought perhaps we would cry over some and laugh over others. I had always thought that as long as my mother was alive, there would be a place for my feelings to find a home. On the day my mother died, I had to face the fact that I had left the house of my feelings a long time ago when I left my mother for marriage.

In the weeks after news of her death reached me, I felt bereft. I didn't want to call my sisters and hear their cries. I didn't want them to hear mine. I thought we needed each other but wasn't quite sure how to speak of this new grief with either of them. In the weeks after the knowledge that my mother was no longer to be found across the spaces of this earth, I felt like I hated the fact that Npis had a mother, that he's had one all these years and I hadn't. I didn't want anything to happen to his mother, but I was caught up in the death of my own. It was clear to me that my children and Npis did not know my mother and thus could not mourn her with me.

On the phone, Soob had been solemn. He outlined the funeral plans. He said my mother would be buried in the backyard of his house—as our father had been years ago in Dej Tshuam. Soob had gotten the authorities to approve of this unprecedented move in Kilometer 52 where they had been living with my mother since their reeducation after the war. The funeral would be a standard Hmong-Lao funeral. On behalf of all Mother's children in Laos, the three surviving brothers and Maiv, he thanked us for the money we, his sisters in America, had sent to help with the funeral expenses. He told me, "Don't cry. Our mother is dead." He told me not to cry but he cried to me. I cried in response. At the end of the call, we said, "Ua li os, ua li nawb." This is it. This is the way it is.

For long minutes after I hung the receiver back on its hook in the kitchen, I returned to the darkened bedroom Npis and I shared with the younger children, saw the full bed that was no longer on milk cartons but now sitting atop a metal frame, the baby crib on one side. On the floor, beside it, in the narrow space between the bed and the sliding doors of the closet, the makeshift blanket bed that Kablia had made for herself. News of my mother's death had triggered her fears of the dark. I thought to myself, this is my adult life, a life so full and yet so empty at the same time.

It dawned on me, sitting in the quiet of the room, that I was now an orphan. In the old country, I'd seen orphans passed from relative to relative. I'd heard stories of how much orphans ate, how bad they smelled, how desperate they were for love and affection. How insatiable their yearning. And how hard it was, even for people with good intentions and kind hearts, to reckon with their grief. In the old country it was understood and articulated: the grief of an orphan is impossible to surface from. Because of my mother, even though my father had died when I was a child, I had not been an orphan. I had grown up under the care of my loving siblings. I had gotten married despite the tumult of the times we lived in. I'd left one country for another and then another. Across all these years, I had left my mother refusing to accept that one day she would be the one leaving me.

The truths assailed me. I had not visited her. I never had the money to buy the plane tickets and go visit with my sisters Xis and Nplooj when they had gone. I said nothing when I saw the pictures they had returned with, photographs of themselves standing beside our elderly mother, each holding a hand. Xis, standing with a hand to her back just as she had done when she was a girl. I felt things I could say to no one. I kept thinking, even if I had found the money for the plane tickets, how was I to face my family with nothing to give? I had salvaged my heart by believing that perhaps there would be time still for me to save money, raise my children, make sure they could survive a couple of weeks or a month without me before I would go. Had I made a mistake I would regret forever?

I took out the two brown photo albums I kept inside a wooden nightstand we'd found at a garage sale and placed behind the crib for the baby bottles and Npis's nasal spray. I flipped through the pages of my children laughing and playing, posing before flower beds and in playgrounds, of Npis and myself standing beside each other, me some- times smiling, him usually not, to the ones that my sisters had shared upon their return from their trip to Laos. In the pictures they gave me, my mother, though old, is significantly taller than her daughters, me included—if I had been there. Her hair is thin and white. She pulls it back from her face. She is wearing a new flowery skirt and a new shirt tucked in, neat and clean. I am sure her clothing were gifts from my sisters. Xis and Nplooj both told me that on their trip, she had asked about me and said she missed me and wondered if I still missed her, too. Had I sent along a hundred dollars or two back for her? I can't remember. Nothing I'd done was enough to fill the empty space where she had been.

It isn't my children.

It isn't Npis.

It isn't even the forces of war.

In the days, weeks, and months after her death, I felt it was just me.

I had failed my mother as her daughter. I had not kept my end of the unspoken promise that mothers and daughters make. By entering

into her world, living in the circle of her love, growing up within it—
even as the years and distance flooded on my end, I should have been
smarter, more able to earn the money to return to Laos and visit her. I
should have been stronger, more capable of leaving my children for a
short time, to be with the woman who loved me most. In my life as my
mother's daughter, I had never questioned her love for me, her devotion,
her loyalty, her anything, and she'd let me believe that it was enough
that I was alive, that I had a husband who was at my side and children
to call my own. I knew it was a lopsided equation. And this fact hurt.

In that heavy season with the sun glaring above, beneath its unrelenting heat, there was no respite from myself. I did not think of myself
as a good mother. I could not bear to think of myself as a mother to
daughters. All I could think of was how undeserving I had been of such
a good woman, a loving mother. No amount of tears could make me
believe otherwise.

Yes, I sent money to help with the funeral expenses. It was nothing.

Yes, I told my children when they asked, "Niam Tais died because
she was sick. No, she wasn't quite as old as your grandmother."

The painful reality that I met each time they asked me a question to
try to get closer to this woman who I belonged to before them was this:
my mother was not the grandmother they knew and loved, the one who
visited in the summers, the one who had moved to Minnesota and came
to our house in the rotation of houses she shared with her children, her
thirteen suitcases full of gifts, mementos, healing herbs, and an assortment of balms and oils.

I stopped caring about the trips to the garden by the highway of the
speeding trucks or whether the plants remained alive. A piece of my
heart would have been happy to see them wither to the ground, sink
into the cracks of the earth, and disappear forever. But they did not. Npis
drove to the garden and watered them by himself, weeded in his haphaz-
ard way, and some of the vegetables survived.

I wanted my children to know my pain. They could not. They just
stared at me with concerned eyes, reached for me, clung fast, pressed
their ears to my beating heart.

I wanted to explode time. I wanted to go back to that jungle in Laos. I wanted to never meet Npis. I wanted to choose my mother that day when I left her standing there, on her way to the stream. I wanted the impossible.

I cried until my tear ducts looked like wounds. I cried for all the things I could not give my mother, among them, me. I remember my grief for my father in the pink light of memory, with the clean scent of citrus blooms around us. The reality of the grief I felt now with my mother's death was ugly in comparison; I wanted to smash everything in the house, break every piece of glass, I wanted to walk on the jagged pieces, feel them cut into my flesh. I wanted what I could not allow my children to see, their mother bleeding and fallen.

The harvest that fall was slim. Without my presence and assistance in the process, the weeds snuck in between the vegetables. The prairie grasses, native to this part of the world, grew taller than the mustard greens whose seeds we had carried across oceans. The vegetables that Npis was able to keep alive, the ones that managed to thrive in the mess of the hot summer, were without flavor in my mouth.

Relatives handed us big pumpkins full of orange flesh, strings clinging to fat seeds so that we might be able to save the seeds and have a better garden next year. The different sisters-in-law, a few of them having known their own losses, gave us bags full of cooked glutinous corn for the children because the few we had planted hadn't produced. I didn't harvest my cilantro, chili, or mustard seeds. I let them dry out in the sun on the stalks and then fall to the ground, ground that would lease to some other family next year, or perhaps be plowed over and planted with corn or soy by the white farmer who owned the fields, the one who took our money at the beginning of the growing season and came to pull out the sticks with the T-shirt remnants we'd tied once it ended.

In the recesses of my heart, I'd always known that when my mother died, I would want to begin my life all over again, and so I did as much as one can do such things. I couldn't make changes in the life I shared with Npis or my children. I endeavored to make the changes in myself. I fashioned a woman out of the process of my grief. I came to understand what a bad luck woman was. It had little to do with men. It was in fact the reality of so many women before me: a life in which we had to give up our mothers far too fast, long before we were ready. I promised myself that I would give my daughters all of me, as much time with me as possible, teach them how to navigate a world in which they need not choose to leave their mothers behind to find their partners. I learned how to accept the fact that I was not only a descendant of bad luck women and that I was in fact one myself, but that the cycle would break with me.

I bought boxes of oranges from the Asian grocery stores. Their labels said they were grown in Florida, Texas, California, or Arizona. I did not know these places. I could imagine them as versions of Dej Tshuam, places where families lived together, played beneath the orchard trees, breathed in its blossoms and blooms. I peeled these oranges for my children. Using a knife, I maneuvered around each segment, took away the pith, until what remained was the clear juice sacs, shaped like tears on the palms of my hands. I tasted to make sure that they were filled with sweetness, then I fed it to my children by the spoonful, from the oldest to the youngest. I did this until there were no boxes left, and the store managers told me, "Next year there will be more."

The Last Girl

The last of my girls was born after the death of my mother. She was born looking more like Npis's mother than any of my children. She had her grandmother's wide cheekbones and small round nose, her thick eyebrows and steady eyes. We named her Ntxhais, the Hmong word for "daughter." When she was delivered, Npis and I believed she was our last child. Ntxhais made us a family of eight.

Npis carried her on weekends to the couch so she could enjoy Saturday morning cartoons, a soft blanket tucked around her plump legs. I made rice porridge on low heat and sweetened it with sugar, blew and blew until it cooled before I brought it to her lips. As soon as she was strong enough, even Zuabli, only a year and nine months older than Ntxhais, carried the baby on her back across the stretch of the moldy house we lived in, singing lullabies, bouncing the child up and down.

And yet: my last daughter was not spoiled. She, unlike the rest, found in the busy of our home spaces where she could be alone. I'd find her sitting in the corner, a notebook on her lap, a set of crayons by her side. She drew elaborate pictures that covered up full pages, a giant blue whale the backdrop to everything. In front, cartoon figures tossing a ball, a fish leaping afoot. She was an agreeable child with a clean, comforting scent. Her hair was cut in a bob like her older sisters' was when they were young and had not yet declared a separate vision for what they wanted to look like. She did not fuss about her clothes or the food on her plate. She enjoyed naps and voluntarily took them during the day. Where her siblings might refuse to fall asleep at night, it was never a problem for my Ntxhais.

The world she lived in had many influences, from Npis and me to her older siblings who read her piles of library books and related obscure facts about the world that they had learned from the television shows they watched, such as the fact that the coinventor of the cotton candy machine was a dentist or that camel milk doesn't curdle. Ntxhais believed these things they told her, and she created her own beliefs. She thought that the clouds above our sky were created by the large factories on the edge of the Mississippi River near downtown St. Paul, so every city had its own cloud-making centers. Though by the time she was born, her grandmother was much older and had slowed down on her foraging for healing herbs and remedies, Ntxhais took to nature in the same ways. In the dismal thaw of winter, she found bits of dried grass, evergreen, crab apples shriveled on the branches of small trees and created bouquets as gifts for her older siblings when they were unhappy with themselves or others. When Ntxhais learned how to talk, she spoke seldomly, her voice uncommonly deep—like the grandmother she knew and adored, Npis's mother.

When Ntxhais started school, we learned that the moldy house Npis and I despised hated us. Its paint chips flaked from the windowsills and scattered like confetti around the house with the trampling of bare feet. Our youngest child had started eating them unbeknownst to us, licking her fingers, picking up the white bits, and then putting them on her tongue. What I saw was that my once chubby and mild daughter had become a child whose skin was pale and temperament irritable. She didn't have much of an appetite, often complaining of stomachaches. When she started school at age five, her teacher soon realized that something was wrong. Ntxhais was not able to keep pace with simple lessons.

The school notified the county. A public nurse visited our home with a Hmong interpreter on an autumn day, kicking at the fallen elm leaves on the sidewalk up to the sagging porch of our little house.

I kept a clean house. The house was small. We didn't have much. Npis vacuumed the carpet every day. I kept the sinks and counters bleached. The children's clothes were folded in baskets. They shared beds and rooms; the house only had two bedrooms, a third if you counted the closet-less room that led to the single bathroom. I hated that the walls were moldy. I hated that the carpet felt damp to my bare feet whenever I tested, though as my habit, I wore slippers all the time. I was embarrassed when guests came to the house. It swelled with our voices and the children's play and I was afraid that its thin walls would crumble and fall. But I kept a clean house.

We didn't abuse our children. Npis and I used to both work the night shift, and the older girls would have to take care of their siblings when we weren't home. For several years now, we were working different shifts. An adult was home to supervise and care for the children most of the time, and now Dawb and Kablia were old enough to take care of them legally when we weren't home. We didn't have much disposable income. While Npis and I both worked, I was in charge of how we spent the money. I paid the household bills. When the girls really wanted something and I knew of it, I tried my best to get it for them. Kablia wanted a jacket from Macy's on a visit to the local mall. It cost $300. I got it for her because she was afraid of asking for anything expensive. I wanted to teach her not to be afraid of costs in the ways that her father and I were. Dawb had full access to our bank accounts and had built herself a sizable CD collection of country and hip-hop albums. All of our children loved books, and from library sales and Scholastic school orders, they'd amass piles of books that stacked up taller than they were in the corners of the house. We had nothing to hide, and yet I'd watched enough Oprah and heard enough community stories of women like me who didn't speak English losing their children that I felt nervous and even guilty for not being able to give my children more.

On the appointed date and time, when the doorbell rang, I got up to let the public health nurse and the interpreter in. I invited the tall woman in the suit jacket inside and the shorter Hmong man beside her. I invited them to sit on the sagging sofa. Npis and I sat on our green metal folding chairs that we took out only when we had visitors. Npis kept his hands clasped in front of him, his thumbs circling each other. I thought he looked too nervous. I tried not to move a muscle, so I didn't appear the same. At least he was breathing. I could barely get enough air in.

They asked us questions, first in English, then interpreted in Hmong.

How old is the house?

I answered, "It was built in 1894."

Did you receive a lead disclosure when you purchased the house?

Npis answered, "Our oldest daughter, Dawb, who was then sixteen years old, negotiated the house for us. We bought it from a Realtor whose father owned the house. We never got anything about lead."

Do you know what lead is?

We both shook our heads.

They told us, "Your daughter Ntxhais was tested for lead. Her levels are significant and dangerous. We have come to help."

We both asked, "How?"

We both asked, "How did she get lead poisoning?"

We both asked, "How will it impact her life?"

We said, "How can you help?"

They told us that there was a program through the city of St. Paul. We could take out a loan to get our windows replaced, to get the lead windows out of the house. We'd have to live in the house for ten more years for the loan to be forgiven or else pay back the loan if we moved before then. Neither of us had a choice. We agreed to the terms they administered.

For a month, we were sent to live in a basement apartment with little windows near the ceiling, the scent of old cigarettes coming off the floor in a brown brick building on the edge of a parkway close to a grocery store where men and women sat outside along its walls with thick jackets hanging loose about their shoulders dosing away, bottles hidden in brown bags beside their slack bodies. The children thought it was a great adventure. They packed for our time away in the spirit of the people on television going on vacation, choosing among their favorite toys and books, asking if the apartment would have a television set and a pool. They'd only ever slept over at their uncles' houses on rare occasions. Npis and I told them, "Just pack what you need."

We felt we had let our child down. Who were we? What had we done? Why couldn't we have bought a better house, a safer house for the kids? Yes, it was $36,500 when we bought it in 1995. It was more than we could afford. We had reasoned that a lower monthly mortgage would give us more money to feed the children healthy food, fruits and vegetables. I wanted to be the kind of mother who could make the meals that her children wanted to eat. Npis, like the other instances in our lives, was afraid of the math and wanted to make sure we could pay the bills and keep the rain and snow away. Living on the East Side of St. Paul, we were afraid of gun violence. We had heard stories of gangs shooting each other, making mistakes, sending bullets through the walls of families like ours. Of all the things we were aware of and concerned about, lead was not one of them.

We worked in the factories. There were all kinds of particles in the air. Npis had moved from the small company close to the house to a bigger company on the edge of Minneapolis where he spent nights polishing metal. He knew coworkers with hard metal lung disease. Both of us had lost our hearing because of the loud machines we worked with. We suffered from carpal tunnel in our hands and arthritis in our legs because of the repetitive work we did every day, standing on the hard concrete floor, trying to keep up with the lines; this repeated itself hour by hour, year by year. But we had believed it was worth it. Whatever damage the work caused our bodies, it was worth it if we could save our children from similar futures, let them go to school, let them study hard, let them get degrees, let them get good jobs. But now we had discovered that we had reasoned our decisions without all the facts, and it would be our youngest daughter who would have to pay the price of our ignorance.

In the whole month at the apartment, we despaired with each other.

We talked about how it was our fault. With Ntxhais asleep between us on the full bed that came with the apartment, we took turns sweeping her hair away from her face, speaking our regrets, making promises.

I said, "Get better. Recover. Your mother will get a cow and we'll call your spirit home if it is sad because your mother and father did not know how to protect you from the poison in the paint."

I said, "I'm sorry that your father and I could not have done a better job of looking after you, making sure you didn't lick the windowsills, pick up the paint chips and other debris in the house."

I said, "My little daughter. Your mother will take the lead poisoning into her own body to save yours if it is possible. There is nothing I wouldn't do for you."

Nothing I said changed our circumstances. In the small, dusty apartment, lit with bulbs that glowed orange, our orange-tinted children lived and played their made-up games. Hlub and Txuj were spiders crawling on the carpeted floor, their bottoms high up in the air, shoulders raised close to their necks, eyes shifting left and right. Zuabli painted on the paper plates we ate from and made flowers that bloomed in red and yellow and taped them to the walls, high as she could reach. Dawb and Kablia found chairs and placed them in different corners of the living room and did their homework and read thick books with no pictures. At night, the quiet apartment roared with laughter or resounded with anger from the different rooms above us and beside us. After nearly a month away, we moved back into the moldy house with both relief and exhaustion.

The moldy house we lived in smelled like fresh paint although nothing beyond the windows had been replaced. The paint on the wall was the same dirty beige, streaks of mold coming down from the ceilings and climbing up from the floor. The dingy carpet was exactly as it had been. To help it stay clean the construction people had laid down plastic while they worked; this fact tickled me, but Npis could not find reason to laugh. The children ran around the house touching the new windows with their hard plastic sills.

Although there was no joy to be found in the circumstances we lived in, Ntxhais gave us cause for celebration in the moldy house with the new windows. She slowly learned how to read and write alongside her peers, working harder than any of her siblings, hands holding tight to the stretch of her pencil, tracing again and again the numbers and letters that switched in her head. We could see how the lead had affected her memory. She didn't remember facts well. On tests, where she had to memorize dates and times in history, she scored low. She got confused easily when she worked with numbers. Even when she followed the teacher's directions, often her answers were incorrect, a number here or there had gone missing. Still, she worked hard, and Npis and I never pushed her on her grades. We were relieved when she moved from one grade to the next, growing in her understanding that her challenges were different from others, but she was not less than anyone else.

Npis and I had few dreams for ourselves in America, little space to imagine alternate possibilities holding fast to pennies, but for our children we had big ambitions. Ntxhais's experience with lead poisoning and its impact on her educational journey humbled us. I didn't say this to her, but I promised myself that I would never pressure her to excel in school. At bigger family gatherings, when tasked with counseling the children to work harder at school, Npis started saying things like, "If your children are not good at school, you can't be sad about it. If they choose not to go school, that is a different matter."

I kept my promise. When Ntxhais graduated from high school and her older sisters offered to help her with college applications, she said, "I'll do it on my own." In another situation, I might have pushed but with her I did not. In the end, we all found out that she had only applied to one school, the University of Minnesota Morris. To her excitement and our relief, she was accepted.

Everything that happens to my children in college happens far away from me and the reaches of our everyday life. Npis and I drop them off at the different places: Hamline University, Carleton College, University of St. Thomas, St. Cloud State University, Stanford University, and the University of Minnesota Morris. We see them run in and out of impressive buildings made of thick cuts of stone or shiny walls of glass. They

come back to us with their laundry baskets from home full of dirty
clothes at semester's end. Each time we drop each child off, we look forward to the day when we might return to campus for their graduations.
On the telephone, we ask them how they are doing and they tell us they
are fine; sometimes we can tell in the slowness of their words there are
things they do not want to share with us.

I tell all of my children, each in turn, "When you want to do something, please ask yourself first, 'Would my mother want this for me?'"

They respond in different ways.

Dawb and Kablia, the two we brought from overseas, both nod
their heads and tell me what I want to hear. They say that they will
not do anything risky. They know that there are no safety nets for first-
generation college students from refugee households. They know that
their very presence in college already defies the statistics in the papers
they read. I know that Dawb will do what she pleases because she
always has, and that her sense of responsibility will guide her when it
matters because she has always been the oldest, tasked with doing all
that we cannot do for her younger siblings with our limited educations
and experiences. Kablia will listen because she is scared of a lot of
things like an empty sidewalk beneath a darkened sky, or the sounds
a library makes when there are few warm bodies moving between the
rows of books. Her fear index is strong; it guides her where and when
we aren't there.

Txuj, Hlub, Zuabli, and Ntxhais are our American-born children.
They also nod their heads, but they do not offer the words to assuage
our hearts. They tell us that America is a racist country. They say that
bad things cannot be avoided in a racist country, that innocent people
are punished every day for being different. I know that each of them
weep when they are mistreated at school, but they don't let us see their
tears. When Txuj is hurt by a group of boys in a hallway, when they
tear at him, send the buttons of his shirt flying, he comes home with
the bruises, never the names or the stories of his pain. When a group of
students tell Hlub she is stupid, when this group of students take charge
of a lab assignment and they do it without her, she bites her lip and

tries to act like it doesn't matter. When Zuabli is in a conversation with a college professor who assumes that she is from a prep school on the East Coast, not the public school she comes from, because of her strong writing and critical skills, she won't correct him. Instead, she will huddle in her dorm room, uncertain of how to be herself in a place where the people whose job it is to help her, carry stronger assumptions about her than knowledge. When Ntxhais learns that there is a strong stigma about people with learning disabilities, she will push herself to the very edge to see if she can overcome the lead in her system, until she sinks to the ground, exhausted. These children, born in America, talk to us of the systemic racism of America, and somehow, they feel like it is their job to be able to deal with it on their own, that the weight of their experiences will crush our vision of this new country.

My children were born in different places, in different times, each influenced by the cultures and governments in power. While they are one group, one team as Npis likes to remind them, each plays a lonely game. For Dawb and Kablia, there is no room for mistakes, for exhaustion as refugee children living in America. For Txuj, Hlub, Zuabli, and Ntxhais, the immense pressures of living in a country where one's race and circumstances are used to not only judge but levy justice is a burden they bear as people who are not white, who do not share in the histories and privileges of the powerful. The thing that binds my children is that they are all Hmong, and they are all mine.

When she was a little girl, shortly after her diagnosis of lead poisoning, Ntxhais had gone with Dawb and Zuabli to visit Kablia in New York City at Columbia University. When they returned, Zuabli said out loud, "One day, I want to apply to Columbia. I want to go to a big school in a big city." Ntxhais said nothing. When I asked her about the trip, she answered in her deep voice, "New York City is beautiful."

New York City is beautiful, I agree. When Npis and I went to New York City with Hlub as our interpreter to attend Kablia's graduation from writing school, I felt the same. I loved the busy, dirty streets. Chinatown spoke to my heart with its vendors at each corner, its handbags hanging in little closet-like shops. My heart hammered just like on that trip to Long Tieng and that first trip to the Mall of America. Npis naturally hated New York City. He wept when we entered the city on the highway and saw how on either side of the highway there were cemeteries; he turned to me in the back of the yellow taxicab and said, "We've sent our child to study among the dead." I didn't want to laugh as he cried, noting how in old age his tears live closer to the surface, remembering my mother's words about how some men take lifetimes to learn how to cry, and thinking about what it means now that my husband cries for his children openly. When we walked in Downtown Manhattan, Npis looked up at the high buildings and said, "They go so high into the sky, they make me dizzy." He yearned for green space but was not impressed with Central Park—now used to the many large city parks across the Twin Cities. But to me, New York City was beautiful, a place where movie stars walked among the newest refugees and immigrants, and it reminded me of how far my daughters have traveled, how far the pieces of me had adventured. After Kablia's graduation, I didn't know that there would ever be another opportunity to return to New York City.

How could I have known that the next time I would be in New York City would be because my baby girl, Ntxhais, would graduate from Columbia University's School of Social Work? There had been magic in the jungles of Laos, leading Npis and his brothers to each other and us after we were captured. When Txuj was born, I knew that pieces of my life were miraculous. Since then, I've learned that there was a different kind of magic happening in an imperfect America, and I saw it in the journeys of my children.

I started wondering if there had been moments in my mother's life with her children where she felt a similar triumph. Maybe it was not with me because I left her so young and was never able to return to her. But with the others? With my sisters, Nplooj and Xis and Maiv and Npib? With my brothers? My heart halted when the thought came to me; what if for her the magic was really in the fact that we were alive despite the bombs and the bullets? What if the fact that I hadn't died in that jungle or that refugee camp or here in America, what if that was the magic of motherhood? What if that was the magic for all mothers?—the simple survival of her children. Watching the journeys they take and believing that life was possible despite what you have seen and what you have experienced.

The year Ntxhais graduated, the ceremony was at Lincoln Center. A giant fountain sat in a square, surrounded on three sides by three buildings, each with tall pillars, windows made of shiny glass. All around us, there were proud parents, relatives, and friends of the graduates. While there were other Asian families, we were the only Hmong family. Npis wore a jacket although it was hot. I wore my soft-soled walking shoes and the pants I had hemmed and ironed so that they would fit me well. We both stood with our baby girl at our center, as tall as we could. In the throng of people, I felt gratitude and joy. There were invisible hands holding me up by the shoulder, pushing my chest forward, and opening my mouth, not to speak to the world but to be part of it.

CHAPTER 24

The Grandchild
with No Grandparents

Your conception was marked by tragedy. Your father's mother died on February 18, 2003. You were conceived then. The possibility of you had not occurred to either your father or me. By the time you came, our baby girl Ntxhais was eight years old already. We had six living children and seven dead ones. I was forty-two. Your father was forty-five. We were filled with sadness when your grandmother died.

I had known your father's mother for longer than I had known mine. She had intimidated me when I was a young woman with her seriousness and her deep connection to the earth, her bold and singular love for her children. In her prioritizing of her sons and daughters, I'd felt the absence of my own mother, and this created a hungry hole in my heart, but with time and maturity, I saw her as a woman of strength and intelligence, as someone who was born under humble circumstances, who grew up as an orphan, and worked hard so that her children might have a mother for as long as possible. Matured, I came to understand that we were partners in our love for your father and our family. I grew to respect her for her stalwart heart, her skills as a shaman and medicine woman, and her ability to live despite all the death that had been delivered in her life.

Your father, used to the presence of his mother, could not wrestle himself from the grief of her departure. I had gone through my own mother's death years ago. I knew what life after losing your last parent entailed, that to survive in a world without my mother, I had to become some other version of myself. Instead of looking to her in the world of the living, I had to find her in myself. I was lost in the old landscape of my life and had to forge a new one. I suspected that your father might have to do the same, so I endeavored to be patient with him as he had been with me in my pain when I became an orphan.

I had been pregnant numerous times before, but I mistakenly thought the beginning of you was the beginning of menopause. My older sister Nplooj had told me of her experiences of menopause, and it sounded remarkably like what I was experiencing: aching breasts, fatigue, a sensitivity to scents of all kinds, a slight spiciness low in my abdomen. When I missed my period, although I was very regular, I was not worried.

I had stopped working at the factory when Ntxhais began going to school full time. I had Dawb help me with an application for a job as a clerk in a mortgage center for a bank. The work was simple, but it was physically demanding because the mortgage files were heavy, and my role was to take them off the shelves and put them back up after clerical reviews. Like the factory work, I had to stand up all day. Unlike the factory work, I was not positioned along an assembly line; in this new job, I walked between long aisles lined with mortgage files. Like the factory, the bank set quotas for us. I ran around all day long in the basement vault where the files were kept beneath the artificial tubes of light. Several times a day, I was tasked with pushing heavy wooden carts full of files, carts taller and far heavier than me. Though my hands had started hurting in the factory job, it was here that my shoulders gave out, and I realized my body would not be enough to sustain my children.

I had just submitted my eighth application for a job promotion, to leave the vault behind and cross-train upstairs to review files for signatures. I had just gotten my eighth rejection. Although all my work performances were strong, the human resource person always said, "We're

sorry but we found a better fit for the position." And always my immediate supervisors would tell me, "Next time, Twsb. You are such a good
worker. We are so lucky you work so hard." That was all I was at the
bank. I didn't fool myself into thinking I was anything else but a hard
worker who pushed herself every single day to meet the quotas. But
each rejection hurt me, took something valuable away from me. I asked
myself, *Will I even have the face to apply again?*

The day I realized that maybe I was pregnant was a hard day. I had
spent eight full hours running along the lines of files worried that I
would not be able to keep up with the pace of the summer hires, people
who were younger, taller, and stronger than me. I was concerned that
when I could no longer do so, I would be fired and would not be able
to feed my children. I was thirsty and shaking and I went to the bathroom to get a drink of water from the fountain. The hallway was narrow
and high. I rested one hand against a smooth wall as I walked, partially
feeling its coolness against my hot palm, partially resting my weight
against its solidness. I realized I hadn't had a period in over a month.
On my way back from the drinking fountain, I started imagining what a
pregnancy might mean for my life.

Yes, I was not getting a new position at work, but if I was indeed
pregnant then I could take up to three months off work to care for a
newborn. I started thinking: *What if I am pregnant with a little boy?
Then, Txuj wouldn't be alone anymore. I'd have two sons and five girls.
I would have seven living children and seven dead ones. The math of my
life as a mother would even out. How nice would it be to raise a little one
away from the danger of lead in that moldy house?* We had moved out
after Npis's mother's death.

When the workday was done, and it was time for Dawb to pick me
up, late as usual, I was nervous with anticipation. The sad rejection had
been rendered insignificant next to the big possibility that at forty-two
years old, I could be pregnant. I asked my oldest to take me to get a
pregnancy test from the pharmacy before we headed home.

Dawb was in her third year of law school. She, like the rest of the
family, had been in a bubble of grief since her grandmother's death. The

chance that I might be pregnant shook her awake. Her eyes grew so big that I laughed. I told her, "I don't think that I'm pregnant, but my period is late and I want to make sure I'm not."

At home, in the brown house on the prairie, Dawb shooed me into the bathroom with its yellowed wallpaper. She followed me in and read through the directions and translated them for me. When I opened the door for her to leave the bathroom, I told her, "Don't say anything to anyone yet."

She nodded. It was, for now, our secret. When did I start sharing these secrets with my daughters? When had they become my friends and confidants? And here again was another gift of motherhood . . . one that I cherished and felt deeply, one I hadn't been able to fully share with my own mother.

When I saw the little red plus come into the face of the tiny screen, time collapsed. Place disappeared. I felt as I had all those many years ago when I learned I was pregnant with Dawb. My breath was cut short in my chest. What did all this mean? What would it do to my life? I wrapped the test in toilet paper with shaky hands and I threw it away in the white plastic trash basket. I wanted to tell your father first before the rest of the children.

But Dawb was waiting outside the door. Her short hair was cut into the familiar lines of her childhood, except she had no line of bangs above her eyes this time. Her black hair was parted to the side. She wore fitted trousers that I had hemmed. She wore a soft blouse, tucked in. How could it be that my oldest was about to graduate from law school? How could it be that I was pregnant again, and yet I was, and here we were standing in the small hallway of our new house.

I said to her, "I'm pregnant. Don't tell the younger kids or Kablia yet. I want to talk to your father first."

I waited up for your father that night. We had our own bedroom for the first time in our lives. The wallpaper was blue, shimmery. The floors were carpeted green. The sliding closet doors on one side of the wall were clad in mirrors. There was a large window to the right side of the room and every night your father insisted that we keep the blinds up so we could sleep beneath the light of the moon. In this way, it recalled our first nights together in the jungle, the moon high above us beyond the canopy of the leaves that sheltered us. I slept on our new bed, bought when we moved to this house, a large four-poster wooden bed that we'd gotten on sale. The mattress was the old one. Your father had changed to the second shift and usually got home after midnight.

I wanted to give your father a reason to be excited. The sorrow of his mother's death was thick over him. When he was sad, it showed on his face, his mouth drooped at the corners like a clown on television. I was filled with emotions, so I couldn't even lie still on the bed. Instead of trying, I got up and walked past the girls' room, whose door parallels ours in the hallway, to the left where Txuj's small room sat beside theirs, past the bathroom on the right, to the brown cabinets of the kitchen with its brown vinyl on the floor, to the eating area of the house, our oval table beside the patio doors that led to the high wooden deck with its unstable boards. The house was a split-level. Downstairs there were no sounds. Dawb must be asleep already. Kablia was still in her final year at Carleton. Kablia, who was still too young to have lived many stories, and yet believes that she has enough of them from her grandmother, her father, and me to become a writer.

I pulled out one of the wooden chairs at the table and sat down in my nightgown. I smoothed and smoothed again the plastic liner I used to cover the vinyl lace tablecloth on the dining table. My fingers looked red and tight. I hadn't done a great job cutting the liner evenly around the curves of the table. This imperfection bothered me. I was about to get up and go get a pair of scissors to see if I could correct my mistake when I heard your father's car. I settled back down at the table and waited for him to open the front door with his key.

After he'd taken off his safety toe boots and hung up his company jacket, he walked up the carpeted steps in his blue uniform. He was startled when he saw me.

He said, "You're still up. Are you sick?"

I shook my head, a girlish tendency.

I straightened the line of my mouth. Somewhere inside me, the girl from the village of Dej Tshuam and from the jungles of Laos cannot escape; she remains and she waits and in moments, she reminds me, I'm still here.

I said to him, "My period is late. I tested. I'm pregnant, Npis."

He made a noise. He had heard me. He walked past me, to the kitchen. There, he put his red-and-white lunch cooler from work on the counter. He walked to our bedroom. He grabbed a pair of shorts. He went to the bathroom. He closed the door. I heard the fan go on. I heard the sound of the shower. I spent the long minutes listening to the old clock we had purchased when we got to America ticking on the wall of the dining area. I heard the shower turn off. I heard silence. Then the bathroom door opened and Npis walked back toward me, a wet towel around his neck, the pair of shorts around his thick waist.

He said, "We can't keep the baby. We are too old."

He said, "My father had me when he was too old. He died and left me fatherless."

He opened his palms in a gesture of helplessness. "I don't want to do that to a child of mine."

He added, "You have to be rational. Ntxhais is already eight. We have six children. We can't raise another one."

The woman I have become stands in front of the girl I was.

I get up. I walk toward your father. I don't touch him. Everything is caving inside me: the feelings of loss—from his mother's death, from the rejection at work, from his fears, always his fears when it is my hurting body that will have to hold the baby inside, my womb that will have to try to keep the baby safe when he knows all too well how easy it is to fail, all of it comes crashing down. Other women can make decisions about their bodies; this was my body, and he would not make the decision for me.

Who did your father think I was? That I would have all those babies die inside me? That I would be the kind of mother to now kill something that might live.

I said in a voice I had never heard from myself, a voice that was deeper than my own, "I am going to have him with or without you. I'm not asking for your permission. I don't need your permission to have a child."

There were so many more things I could have said, how the pressure
of being his son weighed on Txuj's shoulders, pulled them low. I could
have talked about the girls and how they would love a newborn in our
lives. I could have talked to the part of him that loved our children, that
would do anything for them, that toiled away at the factory across the
spread of painful years so that they have health insurance, space to go
to school, room to focus on their education, and not have to work. I
could have said so many things to him but I didn't need to. The simple
fact was that I did not need his permission to have a baby.

That night, I slept with my back to your father in the room we will
share with you. Right up until sleep carried me off, I kept thinking, *How
can this man ask me to kill the child inside me after all the deaths in our
lives, after everything I've gone through because all he can think about
is his own fears, the things he might have to go through? Older men than
him have become fathers and raised their children.*

In fact, a distant relative of his, a grandfather here in America, had
adventured back to Thailand. There, he'd thrown away his US passport
because he had so missed the weather of Southeast Asia and the speed
of life there, the food, the smells, the sounds of the birds in the trees,
the critters that hid underneath the rocks. He also happened to have
fallen in love with a Karen woman in a small town in Northern Thailand.
There, they had delivered a child, a little boy. Unfortunately, the Karen
woman contracted cancer and died, and now this relative who must be
in his late seventies was raising a young boy himself. Every once in a
while, at family events, when I met the grandmother he'd abandoned
here in America, his longtime wife, she told me, both her hands gripping the purse on her lap, "I don't care about him anymore but the kids
tell me he is poor and unable to work and has called asking for money,
asking if there is a way to make a passport for him to return to America
and me, and to sponsor his kid."

Though your father never said anything more about aborting you,
every once in a while, I brought up the story of the old grandfather
and his young son in Northern Thailand, a reminder that even elders make mistakes, and sometimes their actions have lifelong conse-

quences. Whenever I brought up the relative, your father grimaced but said nothing.

In fact, he acted as if our conversation about terminating the pregnancy had never happened. I shared the news of your coming with your siblings. They were happy. Txuj, when he was younger, used to ask about the possibility of a brother. But he'd stopped as he aged. He loved his sisters and did not want them to feel bad. They, the younger girls, had thought that we were done, that we would be a family of eight. They rejoiced not quite remembering the demands of a new baby on the family. On the telephone, Kablia marveled about what a new baby in our lives might mean. I knew I had made the right decision for me but seeing their happiness helped fortify the fact that one more person on their team would be a good thing, and that a new child might give your father and me more reason to stay young for a while longer.

I knew that you could be a girl. I knew that the chance of you being a boy was low. When I started seeing the doctor, near the twentieth week of pregnancy, she told me that I was now considered a high-risk pregnancy because of my age. She was the one who asked if I'd like an ultrasound to make sure that you were healthy.

On the day of the ultrasound, a very excited Dawb took me to the appointment. Your father was home. I didn't ask him to come with us and he didn't offer. On the examination table, in the dimly lit room filled with electronic equipment and screens, Dawb stood by me full of giddy joy as the technician squeezed the warm gel on my soft stomach and then turned on the monitor. She adjusted the volume. The sound of your heart entered my world: swoosh, swoosh, swoosh, like the ocean waves your heartbeat traveled through to the island of grief we were stranded on in the wake of your grandmother's death. It was Dawb who asked, "Is it a boy or a girl?" The technician moved the scanner around my belly, pressed a few buttons, made some measurements, then said, "It's a little boy making his way into your family."

Dawb left the room. I understand that she called your father with the news. I didn't ask how he responded.

Throughout the pregnancy, while I knew a miscarriage was possible,

I also felt healthy enough to sustain you. Although I was older, I had also had a long break between children; there were eight years between you and Ntxhais, and in the space of those eight years, there were no miscarriages or pregnancies.

When my belly grew thick and the bigger family realized that I was pregnant, some remarked, "He's going to be the only grandchild that his grandmother will not meet." I nodded. I didn't say what I knew to be true, "He will not know what life is like with a grandparent at all." I thought, *My love will have to do. My love will have to be enough.*

Your grandmother died in cold, windswept February. You were born on a gray November afternoon when clumps of snowflakes flew from the sky like bits of cotton. You were born on the twenty-sixth, the day before Thanksgiving that year. Your father left the hospital room right before you entered the world, unable to bear the tension inside the delivery room. Your oldest sisters were there with me. Kablia had returned to Minnesota for Thanksgiving in time for your birth, and Dawb had said that she wanted to be one of the first faces to welcome you into the world. When your father came back into the room, the intensity that had driven him out was gone; you were already in my arms. Of all my children, you were the easiest birth, even easier than Hlub. The moment your father saw you, he said, "I have to memorize him in case the nurses and doctors make a mistake and give him to someone else."

I said, "What are you memorizing?"

He said, "His hairline."

I saw it then. You were born with an old man's hairline. Your hair grew far from your face. In fact, your face, scrunched and red, looked like a tired old man's. Your brows were wide and light and your eyes were open, single-lidded. You stared at us, your mother and father. You studied us and we studied you.

Your father said, "He's here. My second son."

Your older sisters said, "Can we hold him? Can we hold him?"

We held you, all of us. We took turns holding you. Even Ntxhais, when we took you home, held you close to her heart.

When you cried for milk and I took you from her arms, she said, "He's the new baby and I'm the old one."

The only one of your siblings who had to warm up to you was Kablia. Kablia who had been part of your birth because she'd returned home from New York City to celebrate Thanksgiving with the family. She, who had been gone, for most of my pregnancy with you. She said on the phone, once she'd return to school, "He looks a little weird. It takes a bit of time to grow to love a baby, I think."

I knew that one day when Kablia became a mother, she would learn how love flowers in a heart, how a child in their mother's arms speaks to the empty in those arms, no matter how full they had been previously. She would learn how a mother's love worked, as I have with each miscarriage, each birth.

Now you are eighteen years old, and I'm sixty-one. Your father is sixty-four. Now your graduation is months away. You are waiting to hear from the big universities that you've applied to. You've already heard from the small ones. I understand that they are all good schools where you will have time to grow into yourself. Now that old man's hairline you were born with has extended so far that you have decided to shave your head clean to the scalp. Now your ability to speak Hmong has been halted by the time you've spent away from your father and me, but you tell me that you can still understand us. Now your father will never agree that he once suggested we abort you. Now, when you are home with us on the weekends, he can barely keep his hands off you. Now you are the only one of my children who stands beside me at the dining table, puts your arm across my shoulder, and pulls me close. Now I still call you Baby—although you are no longer one.

Soon enough, you will be gone. When you hear the good news from the big schools, you will choose one of them, far from me. I won't stop you. Your father has tried. His eyes fill with tears at the thought of you leaving us for this next part of your life.

He says many things to you: "The colleges and universities here in

Minnesota are good enough to take you anywhere you want for graduate school."

He says, "If you choose one of the schools here, your mother and I are still young enough to drop you off and pick you up on the weekends. You don't have to miss anything, New Year's celebrations or birthday parties, the nieces or the nephews. You won't have to miss me, and I won't have to miss you."

He says to your siblings, "I know Hwm is eighteen years old but we've all loved him and protected him. He knows nothing about protecting himself. He would be safer closer to home."

Your father has said many things, but the truth is that he won't stop you. He is his mother's son. She, too, said many things when he was going to leave Ban Vinai Refugee Camp behind for America, but she didn't stop him. We have never been interested in stopping you. This moment is what all the sacrifice has been for.

You were six years old when we agreed to send you to live with your sister Dawb and her husband and their kids. We still lived in that house with the yellowing wallpaper, that brown split-level house on the prairie outside the cities, the house you will know as your first home. The schools in that suburb had failed your older brother, and we couldn't bear the thought of them letting you fall. We sent you to live with your oldest sister and her family so that you could go to the private school in St. Paul.

In those early years of separation, you'd grow sad as the weekend dwindled down, as I began gathering your backpack and folding your school clothes and packing them. In those early years, the light in your eyes would shine bright—perhaps with unshed tears and perhaps with unspoken anger—when your father and I told you to get into the Tacoma pickup truck, put on your seatbelt, and prepare for the trip to your sister's.

On the Sunday nights when neither you nor we could endure a parting, we'd have you stay the night and wake up at dawn. By then, the bank where I worked had let me go because of the shoulder surgeries, so I was home, though your father continued to work the second shift so we could have health insurance and income. Your father knew his morning sleep was important, but he never complained about having to wake up early to drop you off in time for school. In fact, it was always he who said, when he saw the shimmer in your eyes, "My son, do you want to stay one more night with me? Your father can drop you off in the morning."

In my memories of these early-morning drives, the earth was always wet, the green traffic signs with glowing white letters blurry, because of the drizzle of my own tears. It took us forty-five minutes to drive to St. Paul to drop you off outside the tan building with an American flag flying high outside, our headlights now in a line of many, the mufflers from different cars coughing pollution into the still blue of early morning.

As you advanced from first to second to third grade, you moved from Dawb's house to Kablia's because she'd gotten married and was building a home. Without young children, she and her husband had more time to work with you on your studies. You were nine. You believed you were "an indoor kid" and your cheeks were plump and full, your belly a small mound underneath the long-sleeved polo shirts your school required.

One Friday night after picking you up from a week away at school, as we pulled you close after dinner to hug and hold and asked, "Did you miss us?" you answered, "I don't know how to miss you two anymore. I'm used to being away from home now."

Your father was too stunned to answer.

I said something like, "That's a good thing. Then, it will make it easier as you grow up and prepare to go to college."

I couldn't bear the thought of you no longer missing me, but it was not lost on me that you were also angry. I feared that our big sacrifice for your future had been yet one more mistake with a lifetime of consequences unfolding beyond our gaze. Each time you left, you showed me with your stiff shoulders that you were just fine getting into the car, leaving me. I understood. I was never mad at you. I want you to know this. That in all the world, of all our children, you were the last one, the one we wanted to give our whole lives to but knew we couldn't because you were born later than the rest. You were the grandchild without grandparents.

The time that we have all been waiting for is upon us, Hwm. You will make a big decision this time about where you go to pursue the next leg of your journey. I want you to know that I've missed you for a long time and will continue to do so for always. All the time we've had together is not enough. I now know how my mother felt when I left her. How blameless I was in her eyes. How forgiven I've been.

In the chasm between heaven and earth, all the mothers stand, holding the sky above their children. When the load is heavy, their knees bend, their arms shake. The earth trembles with their exertions. They do this so that the children remain protected. Even when the mothers are gone, the force of their love lingers in the light of dawn and dusk, beneath the sprinkles of sun and rain. May it always be so.

Part IV

RETURN OF THE REFUGEE

CHAPTER 25

The Unraveling

L ong before I am on a plane, Laos comes to me in the form of shadowy animals running across the terrain of my life and then, in my dreams, I start the return.

I am wide awake. I am sitting on the sofa massaging my red hands, one on the other. The ibuprofen does not help alleviate the pain. My shoulder aches. It waits its turn for a touch.

The surgeries have failed. The operation to help treat the carpal tunnel in my hands so that I can continue working. The procedure to remove the bone spurs on my shoulders so that my hands can still pull and push the mortgage files onto the high shelves. At first, I take medical leave, hoping that rest will help bring back what the surgeons could not.

When I go to work with the doctor's note saying that I shouldn't lift anything over ten pounds until I get authorization, the bank tries to accommodate at first. They send me upstairs to review files for signatures. I'm slow and meticulous. For two weeks, I get to rest my shoulders, flipping the pages of documents with my index finger capped in a rubber tip. Then, my supervisor tells me that I must return to the vault. When I cannot make my daily quota, she tells me they are going to give my position to someone else who can meet the demands of the job. I'm sent home like a student who has done something wrong in school and their parents must now work with them on correcting their behavior.

Instead of parents, I come home to my children. They tell me, "The doctor says the healing will take time. You only need time, Mom."

Time is the only thing that none of us gets, no matter the need.

One day when I see the mail woman drive up to our mailbox in a car that looks like a toy, I think it might be a good idea for me to take a short walk to the mailbox, feel the sun on my head. I take off my house slippers, which are now a pair of pink Crocs because Dawb has discovered that while they are thick and chunky and look like cartoon shoes, they offer good support. Every night after work, I came home with swollen feet, aching like small needles were embedded deep inside my flesh. Although I have not been working, my feet still suffer from the ghosts of working in a factory and a bank vault. At the front door, I put on a pair of light plastic sandals I've purchased from the Asian grocery store. I open the door with both hands. The day is bright and as perfect as Minnesota gets. The sun is everywhere. Beneath the trees in the yard, the shadows look like puffs of cloud on the green grass. I walk the length of the unpaved driveway to the black mailbox across our street slowly, savoring the sun and the breeze. When I get there, I stop to admire the cluster of daylilies that grow at the base of the wooden post that holds up the mailbox. I'd transplanted the flowers there when we moved into this house after Npis's mother died. The base of the mailbox is now surrounded by a thick circle of long green leaves, and at its center, the yellow lilies in bloom, six petals pushing out. I breathe in, but their scent is too light to reach me. I know that each flower only lives for a day. I open the mailbox door. Inside, there is a single white envelope with my name on it.

If my mother's death had opened me up, this letter sealed me in. After school that day, when I hand Dawb the white envelope, she opens it. Dawb translates the letter for me as her eyes scan its contents quickly, her face frowning when she gets to the end of the page. The white paper in her hands say that I am now unemployed, and that the bank I work for has invoked my long-term disability.

I despair.

My children don't understand.

They tell me, "At least you don't have to deal with the racists anymore, Mom."

They don't know that there is no version of my life in America that is free from racism. Yes, there is a pile where I keep all the rejections I've received for a job promotion, but the children don't seem to understand that I have to do it for them. I see my old bosses, their mouths moving with slow exaggeration, lips stretching, teeth showing, their heads like balloons float across the screen. The film of my life has slowed down and somehow gravity is not working anymore in my world. The old bosses, they talk to me like I'm stupid, mouths wide open, faces grimacing and frowning at the same time, again and again. Their hair floats up not down. All this time, my children thought I was swimming in America when I have in fact been slowly drowning in the sea of racism. If only my drowning could help them float, but it does not work that way.

My children say, "Mom, you can rest now. You've worked so hard for so long."

They don't know that it is not yet my time to rest. They do not know that they will need financial support I cannot give. They do not know that without my income, the roads we are on grow narrower by the day. Their father does not earn enough. His job, his hands, his feet, his back, his lungs, his heart—all of it can give at any time. All of it has given at different times. They don't know that Hwm is only five and I am just forty-seven and although my body is falling apart, the engine within me is still roaring with nowhere to go.

The children say, "Mom, we'll take you to the doctor and see what's wrong with your hands and your shoulders, see if there is medication to help."

They take me to the doctors. The doctors have me do questionnaires. The questions ask me about my pain week after week. Nothing changes. The therapies, once or twice a month, do not help. These other professionals tell me things that I wasn't told before the surgeries. Carpal tunnel can return. Shoulder surgeries are notoriously hard to recover from. The doctors who can give me pills because I can't sleep and my body hurts. The pills do not change how I feel about my life or stop the throbbing of my hands at night or the burning in my shoulders; they do not help me put my arms behind my back to clasp my bras or hold a mixing spoon over a pot. The pills make me see things and feel things I don't want to tell my children about because I know it will scare them.

In broad daylight, I see shadows run across my peripheral vision, creatures the size of cats. They race around me, barely dodging me. These animals trigger me in the ways that the old bullets in Laos once did. They shake me, make me twist and turn my head to follow. I dodge to try to get away from them. They have returned me to the paranoia of the war years. My movements agitate my children.

They ask, "What's wrong?"

At first I try to say nothing, but the shadowy animals continue their race around me at unpredictable intervals. I don't want to frighten them so I start telling the children, "The pills make me see things."

They want to know, "Are they scary things?"

I tell them, "No, they are animals the size of cats. I am not scared of them. I know they are not here in our home. It is just the pills."

They don't look convinced.

At other times, I feel I cannot breathe. I wear knit shirts with wider necklines. But it does not help. My breath is always short. Breathing is never satisfying; I cannot get enough air inside me. Parts of my organs are dying at the dining table with a spoon to my mouth. Parts of my organs are dying in the steam of the shower. Parts of my organs are dying as I lay in bed beside Npis who snores to my left, facing his open window, the stars above in the black sky blinking at me. I try not to panic. I panic anyway. My heart starts to beat faster and faster and I get worried that it might beat itself right out of my chest. I feel suffocated in my body. My skin grows clammy. My spirit wants to free itself from this dying body I now inhabit.

Npis suggests that we call a shaman.

I tell him in the winter when the snowbanks are taller than I am at the end of our driveway, "Let's wait for spring when people can park easily on the streets."

In the spring when the daylilies I love by the mailbox are in bloom, I tell him, "In the hot summer months, it will be easier to gather the family and do the cooking in the open air."

In the summer when the winged insects gather around the lights outside our door, I tell him, "Let's wait for the fall when the cold comes, and the gnats go away before we do a ceremony so the children don't get bitten."

Come the fall when the maple trees in our yard let go of their flaming leaves of red and orange, I let him know, "Everyone is busy now with the preparations to send the children off to school."

Then, it is winter again.

Npis does not push, and I do not plead with him for breath.

I'm home every day. My baby Hwm is not with me because he lives with Dawb in St. Paul so he can go to a school where other kids will play with him because they know about Hmong people. In the beginning, I keep the house clean by picking up small things, finding places for them on shelves, boxes in the garage and basement. I organize and reorganize shelves in the kitchen. My hands hurt whether I work or not. I cry to myself. I feel useless and sorry. Even when I mix the food simmering on the stove, the circular motions of my wrist, the grip of my hand on the handle of the spoon, all of it pains me. My fingers feel tight and my tendons feel sore. I wear hand braces, but they feel unnatural and all they manage is to keep the pain consistent, my range of motions restricted. I wait for my younger children and Npis to come and go from their different schools and their jobs, my older girls to visit from their houses in the cities. The ticking of the clock in the quiet house makes me feel ever closer to death. I start thinking: *If I cannot do my work as a wife or a mother, why does anything matter?* Dust builds on the windowsills, the top of the television set in the living room, on the arms of the furniture, and the floor underneath our very feet.

I don't want to die. I am in a bad state because I want to live so badly. I want to be here for my children, for Hwm, my baby boy. I want to take care of them all. But I can hardly take care of myself. Npis helps me clasp and unclasp my bras in the mornings when he sees me struggle in the privacy of our bedroom so our children don't know that their mother can no longer do this simple task. When he is not around, I circle my waist with the bras. I turn them backside front. I clasp the hooks into their places with stiff fingers over the soft, white skin of my belly. Then, I turn the thing around, flip it the right way, and I shimmy it up my torso, put my hands through the armholes. The process leaves red lines up my body like I've been tied. Unlike the children, Npis does not offer me assurances or need me to assure him of anything. It was as it had been after my mother had died and the miscarriages in America; he simply waited for me patiently to get through whatever it was that I was going through. I think to myself: I don't want to leave a man like this.

Npis and I have shared many agonizing moments. We have shared whole seasons, years and decades of heartache. We are not yet old on paper, but our love feels old. Like many elderly couples, we have to watch each other break down. He has to watch me fall apart, suffer through the days and whimper in pain across the nights and I watch his face turn into an old man's face, the remaining hair on his head turns white and stiffens, the lines around his mouth and on his forehead sink deep. My situation ages both of us.

At night, I dream of returning to Laos. The land is sunnier than it has ever been. I see the spread of its karst mountains from a place in the sky. I see little villages clinging to mountainsides. Yellow dirt roads climbing up the bodies of mountains like Christmas lights around Christmas trees. I see rivers meeting and diverging across the deep green landscape. I see the village of Dej Tshuam. In the earlier dreams, there are no people but this changes in time. Slowly, I see figures walking, talking, children laughing and running around. Each night, the village gets more alive, and soon even the dogs, chickens, ducks, pigs, and cows take their places.

On the first night I see my father; I race to him from my place in the sky. He stands at the edge of the citrus orchard in glorious bloom. A heavy breeze blows and the white petals rain down from their trees and all of them fly in his direction, swirl about him. He is the father I remember from my youth: thin and graceful, an old man whose cheekbones remain strong, the line of his jaw clean, and his eyes are so very clear. When he sees me running toward him, his face lights up. He remembers me. I am his daughter. I have returned home. I don't see his wings until I'm just an arm's length away. Up close, my father resembles an American angel. The wings are white and majestic. Errant petals float on the soft feathers off his shoulders.

He tells me, "Tswb, if you want, you can come into my arms, and I can fly you away."

I want to so badly. I want to run and hide in his wings, behind his back. But even in the dream, I remember that I have children.

I tell him, "I have children now, Father. I would miss them."

The father of my dreams tells me, "Daughter, in my arms, in the arms of the sky, you'll be able to see them every day on earth. You won't have to miss them."

I'm not scared of my father but I start to back away, exit from the hold of the dream. My back moves from the light of my father's presence toward the familiar shadows of the room I share with Npis. There are no more children in between my husband and me, just his warm body asleep, hands above his head. I awake to intense emotions. Tears flow out of my eyes and the fabric of my pillow soaks them up. My mouth opens to the night air and the current of my cries shakes me and forces me to curl into myself. Outside our window, a moon sits in the low sky. It sees my pain.

The night dreams shift on me.

There are nights when I don't see my father at all. Instead, I see myself as a young woman again, as I had been when I'd garnered the admiration of the Chinese man in the war years. I'm beautiful and I stand by the side of a dirt path, my feet lost in the green grass of the rice-planting season. Handsome men on white horses ride by me. Men who are tall like the Chinese actors my daughters admire in movies stop their huge horses in front of me. They dismount gracefully. They offer their clean hands. They tell me that all I need to do is give them the word. They will hoist me into the waiting saddle. They will take me away from every-thing. They smile with their straight teeth. They bow their heads of dark hair. They are gallant, each and every single one of them. Their offers are generous and sweeping. I am overwhelmed by all the right choices in front of me. How can such men exist? My heart hammers in my chest, so fiercely that I awake to a feeling like my lungs are collapsing inside me.

I am embarrassed by the power of my dreams.

My hair, which I had kept short while I was working, grows long.

I get a perm. I haven't had one in decades. The loose curls form a halo around my face. My hair is not as thick or smooth as it had once been, or maybe the Hmong woman who gave me the perm is simply not as skilled as those other women in the past. I had hoped it would cheer me up, make me feel fresh, but the new hairstyle only makes me look more unhinged. In this, there is truth. When I see myself in the mirror, I want to laugh.

The lines across my face. My skin has a pale-yellow undertone. I don't sweat and it looks like there's liquid underneath my skin, unshed tears, old perspiration. I open my mouth. My smile has never been per-fect. But it was—long ago—a nice smile despite my crowded bottom teeth. My smile looks uneven, like a fence after a bad storm, twisted by the direction of heavy wind. My teeth are also yellow now. I want to bleach them, but I imagine what white teeth would look like on my pale-yellow face and I think of the cost, and I decide I will not do any-thing about my face after all. All the lines on my forehead, beside my eyes, my mouth, along my neck.

My medical doctor refers me to a psychiatrist, a talking doctor. I am nervous. I don't know how I will ever be able to talk about all the things inside me. But there's no reason to be nervous. When I am called into the office with empty walls but for three degrees, all framed in dark wood, when I take the patient seat with my back toward the open window, and I face the big desk, there's a tall white man in front me. Beside him is a woman my age in a tight skirt with a pretty blouse. The interpreter tells me that the woman is still a student studying to become a doctor. The man, the doctor, smiles. He pretends to be kind. I know it isn't real, but I choose to believe him. His head is full of gray hair, but his face is unwrinkled. He towers over all of us women in the crowded room: the white woman beside him, me, and my interpreter, who is wearing a black sweater, the snot of young children smearing across her shoulders, and Kablia in a seat behind us.

He says, "What's going on, Tswb?"

I shrug my shoulders.

I say, "I don't know. My hands and shoulders hurt. I can't sleep. I see things."

He says, "Talk to me. Tell me your story."

I start to cry. My tears, once buried deep inside me, now live in my pores. At the slightest squeeze, they seep from my body. I shake my head to try to stop the tears but they are now awash in a current beyond my control.

The doctor retrieves a box of tissues from somewhere in his big wooden desk. I pull out two and I push them into my eyes. The room is silent. Everyone is waiting for me.

I swallow my hurt.

I say, not looking at my daughter or the interpreter, "My father died when I was young."

The doctor nods his head. "Go on."

I say, "There was a war. I was young. I met my husband. I left my mother to be with him. And now . . ."

The doctor says, "And now you need help."

I nod.

He says, "I'll put you on a stronger dose of the sleeping pill than what your doctor has already given you. The side effects shouldn't be significant, but if you have any issues, let me know. It'll help you rest."

He flipped through the thin file in front of him. "I see that your doctor has tried Wellbutrin, Prozac, Zoloft, Paxil, Effexor, and Cymbalta."

He looks at me like we are both in a joke together. He raises his eyebrows.

He says, "What's next?"

He says, "What are we going to do with you?"

It isn't a question and the interpreter's voice is light communicating that the doctor is teasing me but there is nothing laughable about my life.

I tell him, "The problem is that I don't know what to do with myself."

He clicks something in his mouth. The joke is out the door. He takes a deep breath. I've lived in America long enough to understand this means that the white person in front of me feels like I am ruining a moment of fun. The supervisors at the factory used to do this kind of stuff to all of us refugee workers every day.

I say, "My children need me. I don't want to die."

The doctor is looking down again, but when he looks up, he now has on a very serious face, and he tells me with strong emphasis between each word, "You. Are. Not. Going. To. Die. Tswb."

He looks at the white woman who will also become a doctor beside him. He says in a normal way, "What do you think about Celexa?"

She nods and says, "Why not?"

The interpreter tells me, "They are going to put you on a new medication called Celexa to help you with your depression. We'll make an appointment at the front desk for another visit in three months to see how things are going. If you have any problems before then, you should have your daughter call the clinic to schedule an appointment."

After we schedule the appointment, the interpreter, perhaps younger than Kablia, looks at me and tells me, "Auntie, I am called here to interpret a lot. I get to meet a lot of our elders. People like you and my parents who've lost their jobs and are depressed. Don't worry too much. Compared to many of my clients, you are not so bad. I'll see you again. Bye."

She waves her hands. Her fingers are short and plump. They are tapered at the tips. Her nails were painted red, but the nail polish is all chipped. I don't wave back but I say, "Ua tsaug." I thank her just as I had thanked the doctor and the woman who will become a doctor beside him in the tiny room. I try to smile but it feels painful, like my face has been burned by the sun.

I look around me and for a moment I am wide awake. The waiting room at the psychiatry office is full of refugees from around the world. People my age and older. Men in salwars and women in hijabs. New refugees fill the room. There are Karen women with their sarongs fastened about their waists, carrying their ethnic bags, woven bags with lovely designs, fringes at the bottom. All of them sit by their interpreters, younger men and women from their home cultures. The patients, just as I had when I was waiting, look at their hands and the tan carpet beneath their feet. We are all in the same situation all of us. We come from different wars. I look around me. The three receptionists, all white, at the curved counter like a C on its side, are busy talking quietly into their headsets, each clicking away on their computers. Long ago, I had thought I might be like them one day. New knowledge sinks in: even when we ourselves are no longer worthy of pay, we are making money and work for other people. The familiar squeezing happens at my throat. I try to tighten my lips, but my mouth feels slack, heavy, immovable.

I tell Kablia, "Let's hurry home."

In the car, I am exhausted. I feel as if I've not rested for days. I sit in the passenger side as my daughter drives me home.

On the edge of sleep, I think to myself, *Her home is not my home anymore.*

As I fall into rest, my chest rising and falling with my breath, I hear her say, "It's okay, Mom. You go to sleep. I know the way home."

My stiff lips curve a little on their own accord.

When I had a mother in the world, I knew my way home.

CHAPTER 26

The Blanket Over My Heart

I found out about my eldest sister-in-law's death via Facebook. Vaj's wife. Vaj, the brother who had found me when I was a child, playing at the edge of a puddle on a rainy evening, completely dry. Vaj, who had always been the most expressive and tender of my brothers.

My children had gotten Npis and me iPhones so that we would be less isolated. They started a Facebook account for me. I'd chosen a profile picture of Npis and I on a bright spring day, standing outside our new house, not the brown one with the yellowing wallpaper on the prairie but the one we now live in on a hill on the edge of a small town, hidden by towering trees. Behind us, there is our crooked crab apple tree in full bloom, pink with touches of white in the flowers. We are both dressed up. We were on our way to a funeral. I had pulled Npis close and asked one of the children to take the photograph. In the picture, I'm smiling, and I have on a touch of makeup and I'm wearing a soft maroon shirt that flutters at my arms. Npis, unlike in most of his photographs, is smiling, too. When my account activated and my profile picture went up, nieces and nephews in Laos asked to be my friend. All of a sudden, seemingly overnight, I was connected to my family and old friends again in a way I never could have imagined.

When I realized who each person was, I wrote them. I wrote more people than I had ever written before in my whole life. I wrote in Hmong. I asked, "How is your father?" and "How is your mother?" They wrote back. They called me Tais Tswb, Auntie Tswb. They asked about Yawm Txiv Npis and me and our children. The pain in my hands was constant but I found myself using them to do work that I had been hungry to do.

Beyond my family, the iPhone also gave me a sense of beauty in the larger world. I realized that the Internet was full of pictures of flowers. I spent hours searching for "beautiful gardens." My searches took me to the tulip fields of Holland, lines of red and yellow tulip blooms, and to the cherry trees of Japan, a whole world colored by petals.

I spent hours cropping the images, putting filters on them, and saving them on my own phone so I could look at them whenever I was sad or lonely. One day, I checked and saw that I had saved more than sixteen thousand photos of flowers on my iPhone. I decided to post some of the most beautiful flowers on Facebook, saying in Hmong, "I'm just putting them up here in case you like to see flowers blooming like I do." Family, not only mine but Npis's, nieces and nephews, started liking the images of the lotus ponds in Thailand, the spread of purple heather across the English moors. The people in the community whom I hadn't talked to in years, the group of thirteen sisters who had thought I was beautiful in the village of Dej Tshuam in Laos, started commenting, saying how they, too, wished to one day see these lovely places.

Beneath the flowering images, we remember the flowers from our childhood. Among them, the yellow flowering trees that bloomed at the base of the towering mountains where we lived. How the leaves of the trees dropped when the flowers bloomed in time for the Laotian New Year, and their honeyed fragrance traveled down into our lives and cloaked us in their beauty. The tree? What is its name? Someone comments, "It has been named the national flower of Thailand. The flower is called dok koon." We all remember enough Lao to know that *dok* is "flower" in both Thailand and Laos and *koon* refers to gold drops. What a beautiful way to describe the tree of our youth, the golden flower tree. I have my children help me look for it on the Internet. I am disappointed to learn that the person is wrong. The tree of our youth is not the national flower tree of Thailand. In fact, it is nowhere to be found—not even on the Internet.

Beyond the happy connections, the iPhone brought us news of the world. Npis is also now not working. He and all his Hmong coworkers had been let go from their jobs at the factory because each man on the night shift was being asked to run two to three different machines at the same time when the day workers were only tasked with running one; they wanted to talk about workplace safety but their supervisor refused to have the conversation with them. When they all walked out in an effort to be heard, the company sent letters to say that if they didn't return to work immediately, they would all be fired. As they were working with Dawb, who had become a lawyer, to write a response to the company, they each received a letter firing them—just as the bank had done to me.

This happened in 2012, four years after I was let go. Npis went through his own dark times. We overlapped. Without jobs, we were forced to default on the mortgage payments of the brown house on the prairie. Our older children stepped in and helped us initiate a sale. I saw a house on a piece of land southwest of the Twin Cities. When we visited, which Npis was reluctant to do, he kept saying, "If we see it, we are going to want it. We can't afford anything." He was right. When I saw it, I wanted it. I wanted it more than I had ever wanted anything in America, a place where we could wander among the tall trees, a bit of land where we might raise chickens, perhaps if our hands were able, grow a small garden. Again, with the children's help and the remains of Npis's 401(k), we were able to leverage the new house on the land. A house on a hill, a single dirt driveway leading up, generations of trees everywhere.

Npis and I had lived quietly here, patiently going through the days. It was here where I decided, on a walk with Npis to the back field, that I would stop taking the antidepressant drugs, where I would try to hold the reins of my own life, do my best to accept the facts of our lives, how we cannot change our pasts or even futures, but we could grow old together. Wasn't that also a gift in a life where we've known so much death?

On our phones, Npis and I saw Hmong people from around the world, in different countries: France, Germany, French Guiana, Australia, here in the US, back in Laos, in Thailand, in Vietnam, in China—how all of us were alive and part of different countries now and how we belonged to the world, even if the world didn't know who we were. We saw how our situation spoke to each other's and how our individual lives were like and unlike those of our peers who have also survived that dreaded war. There were Hmong people in Laos who lost limbs and now suffered for these losses. There were Hmong people in France who showed their large fields full of cabbage and other produce, driving tractors and waving from the windows, remembering how their parents used to farm in the old country. We saw how the sorrows of the war had coated all our lives, and yet how those lives continued in directions none of us could have imagined in our villages, our mountains, our long-ago homes.

Npis and I agreed that our primary life purpose now was to be buffers for our children, a place for them to rest and hide when the winds of the world grew rough. Npis and I felt a strong duty to guide and nurture our grandchildren, give them what neither of us have ever had, loving grandparents. From Monday through Friday, we lived like an old couple without regard to the ticking of the clock, a freedom we hadn't known since we came to America. I tended my assortment of flowers by the windows of the house. Npis mowed the lawn and fed his chickens in the yard. Together, we grew a vegetable and herb garden in the brief summer months so our children and grandchildren could experience the flavors of our long-ago homes. We ate simple meals that did not take much preparation: greens blanched in hot water with spicy chili paste, parboiled rice, which the children and grandchildren hate, and sipped hot chicken broth.

We became friends again, offering each other the small niceties. In the mornings, Npis made me coffee though I worried about the amount of cream and sugar he put into the milky cup. When we had avocados

in the house, he sliced one, giving us each one-half, drizzled with honey.
We ate them with small spoons right out of the fruit shell like children,
savoring the creamy sweetness. At night, I washed his CPAP machine,
which helped him sleep soundly, silenced his snores, and made his days
more energetic. I made sure the shade at our bedroom window was
pulled up in this house when we slept, so that Npis could rest beneath
his beloved moon and stars, unchanging after all these years. Sometimes, when it was just the two of us, sitting at the long table, looking
at hummingbirds who came to drink from the sugar water before our
window, we talked of the past and we laughed at how young we used to
be, we spoke wistfully about how cute each of our children were, how
Hwm was still just a baby—no matter that he was a young man now.

One day, after Kablia's daughter, our granddaughter Seeyees, had
gone on a school field trip to visit a place called Bdote, she shared a new
fact that she had learned with us: people who live in the Twin Cities are
near the meeting place of the Minnesota River and the Mississippi River.

I asked, "What is Bdote?"

She told me, "For the Dakota people, *Bdote* means 'where two waters
come together.' It is a sacred site, Tais Tais."

For a moment, I could not respond, the sudden lump in my throat, prevented words. When I could speak again, I said, "Do you know that your
tais tais was born in a village where two rivers meet many years ago?"

Seeyees was in awe. That I had been born in the village of Dej
Tshuam, a place where two rivers meet, and that we were now close to
a sacred site of the first peoples on this land, another site of two rivers
meeting. I was in awe. How can this be? How can I have traveled so far
in space and time to come to the same kind of place?

On the weekends, the children gathered at our house. Dawb and her
husband brought their three children on Friday each week and stayed
the weekend through. Kablia and her husband brought their three children on Saturdays and stayed the day through. The younger kids ebbed
and flowed with the currents of their school and work lives. On the
weekends, our house in the woods swelled with the scent of sizzling oil
on the stove, little ones running underfoot, and talk in a thousand dif-

ferent directions. Npis and I told each other that we were content to live this way. In fact, we were grateful for the life we lived. We saw the blessings of our house on the hill, not only for us but also for our children and grandchildren. We both felt that Npis's mother would have loved to wander through the trees, searching for familiar plants, attending to the expanse of green. I thought how strange my mother would have found my life now, here in America, as an older woman, unable to do so much, but now engaged in many things that none of us could have imagined around that fire ring in that wooden house where two rivers meet.

Our children brought influences from everywhere. Zuabli had gone to Stanford and graduated. She was now in law school following in the path of her older sister Dawb.

At our long dining table, a gift from all our children, Zuabli critiqued Steve Jobs and his impact on the world. Npis responded to her, "The harder critique is to consider what the iPhone has done for people like Mom and me. The country Laos, a place that I thought I would never see again, I now can visit every day because of my iPhone."

When Dawb and Kablia decided that they were going to delete their personal Facebook accounts because they didn't like how Mark Zuckerberg was suing hundreds of Native Hawaiians over property he and his wife had purchased on Kaui, Npis agreed with them, saying that the platform was nothing more than a circus of rumors. I surprised myself by saying to him, "For you, it might be the country of Laos. For me, it is the people. The people I lost in the war. Facebook has returned those who have survived to me."

Our children were sad and angry about racism in America, about Black Lives Matter, and the shooting and disappearances of non-white people across the country. We tried to help them think about the situation by sharing instances of injustice from our experiences in Laos, Thailand, and the early years in America. They saw all they needed to see in our everyday lives, how other people feel their parents have no opinions or ideas about international events, our deep feelings and thoughts about political leaders who take from their people, who steal from them and lie to them.

We tell the children, "The world is not a fair place, and has never been."

They know this is a fact.

And yet they say, "Why can't it be? Why can't we hold each other to a higher standard, demand it be a better place?"

Through our conversations and perspectives, we push each other's notions of the world, our individual approaches to it, and think and rethink the issues on the news, and the realities that govern our lives.

None of us can keep the urgency of the world from knocking on our door, even in our new house among the trees. In fact, the fervor of the world has entered our house. The children tell us we can't go to the gas station in town anymore because Asian hate is on the rise. They show us stories about elders getting beaten in other parts of the country. I try to think back to when I was a girl. Elders were respected in our villages. There were few of them in the world we came from because so many died so young. I remember Npis's mother in her final years and think about how her children and grandchildren respected her and loved her. I am now closer to where she was in age and circumstances. I am now the age of the Asian grandmothers who get beaten up on the streets. All the people who cared for me as a child are even older.

I knew that Nyab Vaj, my eldest sister-in-law, was sick because of Facebook. I checked each day, morning and night. The physical distance, marked by the full twelve hours in between our time zones made my heart ache. Although Nyab Vaj was older, she was not yet old enough to be near death's door. Her children had posted photographs of her online. Her skin was pale and sagging, and in each photo she needed the support of others to sit up. She was not quite the young mother I remember from the past: fast moving, always with a child tied to her front, but in terms of age, she could not be more than seventy. Seventy in America was retirement age for many working people. Though when I asked my children to check what the average age of death was in the world, they told me seventy-two and a half. This meant that not only Nyab Vaj but my brothers were close to that number.

Throughout the years in America, I had received calls from my family. Like other families separated by wars around the world, we lived in different countries, in accordance with the laws of different governments and economies. Although Npis and I have not been wealthy people, we have often been tasked with helping relatives when they were in need. We could never give a lot but we always gave something. For many years, these were the nature of the phone calls across the ocean. A monsoon storm had been particularly rough and someone needed a new roof. Could we help? There was a car accident. A child had died. A funeral had to be arranged. Could we help? I was always happy to help. I know how much harder it was to be the one to receive than the one to give, even in the worst years of our own financial situations; twenty dollars here was not life or death. It was migraines, it was self-doubt. These things were different. I rarely call my family in Laos, especially since my mother's death.

Sometimes, my brothers communicated to Xis or Nplooj that they were happy that I was so silent. It meant that I had a good life. It meant that Npis and I had a good marriage and that our children were in good health. The silence from my end meant that I was doing fine without them, without need of their voices or their words. I never knew quite how to take these comments when they found their way to me. My mother had said the same things to me about my sister Huab many lifetimes ago, when she missed Huab and heard no news, when her heart hankered for a visit that didn't come.

When I found out about Nyab Vaj's death, I knew I had to call Vaj. I waited until the weekend, until my children were around me. Dawb made the call. A part of me, the little sister part who was more used to being cared for by her older brothers than to do the caring, waited for the phone call to drop, unsure of how to approach his grief, but it went through. She had it on speaker mode. When my eldest brother's voice came on the phone, I couldn't find words. I went into Npis's and my bedroom. Dawb and Kablia followed me to lend support. They were no longer young like when my mother had died. They had lived through their own grandmother's death. They knew how the death of our loved ones shook us until the pieces of who we were fell around us, how if there was no one to pick up those pieces, they can be lost forever. I sat on the bed choked by my unshed tears. My daughters, now grown women, stood awkwardly by the door. The voices of their children playing came in from the living room.

I said to Vaj, "I learned that your wife has died. I saw your children post it on Facebook. I'm sorry I am far away. I love you so much."

His voice came to me on a wail.

He said, "Me Tswb."

In all these years, no one had referred to me as Little Tswb.

He said, "If there are words you want to say to me, say them to me now when I can still hear you. Don't wait until I'm gone. I want to hear you, to respond to you."

I covered my mouth with my free hand, the other gripping Dawb's cell phone tight. I slid from the edge of the bed to the floor. I pulled my knees up to my body. I cried into the phone.

He said, "Me Tswb. I want you to know that after our father died, you were the blanket that kept my heart warm."

The call continued but for me it ended on these words. Who else but my siblings knew of those heavy days after our father died? Who in this whole world knew how I used to wander among that citrus orchard, amid the falling blooms, imagining him by my side? Talking to him as if he could hear me? Making promises I would fail to keep. Who but they knew of the cost of our separation, that horrid war, my mother left behind, me on the run for a future no one could see? I don't know how long I wept. I don't know that I was able to say a thing to Vaj in return.

All I know is that after the call, Dawb and Kablia told me, "Mom, we are taking you and Dad back to Laos."

A week before we were to leave for Laos, my half-packed suitcase on the bed, I took a break to scroll through Facebook. There was a short interview with a Hmong woman, the owner of a popular newly discovered variety of oranges, the segment walls of the fruit so thin that it melts in the mouth.

The interviewer asked, "Where did you find the seed?"

The woman answered, "My husband and I found it in what was once part of Xieng Khouang Province but has now been named Xaisomboun, in a long-abandoned village. There were two rivers that surrounded this village, a single road out of it. Few people dare go there because of the ghosts, but we decided to be brave. On this island village, we saw the remains of a citrus orchard. Near the debris of a wooden house, there was a single tree with a single branch still producing. There were three oranges hanging above what appeared to have been an old grave mound. We picked them. We ate one and we knew that we had to salvage the seeds from the other two."

CHAPTER 27

A Cradle of Creation

When the plane flew over Laos, I saw mountains rising underneath us, uneven peaks of green standing jagged across the landscape. I saw the Mekong River flowing wide, green and brown, a return to the colors of our lives when we were children in Laos. Then, I saw the spread of Vientiane, the capital city of the country of my birth.

I told Kablia, sitting beside me, "Your grandmother once visited the capital city when she was a child. When I was growing up, she used to tell me that it was a cradle of creation."

Kablia understood I was talking about my mother, her niam tais, not the grandmother who was now buried in America, but she did not know what a cradle of creation was.

I explained, "It is a phrase that the elders used to say. I suppose so many Hmong people come from the mountains that they could not imagine the flat of Vientiane. When they came here, even during my mother's time, they must have seen the two- and three-story buildings rising in the flat expanse. It was a place in which things could rise. Of course, it wasn't the capital city then. When I was a child, the old kings lived in Luang Prabang."

When I was a child, what I found so incredible was the fact that Luang Prabang, like my village of Dej Tshuam, sat at the confluence of two rivers, the Mekong and the Nam Khan. When I was child, Dej Tshuam could have been the old capital city for all I knew.

The red-tiled roofs of the buildings in Vientiane greeted us from below. The plane tilted forward and sped up. Kablia closed her eyes tight. I reached out a hand to cover the clenched fist beside me. It'd been a long journey for us all, but she was the only one sweating, trying to even out her breathing. I didn't have her nerves, but I felt all the muscles in my body tighten nonetheless.

Npis and I had tried to visit Laos once before. Long after my mother had died, when Dawb and her husband had been working and living in Southeast Asia and were expecting their first child, our first grandchild. They bought us plane tickets to return to this part of the world. When we arrived in Thailand, the baby was not yet due and Dawb insisted that we take the opportunity to visit my family and return to Laos. It had been a painful attempt.

We made it safely into Laos. In the airport, in the line of foreigners, I passed the security station smoothly. I waited, leaning on the partial wall that led to the baggage claim, for Npis, knowing my family waited outside the glass doors in baggage claim. When it was Npis's turn to approach the counter, the uniformed guard called his friends over. They examined Npis's blue US passport, staring hard into his photo. They pointed to his face. They whispered. They got more of their friends involved.

Npis asked, "Is everything okay?" in English.

The uniformed man with a gun at his side spoke back in Lao, "No, everything is not okay."

Npis said, "I don't understand what you are saying."

The man said, "If you want to talk, speak the language I know you know."

Npis said, "I don't understand what is going on."

The guards laughed among themselves.

One of them spoke English, finally: "How old when we kick you out Laos first time?"

One of them answered again in English, holding up two fingers, "This second time."

Npis asked once more, "Is something wrong?"

The man with the gun pointed to it. "Ask my gun," he said in English.

My brothers were just on the other side of the wall, outside the baggage area, waiting for us. I found myself at an impasse once again. The jungle. The wind. The soldiers coming. Npis urging me toward marriage. Another moment. My mother standing in the clearing about to go and get water to start dinner. I found my feet walking toward Npis. He was not the young man I had married. He was an old man, balding, round bellied, bags heavy beneath his eyes. I saw the stubborn tilt of his jaw. It recalled an old defiance, something reminiscent of the young man who tore open his shirt along the banks of the Mekong River.

The guards told Npis, "You walk out this airport, you die."

One of them, a young man no older than Txuj, a young man with narrow shoulders, and long, bony hands, approached us. He raised those hands into the air, laughed as he said, "No guarantee your safety, sir."

I stood beside Npis. I pulled his head close, his body stiff beside mine, and said, "Let's leave while we can, get on a plane, go back to Thailand."

The guards told the two young women, both slender and tall, at the flight counter to increase the fare on our one-way tickets out of the country.

The guards walked us across the tarmac of the small airport to the plane waiting to take us out of Laos. The first time we had fled on foot with a baby, all of us on the cusp of death. This time, we would leave on a plane to return to a country that had held us in behind a fence, waiting for the possibility of a new life to begin. This time, in that country, that baby from the past waits, her stomach now bulging with child, for our return. If a heart could divorce itself from a country, that is what ours did as we walked, me following Npis, accompanied by the guards with their guns, across the heat and rising fumes of that black strip, the air wavering as if we were underwater.

Now, here we were once more, returning again, hoping to gain entry into a country that had kicked us out, not once but twice already. Some divorces can never be final.

All of our paperwork, like that previous time, was in order. This time though, we'd returned with our oldest children: Dawb, Kablia, and Txuj. Dawb had gone through different scenarios again and again. She had devised a plan.

A very simple plan. If the authorities refused to let Npis into the country, then Kablia would leave with him and wait in Thailand for our return. Dawb and Txuj would both go with me into Laos. I wouldn't have to make any hard decisions. If somehow with the help of the ancestors we made it through, then . . .

The then was unclear to all of us.

Before the trip, the children had tried to bolster our excitement by asking lots of questions about Laos, about our childhood, our remaining family, about the past meeting the present. Npis put on a brave face about how he didn't care if he wasn't allowed back into Laos. I knew that as much as he'd talked about Laos, as much as he missed the weather in his beloved village near Phou Bia Mountain, it was also the place where his father had died and he'd grown up lonely for a father. I knew that he didn't want to feel like a refugee all over again, this identity that has marked us since we'd left decades ago. We had both now lived in America for longer than we'd live in Laos and Thailand combined. Npis and I were afraid that somehow our memories wouldn't have a home in this new Laos that had been forged after the fall of everything we knew. He warned the children, "It's very hot in Laos. Your uncles won't have air-conditioning. The government is corrupt. There will be spies everywhere. Suspicion is a ghost of war. It haunts everything. You all have no idea what it is like over there."

For the children's sake, I tried to appear happier, less trepidatious than I felt, too. How do you explain to your children that you are no longer the young woman who left your family all those years ago to build a life across an ocean? How do you tell them the truth: that the reunion will be more emotional than you know how to envision or have ever experienced? That your throat constricts each time you think of returning to a country where your mother should be but is no more?

I told them, "Yes, let us see if we can enter the country."

As the plane descended, I told myself, *Take one step at a time. Don't overthink anything. You can hide, Tswb. You can hide behind Npis's talkativeness and your children's endless questions.* I took note of the things we had already done. We had left America and the rest of our children. We had survived the fifty-hour-long trip to Laos. When the tires came to a screeching halt and the trees at the edge of the airstrip stopped moving, the shaking in my legs began.

We got up and stood in a line with the other passengers. Before exiting the plane, most of us placed our hands together at our heart, a sign of gratitude in Laos. The stewardesses with their long fingers, painted nails, and young women's smiles received our gratitude with their own. It had been a long time since I had done the gesture, since I was a girl greeting my teachers, but I was surprised at how naturally it came to me, this tiny lesson on conduct.

In the airport building, we separated into lines just like the first time we had tried to return. It was striking how similar the Lao and the US passports were: both blue with golden seals. The only difference that I could see was that the US passport seemed to be thicker, its cover made of a more substantial material. I saw some travelers with two passports, and knew they belonged to two nations. I held my lone one with both hands. The US passport was the only one I had ever had. Although Npis and I and the older girls were not born as citizens of the country like my younger children, we had been naturalized citizens now for nearly two decades.

I still remember the citizenship test in the building with thick concrete walls and American flags everywhere. The narrow office with a ticking clock, the slit window that looked down at a parking lot in late winter, dirty snow shoveled to the sides creating ridges like a miniature mountain range. The white woman sitting in a blue sweater behind a desk, saying to me after I had passed the exam (after the years Npis and I had spent memorizing all the answers to the possible one hundred questions they might ask us), "Will you fight and die for the United States of America if you are called to?"

Npis will tell me that he hesitated when he came to this question. He will think about the war and the fighting and what that has done to our lives. He will think about all the other wars we have seen on television since the one that had tried to kill us, the faces of the families now struggling as refugees, and he will want to ask her, "Why do we have to fight at all?"—but he will not give in to the want, and instead he will nod his head and say, "Okay."

When the woman asked me the question I said honestly, "I will fight to protect my children. My children are here in America, so yes I will fight and I will die for the United States of America."

In America, we were still refugees despite the fact that for years we carried cards with pictures of our ears, not our faces, saying we were "permanent residential aliens." Even when we eventually received our official Certificate of Naturalization, with pictures of our faces on it, people still looked at us the same as before. We had lived and worked and grown old in the country. Five of our seven children were born as citizens, and yet no one seemed to know who the Hmong people were outside the states and places where we had gathered in Minnesota, Wisconsin, California, and parts of North Carolina. When other people saw us and wanted to talk, they still always asked, "What are you and where are you from?"

In Laos, the Hmong were an ethnic minority, people from the mountains. Some of the Hmong like my family were remnants of the war, now living far away from the villages where they were born, looked over and checked on by the governing powers. Others, those who had ventured from Vietnam and/or were from families who had sided with the Communist regime and were favored, had better positioning in the country. The Hmong were one of many groups of ethnic minorities in a country still reeling from the destruction of the bombs that had been dropped, the unexploded ordnances that continued to kill at least a person a day all these years later.

I knew standing in the line for foreign travelers that I was more

Hmong American than I could ever be Hmong from Laos now, and yet I did not feel like a foreigner visiting. Despite all the hurt, a part of my heart, the pieces that remained from my girlhood, felt like I was coming home.

Txuj, our born-in-America child, would go first in line. I would go next as I had passed successfully before. Kablia would follow. Then, Npis would proceed. Dawb, our lawyer, would be last.

We carried out our plan. Txuj passed with no issues. Kablia was next. She, too, had no issues. Both of them made sure to speak English commenting on their excitement to see Laos for the first time. I was nervous. The man in uniform at the high counter did not greet me as he had my children. He did not speak English to me. He spoke Lao. "Saibaidee." I understood but pretended I didn't.

He said in Lao, "You're the Hmong people. You've been gone for a long time. How does it feel to come home?"

I understood every word but like Npis on that other trip, I pretended I didn't.

I shook my head and said in English, "I don't speak Lao."

He smirked.

Then, to my surprise, he said, "Nyob zoo."

Hello. Hello in Hmong.

I said, "Nyob zoo rau koj thiab."

I could feel my tones rising at the end of my sentence. My gratitude was real. He waved me through.

Txuj, Kablia, and I stood in the small hallway waiting—just as I had before. Each of us had passed through the line and gotten the proper stamps in less than five minutes. The partial wall was low enough so that we could see that Npis was now at the desk speaking to the man in uniform. The man, the same one who had spoken to me, examined Npis's passport. Then, he got up. He walked away with it, slapping the blue book on his left wrist. He didn't say a word to Npis before getting up. He didn't even look at him. Or he had been looking at Npis and was now concerned about something else. The minutes ticked away. My heart was beating fast. I started to sweat. The children looked at their feet. After long minutes, Dawb went to stand by her father. A different man came to the counter. He gestured for her passport.

She spoke in English: "Is there a problem with my father's passport? Everything is in order. I applied for the visa myself."

This man spoke in halting English, something about the war and his being Hmong of a certain age.

She said, "He was a mere boy when the war broke out. He has not been back in a long time. He is looking forward to seeing the land where he was born, showing us the beauty of this country."

The man walked away in the direction of the guard who had taken Npis's passport standing outside a door. They talked. They conferred with other uniformed individuals. One of them had a gun strapped to his side.

Kablia looked at me and said, "Don't worry, Mom. I'll go back to Thailand with Dad."

Then, Dawb was rushing toward us with Npis racing to keep up.

She said only, "Let's get our bags and out of here before they change their minds."

In her hands she held two passports, Npis's and her own.

Outside in baggage claim, she whispered, "I think they were waiting for bribes. But we didn't offer anything. When the man came back, he had the passports overlapped. He threw them at us, clearly unhappy. I picked them up. I knew we had to move fast."

Outside the airport, through the glass, I caught sight of my brother Soob. I had seen photographs of him through the years. I knew he kept a mustache now. In the photographs, he always wore tailored, button up shirts. Like Npis, he was balding. Unlike Npis, his hair had remained black. He kept it combed to the side. He wore dress pants and dress shoes. I saw him before he saw me. He walked in front of the other driver picking us up, a nephew I couldn't place. They were headed out of the baggage claim area toward the parking lot, perhaps thinking that we had been denied entry, that I'd chosen to leave with Npis and my children.

A thousand emotions rose inside me and tears burned my eyes but I didn't cry, scared he'd leave and I'd lose sight of him.

I called out, "Soob!"

He turned at the sound of my voice. When he saw me, he paused for a moment, and then he rushed toward me. Like a dream, he was before me. He placed both palms on my head, a gesture from long ago. All the time we'd been apart, all the distance, and somehow we were here, in each other's arms. He pulled me close.

He said, "You've returned, my little sister."

He wiped tears from his eyes and shook his head as if not him but I was the dream.

He shook hands with Npis. He hugged all three of my children, now adults, though they stood in a line like children before their uncle.

Soob wiped his eyes again and got to the work of getting us out of the airport.

He gestured to the luggage and said, "Is this all yours?"

I nodded. He started carrying a bag, pointed to the nephew, and said, "Grab a bag."

On the way to the cars in the parking lot, he said, "It's hot today."

The heat we had walked into was sweltering. The sun was bright and hot. The scent of diesel fumes mixed with the dry dust in the air. Everything appeared slightly orange. In minutes, my throat was dry, caked with the heavy air and its particles. Txuj's bald head was streaked with sweat.

I said, "Yes, look at Txuj's head."

Soob said, "The trucks have AC."

We separated into two trucks, both Toyotas but models we didn't have in the States, Hilux and Prado. Npis and me and my brother in one. In the other, Dawb, Kablia, Txuj, and the nephew in a borrowed vehicle.

The drive from Wattay International Airport to the place where the Hmong had been resettled was exactly fifty-two kilometers, thus the name of the place. In the truck, Soob and Npis, both in the front, did the bulk of the talking. They spoke of how much "they had missed us" and "how much we missed them." Npis commented on the highway, observed the many red Chinese flags flying outside the commercial buildings. Soob told us facts. The Chinese businesses have been coming into Laos steadily over the years and now own much of the country's economy. I couldn't help but think of the Chinese man from the war years and how even then a different kind of economic takeover was happening as the bombs were falling. Soob said that the whole of Laos only has fourteen thousand miles of highway, and only six thousand of them were paved.

He said, "As you think about your travel plans in the country, it is good for you to know that many of the roads are rough."

Npis said, "Are we on the old 13?"

Soob said, "Yes, the one the French built when they were here. It remains the only highway going north and south."

Npis asked, "It parallels the Mekong River, right?"

Soob nodded in his brusque way. "Yes."

Npis wanted to know, "How long does it take to get to 52 from Vientiane?"

Soob answered, "About thirty to forty minutes, depends on who is driving."

Npis said, "They resettled the Hmong close to the government center."

Soob answered, "Yes, they did."

Npis asked in no specific terms, "Are they strict?"

Soob answered, "Yes, they are. Very."

I had heard of the dangers of spies in Laos, of how there were ears everywhere across the country. I didn't want Npis or my brother to venture into any kind of danger, even in talk. I cut in with a few safe questions. Is your wife still working her stall at the market? What does she sell there? You have an unmarried son and daughter left at home? My brother answered my questions with short responses. Yes, my wife still has her stall. We sell clothes and accessories like hair clips, towels, and sheets. Yes, I have left my only son and youngest daughter at home. The others all have their own lives now. Npis strung together a conversation for the remainder of the drive about car insurance and traffic violations. I looked out the window, saw how the buildings by the highway were coated with dust.

A vendor sat beneath an old, ripped patio umbrella that must have once been red but now looked like dried blood. In front of her was a large woven bamboo basket filled with bright oranges.

Soob made a sudden stop by the side of the road.

He said, "You two sit in the AC. I'm going to buy a few kilos of oranges."

I would have liked to get out of the car and follow him. Oranges. We both must be remembering the same thing. We must both be recalling the life we lived as children, how we were the ones that sold oranges and other fruits to people. My hand reached for the black handle of the truck, but a gust of wind blew and a sheet of dust flew at the car. Each time a transport truck or a regular truck or even a speeding motorbike passed, we could hear the small particles hitting. I settled deeper back into my seat, trying to swallow the dryness in my throat.

Npis, also staring out the window, commented, "Your brother Soob has not changed much. He is still as business as ever."

I felt unnecessarily defensive.

I said, "We've all just gotten old. We are the same people we were."

I didn't quite believe myself.

I said more gently, "Even in the car, I can smell the dust from the road. It's everywhere."

Npis said, "You have to watch yourself. You can't make observations like that to other people."

I asked, "Why not? I'm not making political judgments."

Npis shrugged. "People might think you are judging the conditions of life here."

We stopped talking. In Laos, a site of so much loss, we both felt a need to protect, ourselves, those we loved, and each other. This was the kind of pressure we didn't know how to articulate when our children asked us about a return.

Soob walked back with a clear T-shirt bag of oranges, small fruits the size of my palms. He opened his car door and handed the bag to me in the back without a word. I accepted it—as if forty years hadn't separated the last time he'd handed me something to hold or put away. As if we needed no practice returning to the work of being brothers and sisters again. I felt the thick mucus in my extremely parched throat. I cleared it.

Soob said, "Niam Npis, peel an orange and eat if you want."

Niam Npis. Npis's wife. I had gotten used to everybody in my life calling me this, and even in the letters it was how he referred to me, but not from him in voice. Not from my family. In the letters, I could glance over it. In life, it was much harder.

I took deep breaths, quietly, as Soob started the engine and moved the truck back into the lane of moving vehicles. The highway we were on had two lanes, one going in each direction, no markers in between. My brother drove fast. Everyone else did, too. My body lurched forward when traffic suddenly slowed. We were passing a crowded market area. There were vendors selling fruit and barbecue meats and other items to the right of the road. They had contraptions with strips of revolving plastic to keep the flies away from the cooked foods. To the left, there were several two-story buildings, one with shiny glass, an odd sight in the dusty landscape, but it was a cell phone store that advertised unfamiliar brands from China. They must have people cleaning it every few minutes.

Soob said, "This is 52. This is the market where my wife works. Our stall is deeper in. All of us live just around the corner."

He turned the corner away from the hectic commercial area, turned once again to the left, through an old metal gate, once white but the enamel had rusted in many places. The other truck was already there. My children stood by a thin old man beneath a lonely palm tree. Tied to the palm tree was an equally thin ox with the longest pair of horns I'd seen since I was a girl in Dej Tshuam. Then, it was my brother Vaj who kept long-horned oxen. He loved them.

My children were plump and pale in this new setting. I made the connection slowly. The thin old man standing with them, holding the girls' hands on either side, was Vaj. He'd seen the truck carrying us enter into the yard. His head had started bobbing up and down. Before I could even move toward him, he was walking toward me, weeping.

Soob said, "He cries a lot these days."

I didn't rush our meeting. I didn't run out of the truck or leave the door open as I raced to my eldest brother, who had told me on the phone that it was me who had blanketed his heart after our father died. I moved slowly. Shyly. I got out of the car. I closed the door. I pulled my shirt with damp hands low over my body. Then I walked toward him, a smile on my face, one of my hands shielding my eyes from the bright sun. A real smile swept over my body as my vision clouded over.

I said, "Vaj, it is you."

We stood inches apart.

He said, "Me Noob, you are home. You are finally home."

Another endearment from long ago. Little seed.

We held each other for the briefest of moments. He wiped his eyes. He dried his tears. New ones fell, streaking his wrinkled face.

He said, "It has been too long."

He shook his head disbelievingly.

He said, "You came too late to see our mother."

I'd returned decades too late to see my mother.

And yet, here I was, here we were, at long last, standing face-to-face. I had left when I was sixteen years old for marriage. It had taken me four decades to return to my family. Then, there were the experiences that years alone could never measure. All the heartache, the hard days, the happy ones, too. The smile on my face wouldn't go away. When I was a girl, whenever Vaj returned from trips, he'd come back with candy. The smile on my face now I knew was the same one that waited for him then.

Suddenly, we were surrounded by nieces and nephews and their children, by my remaining sisters-in-law. We greeted each other. We made small talk. We laughed. Plastic chairs were pulled out of the circle of houses that framed a communal yard. A small table was set up. A pitcher of water and glasses followed. Soob took out the bag of oranges that I had left in the car.

I asked, "Where's Maiv?"

A nephew, lanky with skin darkened by the sun, said, "Oh, she's old and forgetful now, Auntie Tswb. Auntie Maiv is not as she was when you last saw each other."

He said to one of the children in the yard, "Go get Auntie Maiv from her shed."

Maiv walked slowly toward my daughters and me, no taller than the child who'd been sent to fetch her. She was now an old woman. Strands of white hair wrestled out of the traditional blue cloth she'd tied on top of her head. Her feet, clad in flip-flops, were the same color as the earth she walked on, gray and dusty. My older sister, teller of a thousand stories. My gentle sister who had lived through so much.

The nephew said, "She can't hear well now. You have to yell."

He showed us how: "Auntie Maiv! Auntie Tswb! Your sister is visiting from America! With her children and Uncle! Come so they can say hello!"

Maiv nodded her head signifying that she understood. She walked a little faster. I got up off the chair waiting for her to come to me but she walked directly to Dawb. Dawb got up to greet her aunt with a smile, hands out.

Maiv clasped both of Dawb's hands tight. Maiv looked up at her and said, "Tswb, is it really you? Have you really returned to Laos?"

Dawb shook her head as tears fell. She pointed to me. She turned Maiv's body toward me.

"Auntie Maiv, I'm Tswb's oldest daughter. My mom is that one."

Maiv looked at me like a stranger.

She said, "Really?"

The nephew added, "Auntie Tswb, her eyes are also very bad now."

The nephew yelled, "Yes! Auntie Maiv! It is your sister! Tswb! Go so she can say hello!"

Maiv approached me slowly, each step stilling on the ground, as if she were walking toward a figment or the edge of a steep cliff. In front of me, within touching distance, she stopped and looked up.

She pointed a finger at my face.

She asked, her words as slow as those of the tall doctor in that small room I'd visited in my sadness had been, "Is. It. Really. You. Tswb?"

She turned around, and asked the others, "Is this another dream?"

The smile I had discovered and held frozen fell from my face. The wall I had been leaning on toppled. In its fall, the dust of the ages rose up, and in the yellow light of early evening, I became young again, young and hurt, going to my oldest living sister for comfort. Her arms enveloped me. I felt the slow patting on my back, her voice saying, "You are home, Tswb. You are home."

CHAPTER 28

Journey in the Mountains

The whole of the mountain village had lost their electricity. The van we were traveling in had no heating. This made sense because Laos was a hot country for the most part—except when you were in the high mountains. And most of the country was mountainous, about 70 percent of it.

The moment we left 52 behind and the road we were on started ascending, I started reeling. The mountains rose one against each other, one into the other, seemingly higher and higher. I shivered in my seat, unable to look out of the van's windows, afraid of the steep fall below. Npis sat in front by the driver, eyes scanning the line of clouds that floated halfway between the bottom and tops of the mountain range before our gaze. While the mountains stood still, the clouds did not, each gust of wind shaking the van, the clouds outside the window, and the contents of my stomach. The children oohed and aahed in their seats as if they were on an amusement park ride. They clamored for their iPhones to take photos, then looked at the images they captured in disappointment. No picture could compare to the experience of this, they said. They put their phones away and looked out their windows, marveling silently. All the while, I felt like I was flying in the air without the safety of a pressurized cabin. I didn't know when the winds would change direction, when I would soar or sail my way to the deep ravines below. I kept reminding myself: Tswb, you can't complain. You have wanted this. You have wanted this leg of the journey, too, this adventure across the country where you were born, to get to know this place that you knew only as a child in a village, a young person in a war, a place you have only imagined from a distance.

All their lives, Npis and I had told the children of the mountains we came from. I had talked of the white flowering trees that bloomed each new year across Xieng Khouang Province, from the base of the moun-tains right up to the tree line, and the special yellow ones my father loved, both of whose names we can't find anywhere. Npis spoke often of a particular stout palm that only grew in the most dangerous moun-tain slopes, how its tender inner trunk had been a delicacy in the war years. Like him, I hungered for a return to that taste: crunchy and light, a texture that conjured a union between a bamboo shoot and freshly dug jicama. Every once in a while, Npis exclaimed, pointing toward a steep incline, "Children, up there, on that protruding edge, that's the palm. So delicious, the heart of that palm."

He observed, "Oh, they are hard, so hard to get. They only grow in the hardest to reach places."

He didn't say this part, but I know we were both thinking, *How des-perate we were in those years that we risked so much for a taste of that inner palm flesh?*

The driver, a soft-spoken Hmong man with a head of thick hair, his age indeterminable, skin like leather, said, "Yes, Uncle. I've only had it once or twice. Unforgettable taste indeed."

The driver was superb. Unlike the other drivers tumbling down the steep mountain roads or racing to pass us impatiently, he was calm and deliberate, handling the car with slow precision, patiently moving out of the way when possible. Each time his phone rang, he responded in what I thought was a peculiar way, with no greetings or questions. He simply said, "Yes, it is me. I'm currently on the road. Yes, that sounds like a good idea." When Npis complimented him on his superior driving skills, he said by way of an explanation, "When I was young, I worked as a driver for a Chinese company that was mining in the mountains. This van is much easier to handle than those big trucks on these narrow mountain roads."

Npis agreed, "Oh, yes, that would indeed produce an exemplary driver."

Npis commented, "The Chinese flag is all over Vientiane."

The driver responded, "Yes, Uncle. They have taken over much of the natural resources in the country."

Npis wanted to know, "How does the Lao government feel about the Chinese presence?"

The driver answered, "I wouldn't know. The leadership must know what it is doing."

Npis agreed, "Oh, yes. Of course."

Not only were Npis and I new to the version of Laos outside the car window, even the Hmong in the country felt different to us now. They seemed to know much more about us Hmong Americans than we did about them, not just the easy stuff like Hollywood and hamburgers, but personal details like: how we liked to chop our chicken into big chunks, or how easily we get dizzy in high altitudes, or how our tastes have changed, how many Hmong Americans no longer eat fresh blood salad and stay away from bile as a flavoring in our freshly slaughtered pig and cow soups. Even with my own brothers, there was this informational disconnect. They understood that Hmong Americans didn't get hungry as often as their Lao counterparts, how we needed more water to alleviate the power of the sun, how limited our vocabulary in Hmong had become when expressing the distasteful emotions like jealousy, hate, anger, and resentment. It was clear that while we refugees were all struggling to learn about America, they had been keeping track of us from afar. We, who had left, had no capacity to do the same in the wake of the war. There were so few ways for us to see into the country we had fled from other than the stories from the survivors in those early years. We didn't have access for a long time. When we did, many of us had no time, caught in the cycles of poverty and the needs of the companies we worked for. More importantly, the Hmong Lao had met a lot more Hmong Americans here than we had them on the other side of the world. It used to be that we were just once all Hmong, no matter the clan you came from or the dialect you spoke, now we were all Hmong and the countries and cultures that we had been living in.

Before we left 52, in hushed voices, my brothers had cautioned us to be careful, to trust no one. We were told that spies abounded. We were not to criticize the country or make comparative observations between governmental ideologies, and most importantly, we had to look and see the country not as individuals who had fled persecution but as tourists and visitors here for the first time.

To the children Vaj had said, "Remember that if you are not willing to yell at someone who is not afraid to be louder than you, you've already lost. Remember that if you are not willing to hit someone who comes at you with raised fists, you've already lost. Remember that your uncle has survived in this country because he is a man unwilling to raise his voice or his fists."

My brothers said to all of us upon our leaving, "The whole of the government has eyes and ears everywhere. They are looking for old enemies from the war. People who have fled Laos successfully. People who should be dead already but are not."

They didn't need to say the rest: people like us—survivors who bear the scars and carry the knowledge of what had transpired in the depths of the jungle, those of us who believed the histories we had survived, not the ones that have been rewritten.

It was clear that the life we once lived was no more. Although it was now early December in Laos, a time when Hmong villages would be gathering to celebrate the New Year's festivities, most of the village yards we passed were disappointingly empty. I wanted to see young Hmong people still excited about the harvests, but I learned that many of the Hmong families in Laos no longer had fields to tend to. The land was no longer free—as it had been when we were children. A family couldn't just go and clear land, plant food, and harvest it. Most of the country, including the mountains, were now owned by the government or corporations from abroad, countries like China and Australia with their big machines and drills, all mining for gold and other precious resources.

Npis and I tried to impart what we knew to our children, the pieces of our history that had happened here. We tried to do so without bringing unwanted political attention to our talk. We told them that in the old days, only Lao houses were on stilts. Hmong houses were on the ground. Lao folk preferred sticky rice. Hmong folk liked regular rice. They said, "But we like sticky rice." We said, "Yes, you do. We are telling you generalized truths not specific preferences of individuals."

We were at a great disadvantage in what we wanted to say and how we wanted to address the country around us. Whatever deeper sense of Laos we wanted to impart to our children, the things we yearned to see and could not find were impossible to communicate. All we could do was sigh each time we passed a mountain whose sides had been pulverized by heavy equipment to find the veins of gold that flowed within. Some of the streams and rivers we crossed were neon green, contaminated by the chemicals that had seeped into their currents. The land around us was not as it had been; it had been hurt and despite the fact that we had fled its borders for our lives, we felt keenly its pain.

The driver nodded politely each time Npis or I sighed, pressed our hands to the windows, as if we could touch and comfort the landscape with our little gestures, like he, too, was also feeling our grief, acknowledging the hurt in the terrain outside our window.

On the few occasions where we did pass by Hmong villagers celebrating New Year's, each a collection of split bamboo or wooden huts clinging to the side of the roads, single lines of electricity running from one to the other, the display was sad: there were always only about eight or nine girls dressed in their finery throwing balls with each other, or the occasional one or two boys. There were no elders gathered close to watch, and certainly no young men and women singing courtship songs.

I asked, "Where are all the people?"

The driver said, "Working in the bigger cities."

I said, "Oh."

Npis added, "Of course; like many other countries, like Thailand."

The driver said, "Yes."

Npis turned his attention back to the rise and the fall of the mountains outside the window. I looked ahead at the road, curving in front of us, always curving. On the long flight across the ocean, Npis and I had wondered about the possibility of once again tasting the insides of the trunks of the stout mountain palms, the beloved flavors of Hmong chicken in broth from our youth, even the big duck eggs with their rich yolks that looked bright as the peel of clementines. He, like me, saw few places outside the car windows where these tastes and flavors from our childhood could be found. There had been few chickens and we hadn't seen any ducks.

Suddenly, Npis, pointing out his window, said, "Children, look."

I looked with the children. On a steep mountainside, there was a small family of stout palm trees, short and fat, their leaves spiking out. This time there wasn't just one or two but a small grove, a family. The sighting made me happy for the first time, true happiness, no sorrow, no hint of sadness, just the memories of the clean, crisp sweetness of the hearts of the palm filling our mouths.

The mountains, we knew, had waited for us. Some of the mountains stood tall despite the fact that Laos had been the most heavily bombed country per capita in the world. And even with the destruction wreaked by the mining companies, they were still haunting and awe-inspiring. Although I found I could not look at them for long, afraid I'd somehow fall quite literally off the road. I had been a child from the mountains. But I had been gone so long, I'd lost all ability to believe I could cling to it, let alone trust a car to do it for me.

As night descended, a layer of fog floated down. The road disappeared from view. The temperature dropped. Without heating, the fog of our breaths steamed up the insides of the van. We couldn't see what was in front or around us.

The goal was to see Laos. If it were a body, we had been children from its chest. The children wanted us to see beyond the places where we had been born, the jungles we had once lived in. The best way to do so was with a car. The best car to do so with involved a native driver. The best road to take was the one we were on. It was the only way to get to Phonsavan and end up in Luang Prabang, the old capital city. The instinct was sound; all of it was designed to give Npis and me some necessary space and time to reckon with this reunion with my family and the country after forty years apart.

The driver apologized about the foggy car and the cloud we were now lost in. He retrieved an old towel from under his seat and every few seconds started wiping at the foggy windshield and the window beside him. Inside the car, it was nearly pitch black. We knew where each other was seated but it was impossible to see anyone.

Npis, in his fashion, as he'd done in the different cars of our children, started pressing buttons to try to turn on the heat, to get hot air to clear up the glass.

If the driver was startled by Npis's handling of his car's buttons, he did not show it. Npis explained, "In America, in Minnesota where we live, this happens all the time when it gets cold. You have to turn on the air and angle it on the windshield."

It was clear that we could travel no further. Earlier in the day, we'd had several unnecessary delays. We had to pass guard points. The driver had warned us that this would be the case. He told us that each time he would go out and talk to the guards, attend to the situation, show the necessary paperwork. He'd smiled and said, "Offer a bit of money to buy the guards something to drink."

He had said, "It might be helpful if you showed your exhaustion."

Npis interpreted this for the children. The driver would have to bribe the guards. If we didn't see this, it would be less embarrassing for all involved. In a whisper, Npis added, "The less the guards can interact with us, the safer we will be."

Each time we saw a guard station, immediately Npis and the children and I would feign sleep as our driver's unchanging face continued its calm survey of the road ahead. At the first stop, a guard with a gun kept walking around the car, examining each of us in our sleeping poses. Npis, perhaps intimidated, started snoring. It was ridiculous and I tried not to laugh in my sleep but then the only way to cover it up was to cough, so I had a coughing fit as I restlessly moved my head seeking comfort. The children observed this in their pretend slumber. Txuj let out a minor giggle which got the girls going. The guard was not pleased by all these sounds coming from us. He knocked on the glass outside my window and my survival instincts kicked in. The guards were all armed. Hmong Americans had gone missing in Laos over the years. The situation was graver than the children understood. Immediately, we all quieted in our slumber, softened into our positions. Npis and I warned them after this initial stop, "Do not anger the guards."

The feigning of sleep continued several more times throughout the day. By afternoon, we'd learned the more comfortable fake sleep poses, the ones we could hold for longer if necessary, and things proceeded more smoothly. With our heads lulling to the right or the left, our chest rising and falling, and eyes solemnly closed, the guards took whatever monies the driver offered, and we were allowed to pass one checkpoint after the next.

But we were now stuck in the mountains. There was no visibility. No sign of a village in sight. All around us, fog. We knew that to our right, there was a steep valley. We knew that to the left, there was the jagged face of a mountain, grown over by the grass that the elders used to make brooms. Moreover, Kablia said she needed to pee. We'd taken several bathroom breaks throughout the day. A quick run into the brush each time. On one occasion, Kablia and I had peed near a burial ground, only to realize too late in the process to stop. The burial stupa had been mostly covered by the growth of a bush. The area where we had peed was the only area where the grass was kept low enough to safely crouch. When I realized what we had done, a small chill passed through me. The old childish fears had returned.

I told the girls to stay close to the van. No one could see anyone. Just do your business and come back in. I stood outside, took deep breaths of the night air. Npis and the driver spoke in low voices. Txuj had truly fallen asleep. I listened to the cacophony of the mountain crickets and the sound of one daughter peeing, the other humming to herself. I was transported.

The first of my mother's many stories returned to me in Laos, at first in my voice, and then somewhere along the way, it became her voice that I heard, and the telling ours.

On foggy nights like this, when I was a child, many of the children of Dej Tshuam village would gather at the feet of their elders to hear stories. One of the tales my mother often told was about a pair of young lovers who had pledged to be together forever despite the far distance between their small villages.

In the long season of separation, the young woman had grown sick and died. Though her parents buried her body, each night, her spirit would rise with the moon and enter the village to await the coming of her beloved. She wore the traditional dress of death: a long coat with a high collar, underneath it she wore her best traditional Hmong outfit, the heavy black shirt and wide-legged pants, red and green sashes at her waist; her feet were clad in winged shoes, so she might journey safely across the land of the spiny caterpillar on her way to the after-life—only she'd refused to go, unwilling to forsake her pledge.

The sight of her walking around the village, her long hair falling about her face, her hands stiff at her side, sent fear into even the hearts of the bravest villagers. Her family called the village shamans, and they tried to set her spirit to rest but to no avail. In fear, the village emptied, family by family, her grief-stricken parents among the last to leave. In the old days, news of births and deaths traveled slowly across villages.

The young man did not know that his lover had died.

On a moonless night, he traveled from his village to hers. To his heart's joy, at the edge of the village he could see the figure of his be-loved waiting for him. He was surprised by the long coat she wore but otherwise happy to run to her and pull her close. Her cold body fell against his own. He said, "You should have waited at your house. The night is too cold for you to wait here for me." She nodded, her voice—

which she hadn't used since her death—had grown heavy and slow. He
felt for her face but touched only hair. He peered.

*In the darkness of the night, he saw very little but, in his heart, he
made out her eyes, her nose, her mouth*, so he said, "Let's hurry to your
house and build a fire so you can warm up." He pulled her by the hand.
On heavy legs she moved with him. As they passed between the quiet
houses, he asked, "Where are the village dogs? They usually bark so
loudly when I visit." She shook her head, so he shushed himself as they
walked to the front door of her house. Before they entered, he said, "Are
your parents asleep already?" She nodded this time. He teased, "Have
you grown shy in my long absence?" She nodded again.

*At the entry door to the house of her family, he was surprised that
the twine used to latch the door closed was absent.* Inside, he shivered
as he moved toward the fire ring at its center. He was surprised to find
that the firewood stack by the wall was low. On all his previous visits,
the family always kept a full stack of wood at the ready. Still, he set to
work, keeping quiet so as not to wake her parents as she stood stiffly
by the door. The shape of her merged into the moonless night. Soon
enough, the scent of smoke filled the house, and then the embers of a
fire began to glow.

In the light of the fire, he saw that the house was empty of its furnishings. He asked, "Where is everything?" She shrugged. He said, "Why
don't you come to the fire?" She walked toward him. The closer she got,
the colder he felt, goose bumps rising on his arms. When she stood over
him, the flames began to dance. As he looked at her, he saw in the light
of the fire the shoes on her feet, the intricate embroidery on her coat,
and the high collar at her neck.

Before he could move, she crouched low. In the orange glow, he saw
that her face was swollen and blue beneath the tangle of her hair. The
stench of her decomposed body filled his nostrils. He whispered, "What
has happened to you?" She spoke then, her voice hoarse and unfamiliar:
"I've waited for you. Even in death, I have waited for you." The man fell
on his butt. He had no words to offer looking at her, crouched low to
the ground, the object of his love now the object of his fears.

He connected the pieces: the absence of the village dogs, the eerie quiet of the village, the empty house. He whispered, "You shouldn't have." She said, "But I did. Now, we can be together forever as we'd planned." Now, it was his turn to nod stiffly, unsure of how to proceed. For the next hour, the pair sat by the fire. Each piece of wood he poked into the hungry flames meant there was one less on the pile. The night was still young. Soon, he would have to sit with her in the darkness.

As the fire dwindled, the man could only think of one thing to say: "I need to pee." The woman, looking at the man she loved, read him right. She said, "Sure. You can pee right here." He said, "I'm too shy to do so in front of you." She said, "There's nothing to hide between us." He said, "We're not married yet. First marriage and then I can pee in front of you as often as you like." She pondered his words. She said, "Here." She untied the sashes at her waist. She tied the two ends together and made a long rope. She said, "Tie one end around your waist. I'll hold the other. You go pee outside. I'll wait here so I can warm up for your touch." He agreed, tying the damp sash around his waist, its scent the rot of her body. He told her, "You wait here. If you get concerned, pull on the sash so I'll know to come back." She nodded. He walked quickly outside.

By her family's door, he saw that there was an old water gourd hanging. To his surprise, it still held water. He tipped it over to create the sound of pee. He untied the sash carefully from his waist and tied it to the pole holding the overhang of the family's thatched roof up. Then, he ran, as fast as he could, without looking back. At the sound of his footsteps, he heard hers follow in a great hurry, but her legs were stiff, muscles rotting, so she could not keep up. At the edge of the village, he dared himself to turn. In the darkness, he saw nothing, just heard the heavy steps of her stiff legs chasing. No exertions, no breath coming fast.

Kablia said, "Mom."

I jumped. My arms were full of goose bumps.

The man's fear in that dark abandoned house was now mine.

In the car, we managed to drive for fifteen minutes. In those fifteen minutes, we saw that we'd entered a darkened mountainous town.

There were several two-story houses on either side of the road. The driver parked, got out and walked toward the candlelit glow of an open shop. He returned after a moment and said, "We are in the town of Phou Khoun. Their power has suddenly gone out. The shop owner can feed us dinner. There are rooms upstairs we can rent for the night and get some rest." It was our only recourse.

We took our luggage and went into the small shop. There were a few tables. The shop owner was a tall woman with sharp bones highlighted by the large candle she carried in both hands at her chest. She was Lao.

With a curt greeting, she said, "I only have thick rice noodles in pork broth tonight."

We ordered six bowls, one for each of us.

We sat around two of the tables. Each held four stools. The night air was chilly. The sounds of crickets were loud. A cold draft blew into the open door of the shop, causing the candles at the center of the tables to waver.

The noodles when they came to the table in big bowls were stiff and hard, but the broth was warm and we were grateful.

After dinner, the proprietor took us up a narrow stairway on the outside the building. She opened a door into a hallway. Rooms were on either side.

She said in Lao, "How many rooms do you want?"

Npis asked in halting Lao, "How many beds do you have in a room?"

She answered, "Two."

Npis said, "We'll take three. One for my wife and me. One for our son and the driver. One for our daughters."

She opened each room with a key. We asked if she had candles. She left us in the dark hallway and said she'd be back. We listened for the return of her steps, all of us very quiet. When she finally returned, to our collective relief, she brought us three candles, one for each room, each the thickness of an index finger, the height of an opened palm.

Our room consisted of two twin beds separated by a narrow aisle. There were thick floral blankets, its fibers like fine plastic, on each bed that smelled of many other bodies. The pillows were flat. The beds themselves were little more than blankets on wooden platforms. There was a door that led to a bathroom. In the light of the candle, I saw a plastic bucket by a drain filled with water, a plastic bowl sat inside it for hygiene use. The squatting toilet sat on a platform by itself. The bathroom made me particularly lonely. I brushed my teeth with a bottle of drinking water I had tucked into my purse from the 52 Market. Npis shared the water and did the same. The water in the bucket was too cold to bathe or even wash up with. On the narrow bed, I laid down the sheet I'd brought from America against Npis's advisement. "They have sheets in Laos," he'd said. He'd added, "You are insulting the country by bringing your own." I laid down a towel Soob's wife had gifted me from her stall over the pillow. I covered myself with a thin blanket I'd also brought from America, also against Npis's judgment. I lay down on the hard blanket and to my surprise felt myself falling into a deep sleep. Somewhere in the night, Npis woke me up and asked if I could extend my blanket across the small aisle so he might share. I complied.

I had no dreams. The reality was enough. And the reality was: I had traveled halfway around the world for a reunion with my family that I could not have prepared for, to go on a long journey across Laos because I wanted to delay the moment when I would be with my mother again.

The next morning, we woke up to the voices of the children in the hallway. The hallway, which was colorless in the night, we saw in the light of morning that it had been painted in a deep green color. At one end, there was a window. The girls were there, taking pictures.

I walked to them and saw what held them enthralled: haunting hills of green spreading for as far as the eye could see. A layering of sky, clouds so fine and soft it looked silky, pink and blue melting and merging across the land. It was the gentlest and most beautiful meeting of sky and earth I'd ever witnessed.

On the street, still clad in the purple of dawn, the early-morning vendors sold Dawb and Kalia reheated fried doughnuts that were too hard to eat. Without breakfast, we all got into the van and made our way toward Luang Prabang, a place I had never seen, a place I had learned about in school as a site where kings and queens lived, as a place that, too, sat at the confluence of rivers.

In Luang Prabang, the old seat of the Kingdom of Laos, before the communist takeover in 1975, in a gently lit hotel courtyard owned by a French company, our driver, drunk and sad, told Npis, "I'm a spy for the government. My job is to get information from your family and make it useful."

Npis said, "You've had too much to drink, son. I'll help you to your room."

He shook his head of dark hair. He said, "Come."

The driver started walking out of the gated courtyard, with its twinkling ground lights. It was the kind of place we had never been, the kind of hotel on a magazine cover. Its courtyard held a wide lotus pond, full of blooms—just like the photographs I had found on my phone, cropped, and shared on Facebook. The driver's feet were unsteady and he weaved through the manicured walkway like he was a reed in water.

Npis had no choice but to follow him and steady him as he exited the gated door of the hotel and crossed the cobblestone street to where he'd parked the van. He leaned on the side of the van as he walked along its length to the back, a strange continuous hug. At the back, he knelt and felt underneath the vehicle. He took out a handgun and what appeared to be an iPhone. He showed it to Npis beneath the full moon above them, the music and voices from the night market floating around them.

He said, "Look."

Npis nodded and said, "I see it."

The man said to Npis, his soft voice breaking, "There is nothing useful your family can offer this country. The world you lived in died a long time ago. It is now only a ghost. The ghost that haunts Laos. Why have you and your wife allowed the ghost of Laos to haunt you, even in America? Why have you allowed it to chase you across the years?"

Npis repeated these words to me later in the night. After he'd helped the driver put the phone and gun back in their places and cross that cobblestone street, enter into the hotel gate, weave along the curving walkways with its ground lights, and climb the flight of stairs to the room the driver shared with Txuj.

In the quiet of our bedroom, on a soft, clean bed, Npis whispered incredulously, "Our driver is a spy for the Laotian government."

I said nothing.

We had been with the driver for nearly two weeks. He had taken us up and down mountain ranges. We'd started treating him like family. We washed his clothes with our own at the laundromats that charged by the kilo. Still, this was Laos and we had been warned. Why were we surprised? Why did we think otherwise?

Npis whispered, "He showed me the gun and an iPhone he kept underneath his van."

Npis said, "He might have been recording our conversations, documenting our actions."

What was there to record? What was there to document? What could Laos take away from me, learn about me? That I had been a child whose father had died, that I had been a foolish teenage girl who believed in a love story living beyond a war full of death, that I had left my own mother in pursuit of that love story, that in that love story I would become a refugee mother starving for belonging, a poor woman watching the babies slip out of her body, too impoverished to shelter them from the dangers of a bigger world, that I had been in America, been an uneducated woman, working the years through, pushing my hands and my feet until they could push no more, falling apart, afraid every day that I could not be the kind of mother my own had been? What was there to document? How I wish for a record of my life, something to show that I had indeed lived and that I had tried my best not only to build myself but my children up to something that mattered, people the world might see and care for.

I was not mad at Laos. I was not mad at the government in power. I was not mad at Thailand or the fact that it could not be a home to my children and me. I was not mad at America for not understanding my broken heart, my breaking body, and not hearing my pleas, my yearning, my wanting—for how could any of these countries give me what I had lost on my way to everything?

What I was, what I had become, was a woman trying to turn the tides of luck in favor of her children. All along the way, I was not sure how to find good luck for myself because I came from women who others feared and labeled, so I had clung blindly to the idea of love, a love that might have the power to not only sustain but offer comfort in an unjust world.

I said to Npis, "Does this spy really want to know why people like you and I return to Laos?"

Npis shook his head. "I don't think so, Tswb."

I looked at him in the beautiful hotel room with the gleaming light of the moon shining from beyond the window. I heard more than saw the exhaustion in my husband. I relaxed the line of my lips.

I smiled at him.

I said, "No one really wants to know about people like you and me, Npis."

In the silence that greeted my words, I heard the distant rush of the rivers that made a peninsula for Luang Prabang, the Nam Khan and the Mekong Rivers. I heard the rush of the rivers from my youth in the village of Dej Tshuam.

I said, "We have nothing to hide. We have nothing to fear."

Night is falling. My mother, my sisters, and I are bathing by the wide river. It is a cool evening. Steam rises from the surface of the water. I hear my sisters dipping their bowls into the warmth of the river, washing themselves.

I look at my mother, untwirling her long hair.

I ask her, "Mother, are we going to be in this village forever?"

Her lips curve up and she tells me, "Yes, Tswb. Parts of us will always be here."

I ask her, "Will we be here together?"

She answers, "Yes, we will."

CHAPTER 29

Arrival

It was a small yard. I could see my brother's prized bull in a pen at the back standing in front of a darkened shed. Its glossy horns rose proudly from his head like sharp crescent moons facing each other and shimmered in the light of the day. My daughters stood close to the wooden fence holding him, admiring the animal. In one corner of the yard, there was a small stand of banana trees. There were no fruits but several purple cone-shaped blossoms dangled from beneath the leaves. At the base of the trees, a red mother hen pecked at some fallen leaves drying on the ground, her fluffy chicks spread around her. In the middle of the yard, there was a single mango tree, no fruit, but its almond-shaped leaves created a canopy.

In the uneven shade of the mango tree, dappled sunshine danced on two graves. One of them belonged to a respected relative who had died. The Muas Clan could not bear to part with his body, so instead of burying the body where the government had made allowances, Soob had garnered the appropriate paperwork to bury the man in his backyard. Beside his grave was my mother's.

In the tradition of my family, the graves are set in mounds. In the village of Dej Tshuam, the graves were piled with river rocks, but in 52, there is no supply of river rocks, so my mother's grave is covered by a mound of concrete. There is a little door at the end of the burial mound. It faces the east, in the direction of the rising sun. The door is for the spirit of the deceased, so that they may wander free, see the approach of day each morning.

A breeze rustled the leaves overhead. The girls talked to each other in a whisper. The prized bull chewed the dry grass stacked high in front of him slowly, making wet sounds with his mouth. The hen and her chicks walked in a line toward me, pecking at the earth in a random way. There were little red ants crawling over the mound of my mother's grave.

It had been forty-two years since I had last seen my mother in that long-ago jungle clearing. I had feared a return to Laos because I had been afraid of this moment. I had journeyed across the country in the backseat of a van with a spy as our driver over roads that traverse mountains because I had wanted to delay this moment. I had spent most of the day sitting on a plastic chair, holding a warm glass of water, talking to everyone in my family who would talk to me because I wanted to use as much of my voice as possible before this moment.

We had returned to my family in Kilometer 52. The day before, they had killed a cow and held a blessing ceremony to both welcome us back to the country but also send us safely back to America. We would fly out in two days' time. This knowledge tightened my chest in a suffocating grip. I hadn't had enough time with my family. The thought of leaving Maiv and my brothers created ripples behind my eyes, blurred my vision. Why had I agreed to go on a trek across Laos? Why hadn't I asked the girls to ask the driver to take us back sooner? Why? Why? Why?

I had known that my mother's grave was here. No one had invited me to see it and I hadn't asked that first day we arrived in the country or the second, or on any of the other days. It was just footsteps away from me.

From my perch on the plastic chair, I saw that the bamboo gate to Soob's yard was open and that my daughters had wandered in and whatever trepidation I had felt disappeared when I lost sight of their backs, so I followed my girls through the open gate into the yard.

I was fifty-seven years old. It had been twenty-four years since my mother had died, since her body had been buried beneath this mound of concrete. My right hand trembled as I reached for the little door on my mother's grave. I saw my fingers, slow, shaking, arthritic, small sunspots atop of the wrinkled skin. I felt the wooden door, the size of my palm. The pads of my fingers pushed into its rough surface. There was no give. My eyes searched for a doorknob that wasn't there. There was no way in and no way out. This was the impasse of my life.

To be with my mother.

To be away from my husband and my children.

Why couldn't we all be together?

When my tears stemmed and my sobs quieted, I noticed that my daughters were nowhere in sight. The hen and her chicks were no longer in the yard. The prized bull had retreated into the darkness of its shack. It was completely silent in the yard. The leaves of the mango tree had stopped rustling. There was no more breeze. The heavy sun sat in the heavy sky and both pressed down on me. Even the lines of red ants on the grave mound had disappeared. The ocean of words I had saved for my mother were thick in my throat.

I wanted to tell my mother everything that had happened since our parting. I wanted to tell her that my time with Npis had been far from perfect and yet we had made a life and filled it with children we both loved more than we loved ourselves. I wanted to tell her about the seven babies that had died inside me. I wanted a chair so I could sit and tell her long stories of the seven children who had survived. In the end, I wanted to say I was sorry. I wanted to say that if I'd known that by marrying Npis I would not see her again, then I would never have left her. I would have allowed her to grieve with that family in that hut, so I'd never have met that young man with the head of spiky hair, seen a smile that I thought was perfect for three years! It took me that long to see how his two front teeth overlapped just a bit. It took me decades to see the lengths he'd go to keep them even. I'd laugh with her, tell her about how I found him, one day in the garage of our house on the hill, how I came upon him trying to keep his teeth even with sandpaper. I wanted to see the spark of laughter in her eyes, the opening of her mouth, the looking away as mirth erupted. If she found my life humorous, even a moment of it, then perhaps my tears would stop. But as it was, there was no easing, no release. The weight in my heart that had been there remained in its place. All this time, I had wanted to shake it loose. On the unpaved roads of my life, even on the treacherous terrain of the country that had birthed me, I had hoped to dislodge it.

But nothing ever would. And now I knew that nothing ever could. It was the weight of my mother's love; her love had been the anchor that had held me fast to the earth, even when I felt life itself had turned on me, even when I turned on it.

I promised my mother that while the war had taken so much, it couldn't take away my memories of having been born hers, my memories of the house we shared in the village where two rivers met, that place where the scent of the citrus trees are strong and its flowers carpet the earth where my father rests.

I told my mother that the love she gave me in sixteen years was enough to last a lifetime without her, that the river of her love, despite the partings we have endured, has flowed through the darkest of nights and the brightest of days.

Epilogue

By a mountain stream, still flowing, the ghost of my niam tais waits for my mother in a jungle clearing. It has taken me forty-two years to realize that mothers will wait for their children, no matter how long it takes.

In the Hmong culture, when it is time for my mother to begin her journey to the land of the ancestors, she will need the little pieces of water-stained and time-weathered embroidery her mother gave her on her wedding day. She has kept them safe all these years and carried them from one country to the next, one house to the other. They are necessary so that in the world that awaits on the other side of life, she'll be able to find her mother.

My mother will wear a strand of beads in her thick hair, grown dark and long again. She will find her way back through the dense jungle, shed the heartache of the years, cross the rivers of her life one by one, until she makes it to the place where her mother stands. She will run to the older woman who has been waiting, a water pail at her side. Her mother's arms will open wide. My mother will feel the warmth of her mother's embrace.

In the arms of her mother, Tswb Muas will be cherished, nurtured, seen, and adored by the woman who loves her best in all the worlds. Tswb will let go of the hurt that this life has delivered, the mistakes that she has made, the wrongs that have been done to her. She will shine in the light of her mother's eyes, bright and new again.

Together, they will walk that dirt path toward the village of Dej Tshuam, where two rivers meet. The tall grass on either side of the dirt road will welcome them back. They will return to the spread of that citrus orchard and the trees will be alive, full of green leaves and ripe fruit. Pomelos and grapefruits, lemons and limes, tangerines and clementines, the oranges with the segment skin so thin that it melts in the mouth. They will walk, hand in hand, to the door of the wooden house.

They will not need to knock. The door will swing open. Inside, my mother's father, her brothers and sisters, their wives and husbands, their children, all of them will rejoice at their return.

The reunion will be a beautiful one. They will drink and eat and share all the stories that have lived far apart from each other, stories that have been waiting to come together. They will know that they have carried each other's memory for a long time and be happy to set down the missing and celebrate their homecoming.

This record is for Tswb Muas.
For the gift of your stories, for the tenderness of your love.
Niam, through you, Niam Tais's love flows.

Acknowledgments

O ne of the questions I get asked the most is, "How do you find time to write?" I've tried to answer it across the years in a multitude of ways, all true, but this year I've learned that the time I've had to write has come from the generosity of the people closest to me: my mother and father, my brothers and sisters, my husband, and my children. Each, in their own way, has ushered me toward the page, has urged me to do the work that keeps me whole.

This book is a gift of time from those I love and a gift of opportunity from the team of women who believe in its necessity and its truths. Anna Stein, my agent, who I met early in the mess of the COVID-19 pandemic, offered a perspective and experience that solidified the rocking boat I was on as a writer working from the American Midwest, stumbling on the pathway to dreams. Lindsay Sagnette, my editor from Atria Books, who from the very first expressed the confidence and enthusiasm for this project that my heart needed in order to do the work of pushing its depths. Jade Hui, assistant editor at Atria Books, who has carefully and patiently helped bring this book into the world. Tswb Muas, my mother, who has raised me with her truths and continues to feed and fortify me with her courage in sharing the lessons she's learned, the life she has lived, and her spirit of adventure and curiosity for all that life delivers.

I am a writer whose work is possible because of the generosity of individuals and institutions. I am lucky to live in a state that is home to the McKnight Foundation, the Loft Literary Center, the Minnesota State Arts Board, and the Metropolitan Regional Arts Council, and I am grateful for their support.

Thank you. Ua tsaug.

About the Author

Kao Kalia Yang is a Hmong American writer. She is a memoirist, a children's book author, a librettist, a public speaker, and a teacher. Her first book, *The Latehomecomer: A Hmong Family Memoir*, is a National Endowment for the Arts Big Read title and the only Asian American title adapted for the stage by Literature to Life. Her second memoir, *The Song Poet: A Memoir of My Father*, was a finalist for the National Book Critics Circle Award, the Chautauqua Prize, and the Dayton Literary Peace Prize. Her collective refugee memoir, *Somewhere in the Unknown World*, was one of Kirkus's Best Books of the Year. She coedited the groundbreaking collection *What God Is Honored Here?: Writings on Miscarriage and Infant Loss by and for Native Women and Women of Color*. Her children's books, *A Map into the World*, *The Shared Room*, *The Most Beautiful Thing*, *Yang Warriors*, and *From the Tops of the Trees*, have been recognized as Notable Books by the American Library Association and garnered the American Library Association's Asian/Pacific American Literary Award for Children's Literature and a Heartland Booksellers Award. She is the winner of four Minnesota

Book Awards. Yang is a recipient of the Sally Award for Social Impact from the Ordway Center for Performing Arts and the A. P. Anderson Award for her contributions to the cultural and artistic life of Minnesota. She is a Soros, McKnight, and Guggenheim fellow. Find out more at kaokaliayang.com.